THE GEOGRAPHY PROJECT 3

The Developing World

Neil Punnett, Wilberforce College, Hull
Peter Webber, Kingsdown School, Swindon
Stephen Murray, Thomas Telford School, Telford

SIMON & SCHUSTER
EDUCATION

Contents

Pupil's introduction — 6

POPULATION AND SETTLEMENT
1.1 One world — 8
1.2 What are developing countries? (1) — 10
1.3 What are developing countries? (2) — 12
1.4 Pre-colonial civilisation — 14
1.5 A Hausa village in Northern Nigeria — 16
1.6 Newcomers — 18
1.7 Urban life and work — 20
1.8 Urbanisation – Brazil — 22
1.9 Population distribution in Brazil — 24
1.10 Population change — 26
1.11 Millionaire cities — 28
1.12 International migration — 30

PEOPLE AND THE ENVIRONMENT
2.1 Natural environments — 32
2.2 Brazil's rain forest — 34
2.3 West Africa's savanna — 36
2.4 Living on the edge – deserts and desertification — 38
2.5 Irrigation — 40
2.6 Where is the rain? Drought in Africa — 42
2.7 Earthquake! — 44
2.8 Typhoon! — 46
2.9 People upset the environment — 48
2.10 Costs and benefits — 50
2.11 Conservation: African game parks — 52

PEOPLE'S NEEDS
3.1 People on the move – the Fulani of West Africa — 54
3.2 Water for everyone — 56
3.3 Primary products — 58
3.4 Remote sensing — 60
3.5 World trade — 62
3.6 Changing needs after colonialism — 64
3.7 Multinational companies — 66
3.8 Countertrade — 68
3.9 The need for infrastructure — 70
3.10 Transport development in West Africa – rail and road — 72
3.11 The need for aid – the poorest countries in the world — 74
3.12 Raising the money — 76
3.13 Oil brings wealth and problems — 78
3.14 War in the Middle East — 80
3.15 Needs not being met – apartheid in South Africa — 82
3.16 Needs not being met – being a foreigner in Britain — 84

3.17	What price progress?	86
3.18	Half the world's people	88
3.19	A woman's world – the role of women in development	90

PEOPLE'S LIVES AND WORK

4.1	Farming systems	92
4.2	West African farming – a case study	94
4.3	Cash crops cost lives	96
4.4	Land ownership and land reform	98
4.5	Industrialisation or alternative technology	100
4.6	Appropriate technology	102
4.7	The NICs – newly- industrialising countries	104
4.8	Taiwan – a NIC	106
4.9	Global village	108
4.10	Variations in employment	110
4.11	Tourism – a way forward	112
4.12	Tourism – culture clash?	114
4.13	China	116
4.14	China's road to development	118
4.15	One world – sporting links	120

Backtrack What to do in Igrinea?	122
Matrix of concepts and issues	124
Matrix of skills	126
Index	128

Eovy number I have don

Pupil's introduction

Geography is a vital, living subject. Geographers study the world and its people. They look at the environmental, physical and social conditions that affect how we all live. The study of geography helps us understand important issues such as **development**.

This book focuses on the **developing world** – Africa, Asia and South and Central America. The developing world is also called 'The Third World' or 'The South'. If they hear the words 'developing world', most people in this country probably think of poverty, starvation and hopelessness – or of exotic holiday locations. Newspapers and TV catch people's attention by concentrating on the tragic problems of the developing world. Holiday companies, on the other hand, want to present a happy, carefree image. This book will help you work out just how much of either picture is true, by asking questions like: *Is the developing world all problems? Or is it all wonderful landscapes and empty beaches? Is it a combination of these? Or none of them?*

Many people in the developed world (that means us – and *you*) want to help the developing world. They have ideas about how to solve some of its problems. But before we try to tell people in the developing world what to do, we need to find out as much as we can about the situations they have to face; to understand how they feel about their lives; and to consider the choices they have to make if they are to change. It is important to remember, too, that people in the developing world have their own ideas and plans for the future.

We all live in **one world**. The developed and developing worlds are interdependent – that means we all rely on each other and affect each others' lives. We have the same needs and will share the same future.

Look at the *Contents* list on page 4. The four main topic areas are about our everyday lives. **Settlement** means where people live. **Environment** refers to the surrounding area, eg mountains, the coast, the weather. We have many **needs** – for shelter, food, water, fuel, power, transport . . . These needs affect our **lives and work**.

Look at the photograph on the opposite page. A geographer can understand a lot about a place by looking at a photograph like this, especially if it is linked with a map of the area, showing street names, directions and so on. You can probably write something about the photograph already. Try answering these questions:

- Where in the world do you think this is?
- What type of settlement is it?
- What is the environment like?
- What do the people need?
- What type of work might the people who live here do?
- What do you think it is like to live here?
- What could be done to improve people's lives?

To answer these questions you will need to learn the **key words** that a geographer uses. You will also have to practise geographical **skills** like map reading, map drawing, field sketching and graph drawing. There will be new **ideas** or **concepts** for you to understand. Sometimes the subjects you study will not have a right or wrong answer. You will have your own views, but the geographical **issues** will need to be discussed.

The box in the top right-hand corner of each unit in the book lists the skills, key ideas and issues dealt with in the unit. The matrix charts at the back of the book will show you how these fit together and develop as you work through the units. They also tell you where you can find the same subjects, issues and concepts elsewhere in the book.

Geography is important for all of us. It is also fun! So make the most of your opportunity to learn more about the world and its people, so that you can understand the opportunities and problems that face us all.

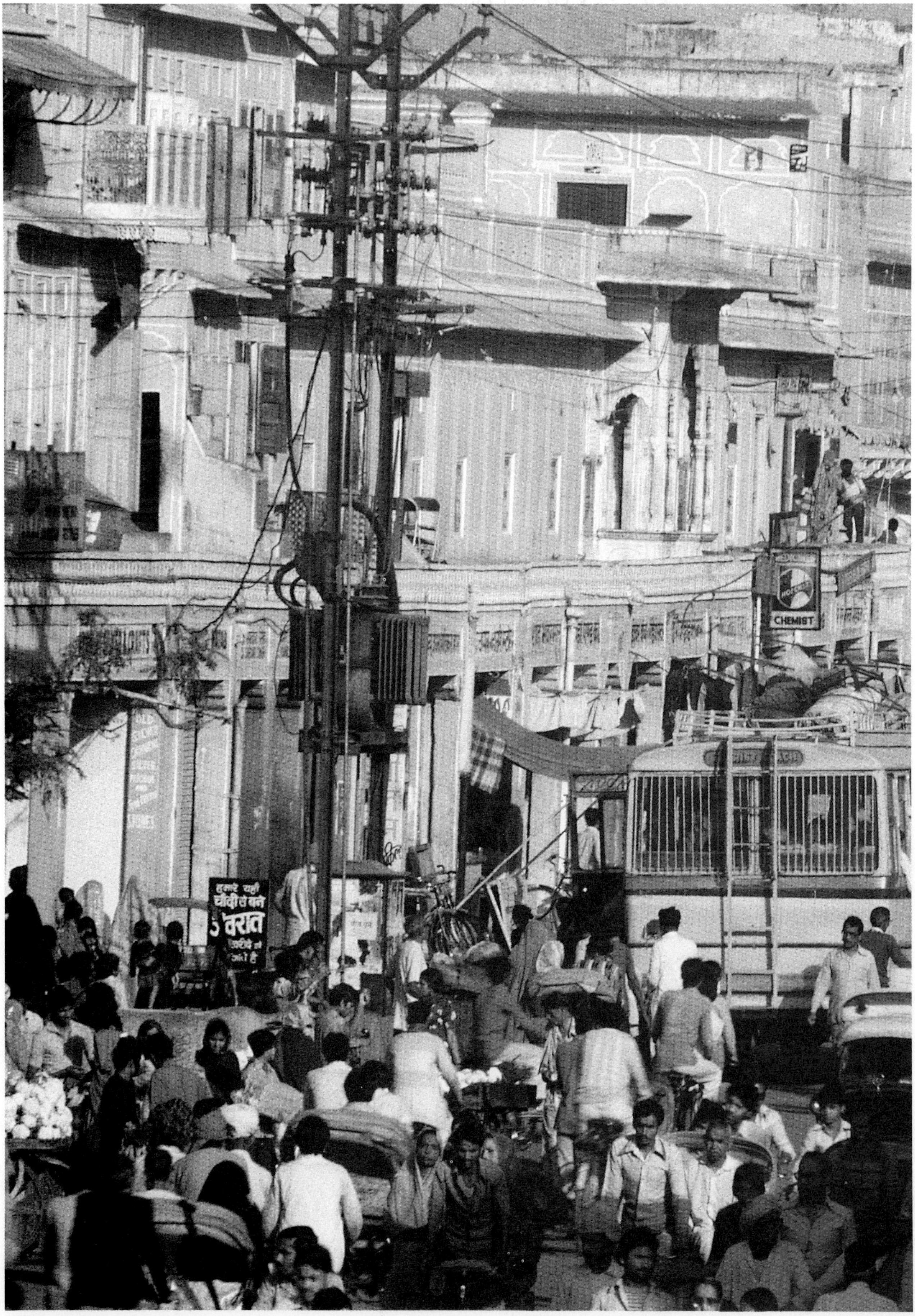
CHEMIST

POPULATION AND SETTLEMENT

1.1 One World

A shows Paula's homework. You can see that she has organised her work well and has made an interesting list. She has followed the instructions correctly. In **B** Paula says, 'What's it to do with me?'. Clearly she has not thought much about the meaning of her homework. If she did, she would realise how important the world is to her **lifestyle** (the way she lives).

Paula uses manufactured goods from the poor world and eats food from all over the world. Some of her clothes are not made in Europe. Her interests are influenced by people from the poor world, eg her interest in African music and reggae.

This book concentrates on the geography of the poor world – the **'South'** or **developing world**. This part of the world is made up of the continents of South/Central America, Africa, and Asia. It covers all the tropical areas and large areas outside the tropics. Unit 1.2 looks at this part of the world in more detail. The continents of North America, Europe and Australasia are called the **'North'** or the **developed world**.

How do Paula's homework and the television news items link up? We all have the same basic needs – for food, water, and shelter. We all live in **one world** even though it can be divided up in many ways. We each depend on many people in many different countries; in turn they depend on us. It is vital to remember this **interdependence** as you use this book. No one group of people or country can survive alone in the modern world. We all depend on each other (see **C**).

A

Name: Paula Taylor   Date: 12th September

Make a list of 'what is around you' that comes from the poorer countries in the world, eg not from countries in Europe, North America or Australia.

ARTICLES	COUNTRY
radio	– made in Malaysia
sports shoes	– made in South Korea
blouse	– made in Hong Kong

FOOD	
tea	– grown in India
coffee	– produce of Brazil
corned beef	– produce of Tanzania

OTHERS	
pop music	– sung by a West African group (Sierra Leone)
tv sport	– athletics – a Kenyan won tonight's 3000 metres steeplechase
floods	– there are monsoon floodwaters threatening villages in Bangladesh

B

- 30 gold miners are now feared dead in the Brazilian mining area...
- The effects of the floods in Sudan and Ethiopia have...
- The President of Indonesia is planning to visit Europe in...
- And finally... a West African dance group now touring Britain...
- Leading American banks have agreed to extend debt repayments
- What's it to do with me?

Skills	mapwork, empathy, research
Concepts	developed/developing, interdependence
Issues	inequality

C Some examples of interdependence

Understanding interdependence

The news headlines in **B** are factual. They concern different events and **issues** in different parts of the world. When you watch the news or read the headlines, ask yourself **why** these events happen. Why was there a famine in Sudan?

As you read this book always be aware that world events do concern you. What happens in one part of the world may directly affect you. For example, if there is a serious frost in Brazil the price of your coffee may rise! Because of the frost there will be less coffee, people still wish to buy the coffee and are prepared to pay a higher price for it. Other events that happen may be a direct result of your own country's policies. For example, many countries are now in **debt** because they are paying back loans from rich world banks. Poor countries sometimes borrow money to build a port, dam or factory. But when they repay the loans they have to pay extra **interest**. Sometimes they end up deeply in debt, with no hope of repaying all the loans.

1 Was Paula wrong to say 'What's it to do with me' (in **B**)? Give reasons for your answer.
2 Study the sketches in **C**.
   a List the examples of interdependence shown by the sketches.
   b Briefly state how the example of Hyundai cars shows that we live in 'one world'.
3 How do you think world trade makes all of us members of 'one world'?

FURTHER WORK

- List ten items you have used or eaten recently that come from the poorer countries and the countries they come from. Organise your work as Paula did in **A**.
- Shade in each country you included on a blank outline map of the world. (There is an outline map in the Resource and Activity Pack).

POPULATION AND SETTLEMENT

1.2 What are Developing Countries? 1

What do you take for granted? A group of pupils made keyword plan **A**.

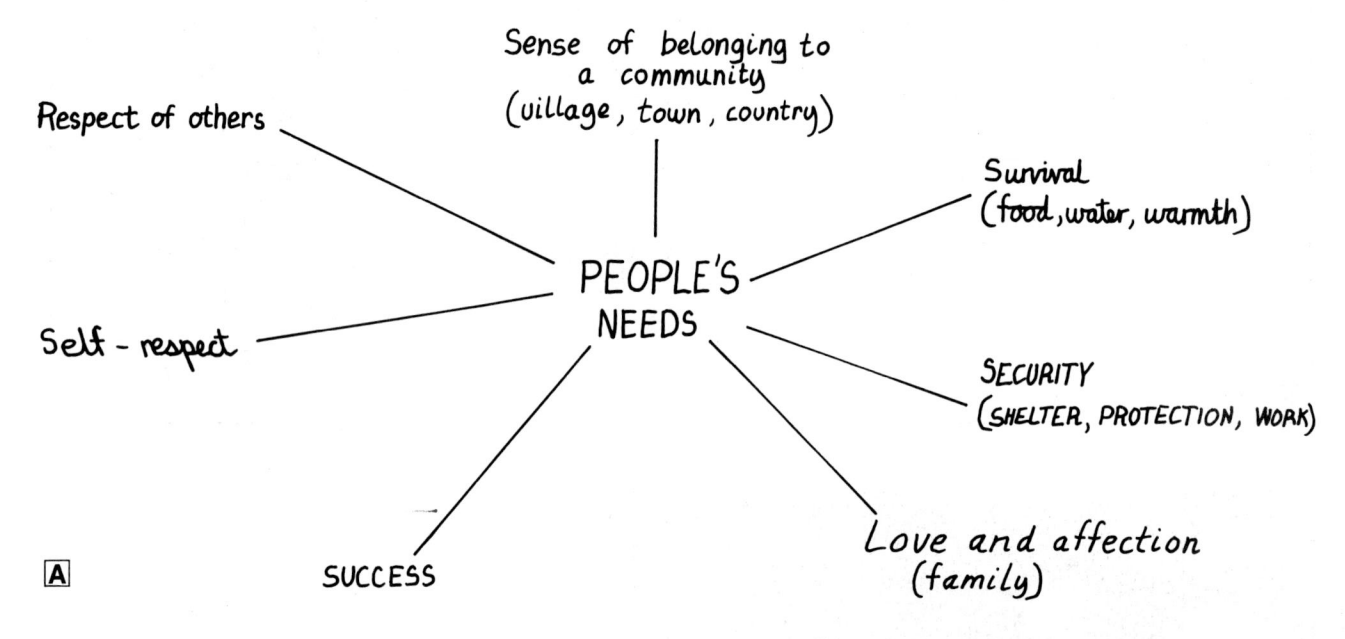

A PEOPLE'S NEEDS
- Sense of belonging to a community (village, town, country)
- Respect of others
- Self-respect
- Success
- Love and affection (family)
- SECURITY (SHELTER, PROTECTION, WORK)
- Survival (food, water, warmth)

Map **B** shows developing countries. You will often hear other terms used to describe this vast area of the world:

- Third World
- Poor World
- The South

---

1 Discuss the keyword plan with your neighbour. Make a keyword plan to show the needs you have now, and also what you want for the future. Then try to rank your needs in order of importance.

2 Look at the photographs in **C**.
   a How are people's needs being met? Note items in the photographs that show needs being met, and items showing needs not being met.
   b How do you judge the well-being of people? For each photograph describe the people and their surroundings. Who do you think is ● rich or poor? ● happy or sad? Give reasons for your answer.

The term **'Third World'** is probably used most often. To the geographer, this is an unsuitable term. It suggests that there are three separate worlds: the 'First World' is the USA, Canada, Western Europe, Japan and Australasia; the 'Second World' was used for Eastern Europe and the former USSR. This series aims to show that we all belong to **one world**, a world in which every country plays its part.

---

3 Why is 'Third World' an unsuitable term to describe developing countries?

4 Study map **B**.
   a Why is the term 'The South' not strictly accurate to describe the location of the developing countries?
   b Use **B** and an atlas to help you decide whether each of the following countries is in the North or the South: ● Turkey; ● New Zealand; ● Mexico; ● Greece; ● South Africa.

Skills	keyword plan, mapwork, using photographs
Concepts	regions, North/South
Issues	viewpoints, inequality

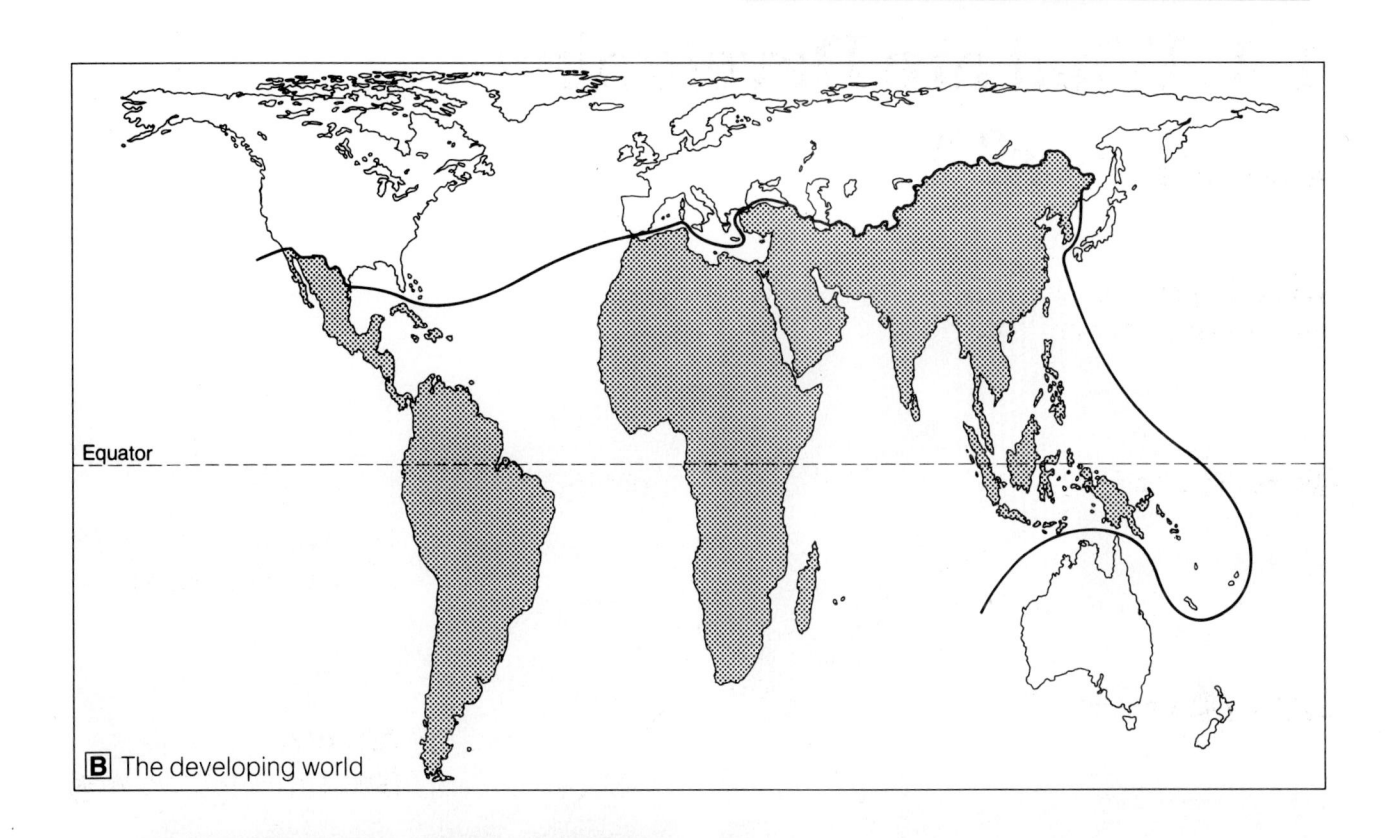

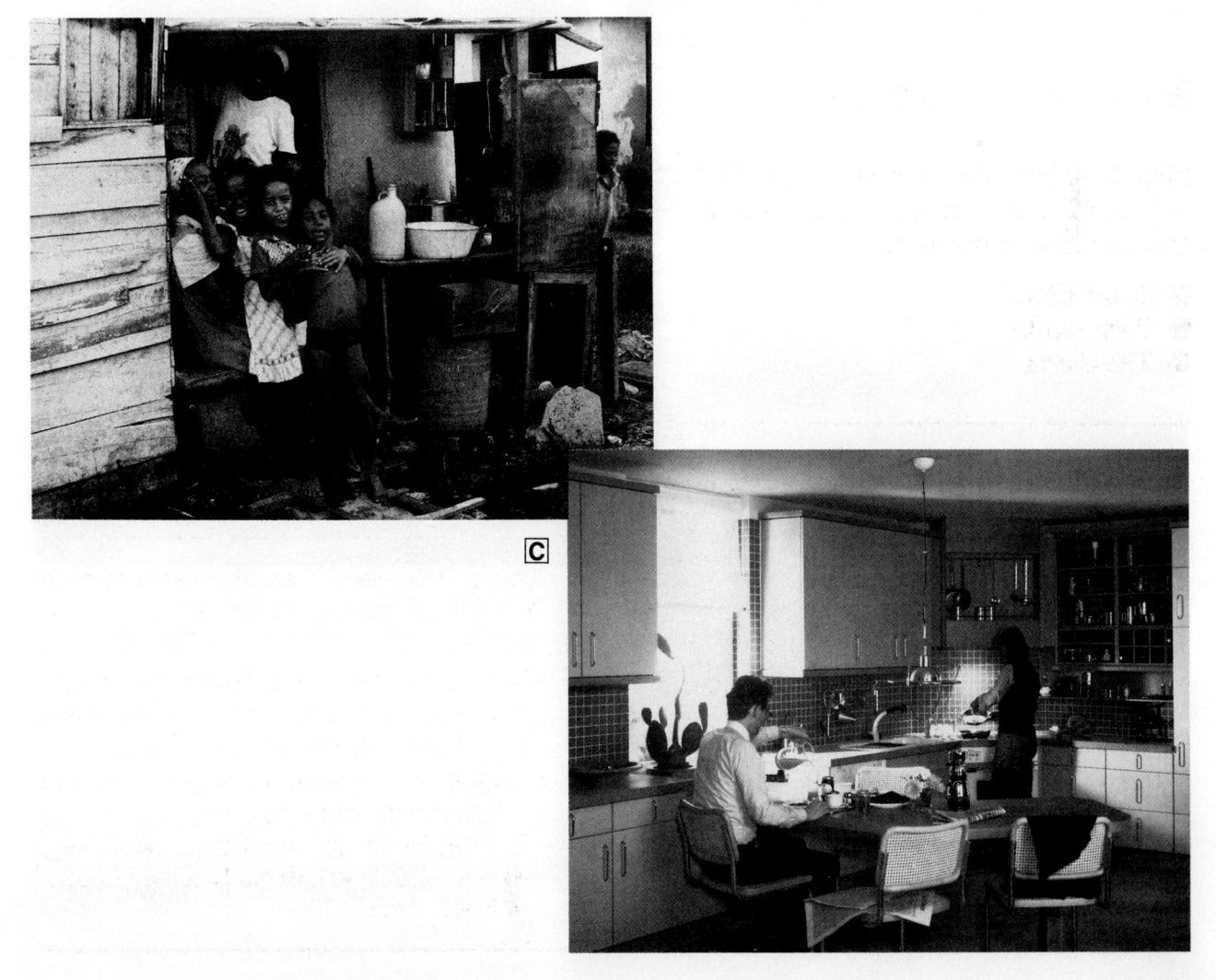

Equator

B The developing world

C

POPULATION AND SETTLEMENT

1.3 What are Developing Countries? 2

How do you recognise a developing country? There is no easy way to do this. Wealth is often used as a way of defining whether a country is 'developed' or 'developing', but this is not enough. Although most developing countries are poor, some, such as Kuwait and Saudi Arabia, are among the richest nations in the world. Although most developed countries are rich, some, such as Portugal and Bosnia, are quite poor.

1 Study photographs **A** to **D**.

   a For each photograph, decide whether it was taken in a developed or developing country and give your reasons.

   b Turn to page 129 where you will find the correct locations of the photographs. Did you get all four correct? If not, why not?

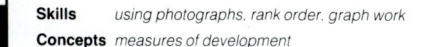

Country	UK	India	USA	Portugal	Saudi Arabia	Tanzania	South Korea	Brazil	Japan	Greece
GNP per capita ($):	9110	260	14100	2200	12200	240	2000	2232	9930	2950
Birth rate (per '000):	13	34	16	18	46	51	23	32	12	14
Infant mortality rate per '000):	13	118	9	30	103	96	29	79	8	20
Life expectancy (years):	74	53	75	71	59	50	68	63	77	73
Cars (per '000):	282	1	522	132	18	0	10	75	215	101
Energy use per person (kg of coal equivalent):	4700	230	9300	1330	3660	3	1450	660	3400	2180

E Measures of development for ten selected countries

In order to recognise a developing country, a combination of things must be considered. First we need to define what we mean by **development**:

DEVELOPMENT means meeting the NEEDS of people and IMPROVING society.

Second, we need some information relating to development. **E** shows statistics for different **measures of development** in ten countries.

2 a Rank the ten countries in **E** for the six measures of development: GNP per capita; birth rate; infant mortality rate; life expectancy; cars; energy use per person. Rank the country with the highest level 1 and so on.

b Add up the ranks of the six columns and write the total in the TOTAL column. This figure is the **development index**.

c Rank the development index totals.

d Shade in the ten countries on an outline map of the world and number them according to their development index ranks.

e How successful has this process been in identifying developed and developing countries? How could the process be improved?

F

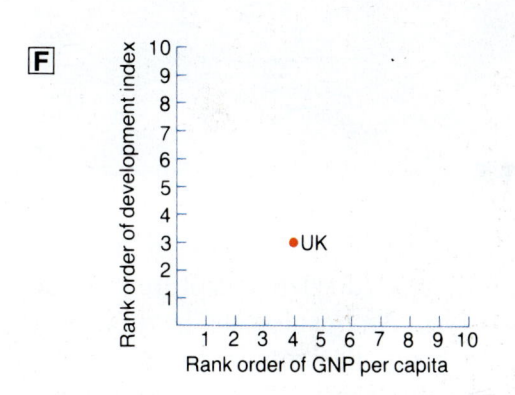

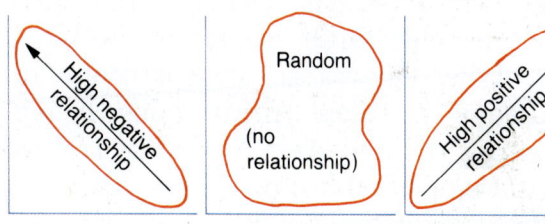

FURTHER WORK

F shows some information about **scattergraphs**.
- Make a large copy of the graph axes. Plot the rank order values for development index and GNP per capita for the ten countries.
- Draw a line around the dots so that the relationship between the development index and wealth can be judged.
- **F** shows what your pattern on the scattergraph means. Does your scattergraph show a high positive relationship between the development index and wealth?
- Were there any odd ones out? Did any of the countries not fit the general pattern? Why do you think this was so?

POPULATION AND SETTLEMENT

1.4 Pre-colonial Civilisation

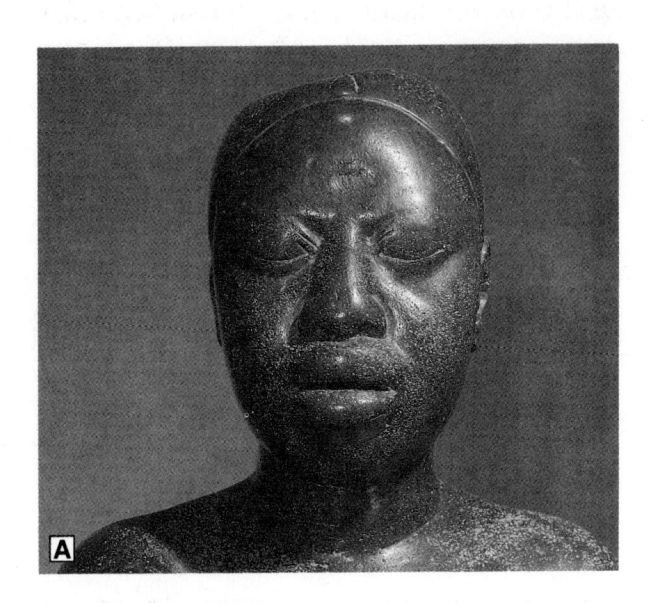

A

The head shown in **A** is made of bronze. This magnificent, life-size sculpture is over 600 years old. Archaeologists have discovered many heads like this in Nigeria.

The head represents a king, or oni, who once ruled the Yoruba people in the kingdom of Ife. Ife was an ancient centre of civilisation in West Africa. Long before Europeans came to West Africa the Yoruba had developed a complex and powerful civilisation (see timeline **B**).

It was a wealthy civilisation, based on rich agriculture, trade and the manufacture of handicraft goods. Ife traded with other areas for goods and materials which were not available locally. Copper, for example, was brought from the Sahara and mixed with local tin to create the bronze used by Yoruba craftsmen. There was a strong army with thousands of soldiers, including cavalry.

Map **C** shows the location of Ife in the equatorial rain forest of south western Nigeria. It is 120 km from the coast. Ife is probably the oldest town of the Yoruba people; it dates from before AD 1000. Another important town was Oyo, which was the centre of a large empire between the 16th and 19th centuries. The most famous of the early Nigerian towns is Benin, 200 km south east of Ife. Benin was founded soon after AD 1000. When the first Europeans visited Benin, over 400 years ago, they were very impressed by the size of the city, which had several thousand people (**D**).

At first the contact between Europeans and Africans was peaceful and constructive.

YEAR	
1000 AD	The kingdoms of Ife and Benin are founded. Towns grow within an ordered and cultured society *Normans invade England and defeat the Saxons.*
1100	Pottery statues made *England a colony of the Norman empire which includes much of France*
1200	First bronze cast heads
1300	
1400	*European sailors start to explore Africa and Asia* The King of Benin exchanges ambassadors with Portugal (1486) Period of peaceful trade *Columbus discovers the West Indies and America*
1500	*Spain and Portugal build empires in South America* Slave trade begins
1600	The Oyo Empire unites the Yoruba lands *English Civil War*
1700	
1800	End of the slave trade The Oyo Empire collapses *Agricultural revolution and industrial revolution begins* British trading companies seek palm oil, rubber and other resources *European empires reach their height*
1900	Nigeria declared a British colony Nigeria gains independence (1960) *The European empires are broken up*
2000	

B A timeline of West African and European history

Skills	map work, research
Concepts	tradition, culture
Issues	viewpoints

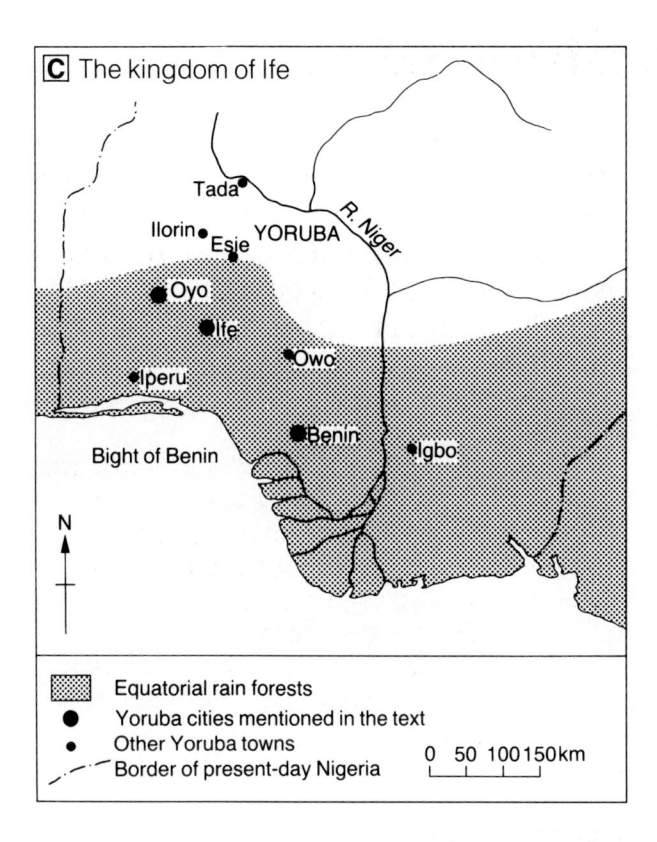

C The kingdom of Ife

Map showing: Tada, Ilorin, Esie, YORUBA, R. Niger, Oyo, Ife, Owo, Iperu, Benin, Igbo, Bight of Benin

Key:
- Equatorial rain forests
- ● Yoruba cities mentioned in the text
- • Other Yoruba towns
- Border of present-day Nigeria
- 0 50 100 150km

A Dutchman, Dierick Ruiters, wrote:

"Benin is a very big city. You go into a big broad street which seems to be seven or eight times broader than our Warmoes Street in Amsterdam. There are many great streets to the right and left. You cannot see to the end of these because of their length. The houses in the town stand in good order as the houses stand in Holland. Those belonging to men of quality (which are gentlemen) have two or three steps to go up, and in front of each there is a kind of gallery where a man may sit dry. The palace of the king is very large, having within it many square courtyards with galleries around them, where sentries always stand."

Another Dutchman wrote:

"The people of Benin have good laws and a well organised police. They live on good terms with the Dutch and other foreigners who come to trade among them, and show them a thousand marks of friendship."

D Descriptions of Benin written by 16th Century Dutch visitors

They traded fairly and respected each other. Unfortunately this did not last long. Later, the Europeans came to conquer and **colonise** (claim territory for themselves). They captured millions of Africans and sent them to work as slaves in European colonies in America.

The pre-colonial civilisations could no longer develop. Many collapsed. Later generations of Europeans knew nothing of the great cultures that had existed. They thought of Africa as an uncivilised place, and called it 'the Dark Continent'. Only in recent years have the Africans begun to re-discover their great civilisations such as Benin and Ife in West Africa, Kilwa in East Africa and Zimbabwe in southern Africa.

---

1 a Who were the Yoruba people?
  b Where did the Yoruba live?
  c Name three of their towns.
2 Study map **C**.
  a Where is Ife?
  b When was the town of Ife founded?
  c From which direction would the European traders have come?
  d How far from Ife are (i) Oyo and (ii) Benin?
3 Why did Ife become an important town?
4 Read the descriptions of Benin (**D**).
  a Who wrote these descriptions and when?
  b Why do you think they were in Benin?
  c Write a short description of about 100 words describing your own village, town or city to a foreign visitor.
5 Why do you think it is important for the Africans to re-discover their great civilisations of the past? (Think about the effects of the colonial period when the Africans were ruled by Europeans).

FURTHER WORK

- Try to find out about other civilisations in the developing world eg the Incas, Zimbabweans, Chinese.
  When you have finished your research, write a brief description of the civilisation.

POPULATION AND SETTLEMENT

1.5 A Hausa Village in Northern Nigeria

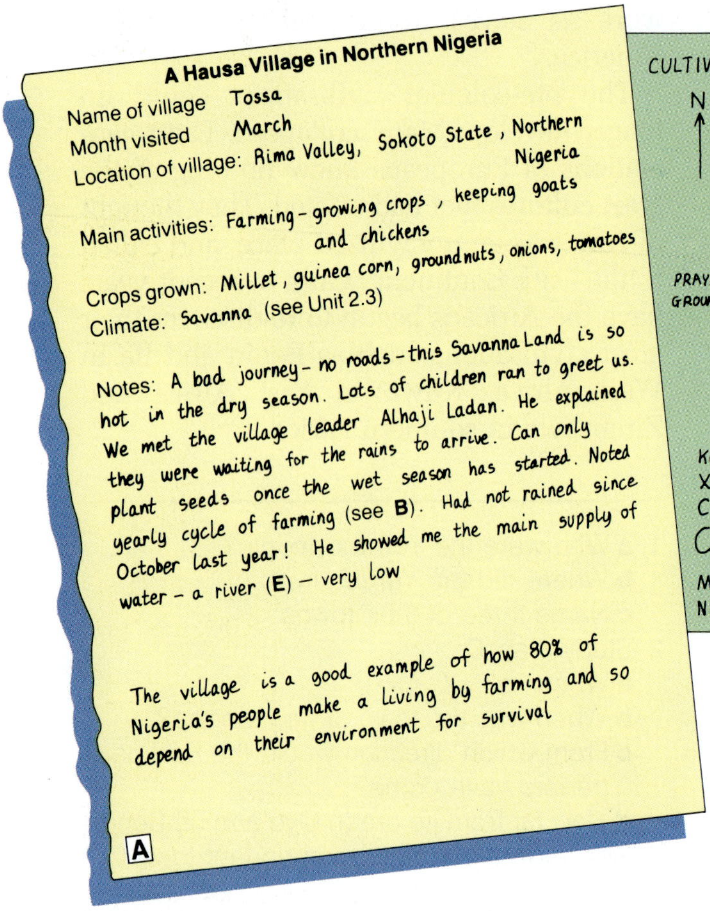

A

A Hausa Village in Northern Nigeria

Name of village: Tossa
Month visited: March
Location of village: Rima Valley, Sokoto State, Northern Nigeria
Main activities: Farming – growing crops, keeping goats and chickens
Crops grown: Millet, guinea corn, groundnuts, onions, tomatoes
Climate: Savanna (see Unit 2.3)

Notes: A bad journey – no roads – this Savanna Land is so hot in the dry season. Lots of children ran to greet us. We met the village leader Alhaji Ladan. He explained they were waiting for the rains to arrive. Can only plant seeds once the wet season has started. Noted yearly cycle of farming (see B). Had not rained since October last year! He showed me the main supply of water – a river (E) – very low

The village is a good example of how 80% of Nigeria's people make a living by farming and so depend on their environment for survival

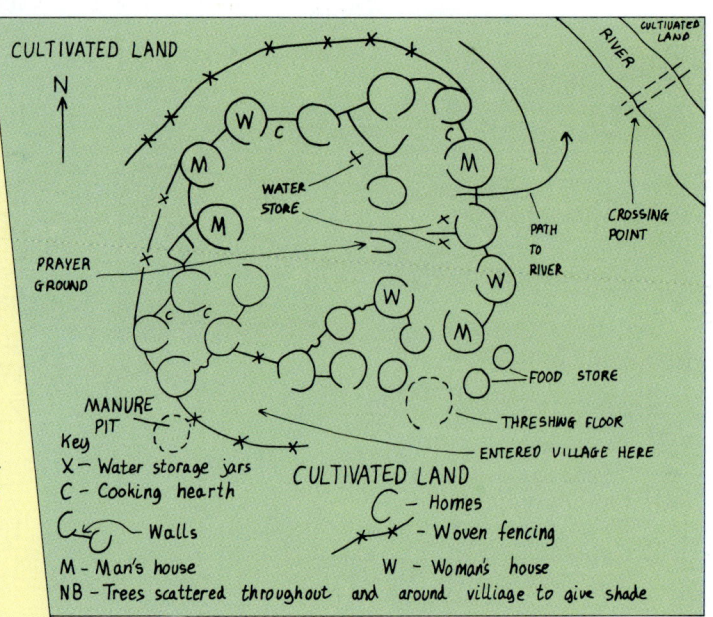

B

Map key:
X – Water storage jars
C – Cooking hearth
(symbol) – Walls
M – Man's house
(symbol) – Homes
✕✕✕ – Woven fencing
W – Woman's house
NB – Trees scattered throughout and around village to give shade

Features shown: CULTIVATED LAND, RIVER, WATER STORE, PRAYER GROUND, MANURE PIT, PATH TO RIVER, CROSSING POINT, FOOD STORE, THRESHING FLOOR, ENTERED VILLAGE HERE

Month	Temp °C	Rainfall mm	Work
January	29	0	Repair work
February	32	0	Repair work
March	35	0	Land cleared of shrubs – vegetation burnt and spread on the land
April	38	8	Millet and guinea corn sown
May	37	69	Groundnuts sown
June	35	114	Weeding
July	31	203	Harvesting
August	29	315	Sow second crop of millet and guinea corn
September	31	130	Continue to sow second crop
October	34	13	Harvesting
November	34	0	Sow vegetable seeds
December	31	0	Harvesting

1 Where is Tossa located?
2 Describe the features of two seasons which affect the region.
3 How do the people survive and make a living?
4 Look at **B** and draw a climate graph (one has been started in the *Activity Pack*).
   a Which months are the dry season?
   b What is the temperature range (difference between highest and lowest)?
   c Use a calculator to find the average temperature (total and divide by 12) and total rainfall in a year
5 Explain how the environment affects the lives of the people who live in the village. You could present your answer in the form of a newspaper article or a radio programme.

| Skills | interpreting photographs, graph work, empathy |
| Concepts | seasonal change, cause and effect |

C

6 What makes you think this is the dry season?
7 Why do you think this is a very hot time of day?
8 What different building materials can you see?
9 Where might the materials come from?
10 Why has the village got walls and fences?

E

16 What animals can you see here?
17 How might the animals be used by the villagers?
18 How is the river useful to the villagers?
19 What might happen in the wet season?
20 What do you think the children do?
21 Describe the clothes worn by the children. How are they different from your clothes? Why might this be?

D

11 What do you think these people are talking about?
12 How are the trees useful to the village people?
13 What do the houses look like?
14 What might the houses look like inside?
15 Why are the houses clustered close together?

F

22 Do you think the clothes were made locally? Give reasons for your answer
23 What might these children need to learn to live in this village?
24 What will they do when they grow up?
25 What do you think they do for entertainment?

17

POPULATION AND SETTLEMENT

1.6 Newcomers

For centuries people have moved or **migrated** to towns and cities (**urban areas**). In the developed world a large percentage of the population (69% in Europe, 53% in North America) is urban (lives in towns and cities). In the developing world the percentage is lower, but it is increasing. In 1975 28% of people in developing countries lived in towns and cities; by the year 2000 the urban population will be 44%

Each year over 25 million people from rural areas move to towns and cities. The vast majority of these people live in the developing world. Developing world cities are growing rapidly (**A**).

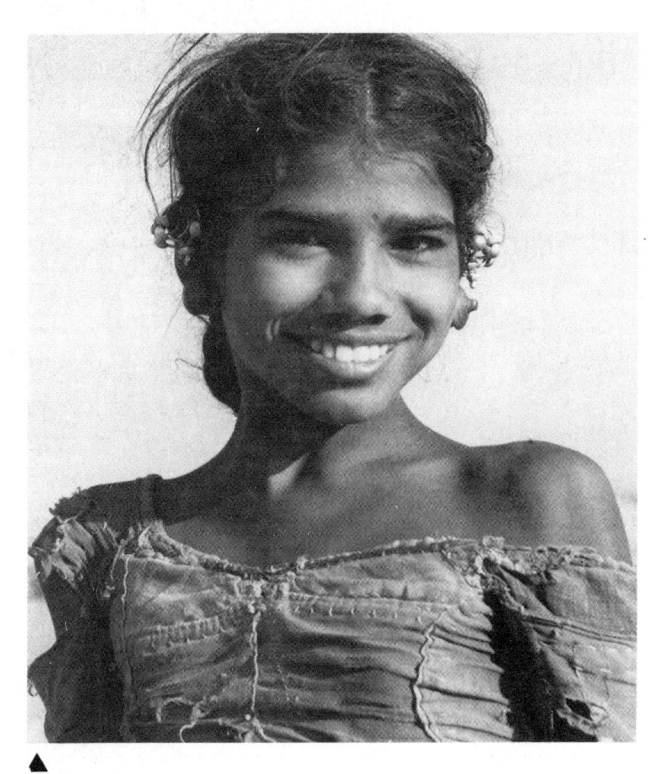

		1960	2000
Calcutta	(India)	2.9	16.6
Sao Paulo	(Brazil)	3.8	24.0
Mexico City	(Mexico)	3.3	26.3
Seoul	(South Korea)	2.4	13.5

A Population growth in four developing world cities (millions of people)

Why do people move to the city?

The comments of these six children may help to explain some of the reasons for the movement from rural to urban areas.

Lima, Peru

TERESA – 14 years
'It was so hard for my family in the mountain village where we lived. My mother almost died when she had my little sister. Now Mama is well and has been to the local hospital. I am hoping to get a job as a domestic servant with a rich industrialist's family.'
▼

Bombay, India

ANJU – 14 years
'I don't want to go back to the village. School is good here. I would have left school at 12 years old back in the village.'

Abidjan, Ivory Coast

BUCHI – 14 years
'I always wanted to move to the city ever since our crops suffered in the drought. It's fun in the city, I love looking round the shops.'

18

Skills	empathy
Concepts	migration, push and pull factors
Issues	quality of life

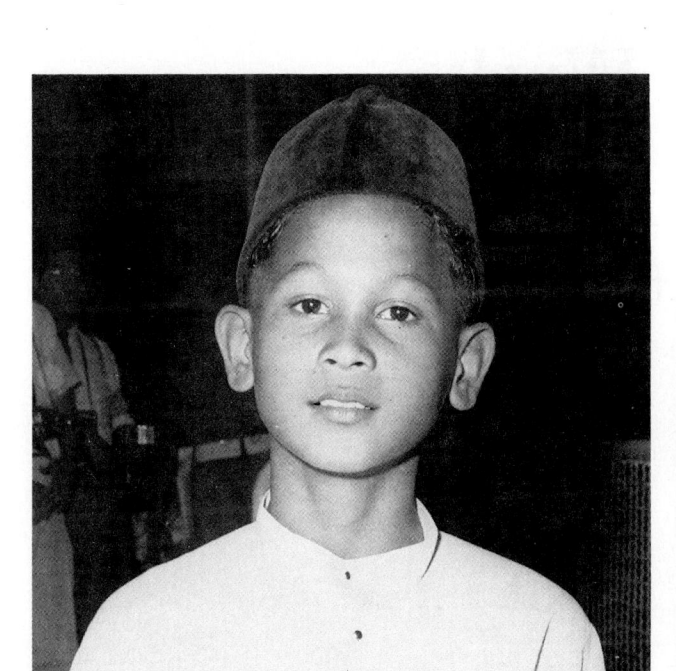

Kuala Lumpur, Malaysia

LEE – 13 years
'I can earn a lot of money here compared with the old village. I wash up, run errands and deliver parcels.'

Lagos, Nigeria

AJATO – 14 years
'I remember moving to the capital when I was 8 years old. I was always ill in the village. Diarrhoea was the worst problem; now I don't suffer any more.'

Sao Paulo, Brazil

JOSE – 15 years
'My family had to leave their farmland as it was taken over to be used as a beef ranch. We all have jobs here in the city and are building up our new home from any materials we find.'

The reasons why people move or migrate to towns and cities are called **pull** factors. The town and cities 'pull' people towards them like a magnet; people are attracted to them.

The reasons why people move away from the rural areas are called **push** factors. Life is often difficult in the rural areas. For example, Buchi's family were 'pushed' from their village by drought and crop failure. There were other push factors which explain why they left the village for Abidjan.

- there was no running water
- employment for the children was non-existent unless they worked on the farm
- medical services were poor
- roads were poorly made up and became impassable in the rainy season
- education was very limited for children over 11 years old
- the new electricity supply to the village was unreliable

1 On an outline map of the world, mark the countries and cities where the children in this Unit come from. (There is an outline map in the *Activity Pack*).
2 Draw up a chart (or use *Activity Sheet* 4) to show the young people's likes and dislikes about the city and their old village.
3 a What is a **pull** factor? Give an example.
  b What is a **push** factor? Give an example.
4 Make a list of possible pull factors which explain why Abidjan was attractive for Buchi's family. (You can base your list on the 'opposites' of the push factors.)
5 Work in a pair to answer this question: Imagine you are two Peruvian children about to leave your mountain village for the capital city, Lima. Discuss:
  - What you are looking forward to and what you are worried about.
  - What you will miss about the village and its life when you have left it.

POPULATION AND SETTLEMENT

1.7 Urban Life and Work

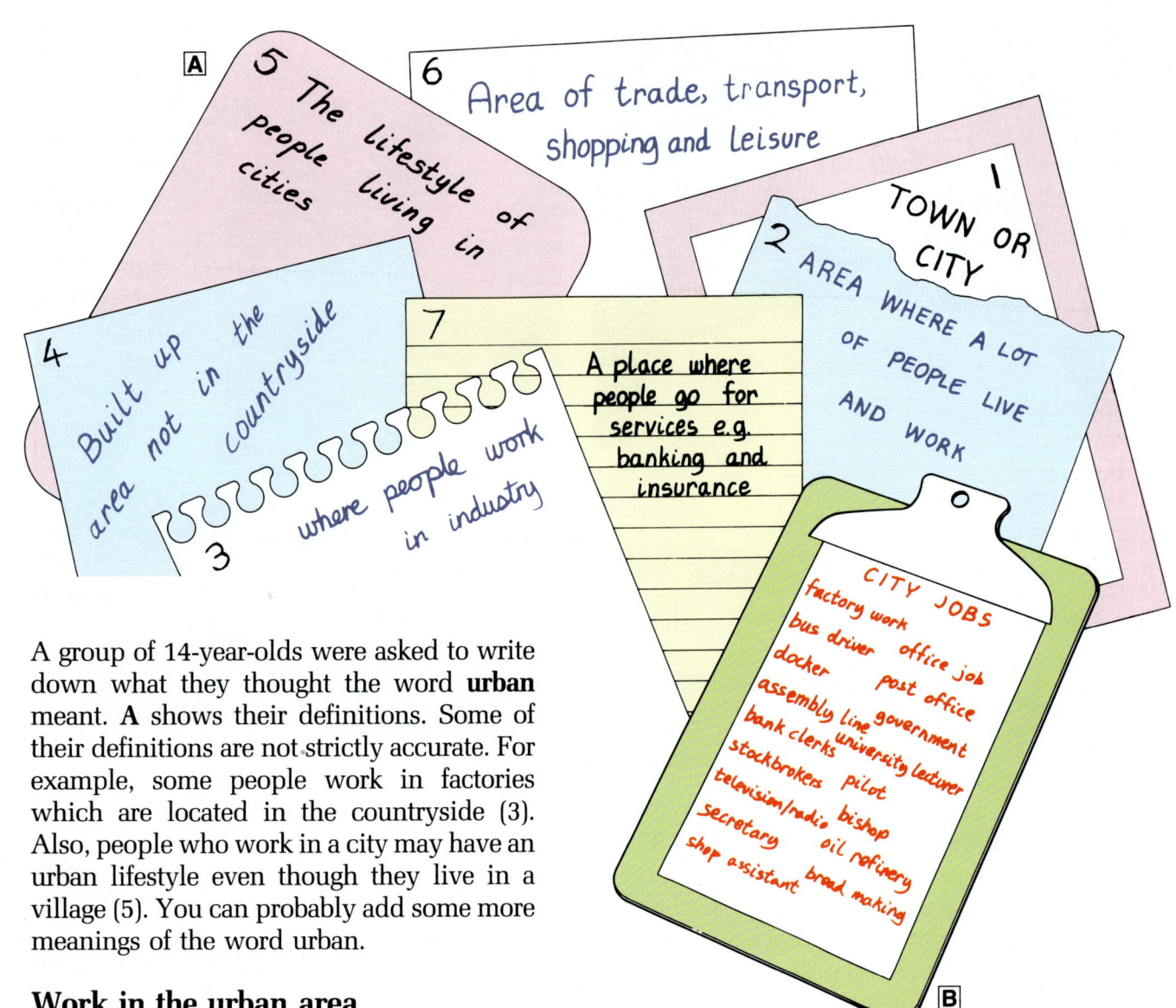

A

1. TOWN OR CITY
2. AREA WHERE A LOT OF PEOPLE LIVE AND WORK
3. where people work in industry
4. Built up area not in the countryside
5. The lifestyle of people living in cities
6. Area of trade, transport, shopping and leisure
7. A place where people go for services e.g. banking and insurance

B CITY JOBS
factory work, bus driver, office job, docker, post office, assembly line, government, bank clerks, university lecturer, stockbrokers, pilot, television/radio, bishop, secretary, oil refinery, shop assistant, bread making

A group of 14-year-olds were asked to write down what they thought the word **urban** meant. **A** shows their definitions. Some of their definitions are not strictly accurate. For example, some people work in factories which are located in the countryside (3). Also, people who work in a city may have an urban lifestyle even though they live in a village (5). You can probably add some more meanings of the word urban.

Work in the urban area

Next the students thought about the types of work people do in urban areas. They decided to have a **brainstorming** session. One person acted as 'scribe' and wrote down all the ideas the group suggested. **B** shows the list they came up with.

The jobs on the list can be divided into **secondary** and **tertiary** employment. Secondary employment refers to manufacturing or making things, such as cars. Tertiary refers to jobs in service industries – such as shop assistants or teachers.

The jobs on the students' list could all be found in urban areas in the developed and the developing world. But the list shows that the students had not studied patterns of work in developing world cities. They had a **Eurocentric** viewpoint, one that did not look beyond Europe or the developed world.

Informal work in the developing world

Many types of work in the cities of the developing world are part of the **informal sector**. Photographs **C** and **D** show examples of this kind of work. These jobs are not

20

Skills	Brainstorming, keyword plan
Concepts	formal/informal work
Issues	urban life, viewpoints

always legal and are not covered by government regulations. Sometimes very young children do informal work, such as:

- making kettles out of tin cans in Bombay
- selling souvenirs on the streets of São Paulo
- cleaning cars on the streets of Lagos
- collecting garbage from the rubbish dumps outside Lima
- selling cigarettes on the streets of Kuala Lumpur
- washing up in Abidjan

People doing informal work do not usually *want* to break the law. But it can be difficult to make a job legal: there may be rules and restrictions, bribery and corruption. Most people just want to get the job done – and they will employ anyone who is willing to do it.

Even some of the jobs which appear to be legal are not. Some large firms employ people illegally, to work at home for very low wages. Electronics firms in Mexico employ women to make parts in their own homes. The labour is cheap – wages are not up to the legal minimum and the firm does not have to pay national insurance.

---

1 Which definitions in **A** do you think give an accurate meaning for the word 'urban'? Discuss this with a partner, then look up the answers (on page 129). Make a list of the correct definitions, under the heading 'Urban checklist'.
2 Look at **B** and write down examples of the following:
● manufacturing employment; ● transport services; ● retailing (shopping); ● financial services
3 What does the word 'Eurocentric' mean?
4 Why was the students' list of jobs Eurocentric?
5 What do you understand by 'informal employment'?
6 Describe the types of informal work shown in photographs **C** and **D**.
7 What type of informal employment is there in your area/country?
8 Why do you think more people do informal work in a developing world city than in a city in Europe?

POPULATION AND SETTLEMENT

1.8 Urbanisation – Brazil

As you saw in Unit 1.6, many people in the developing world are leaving the countryside to live in cities and towns. Many towns and cities in the developing world are growing rapidly. Graph **A** shows this process of **urbanisation** in both the developed and developing worlds. Urbanisation has slowed down in the developed world, but it is increasing in the developing world. **B** gives the percentage of the population living in urban areas in some developed and developing world countries

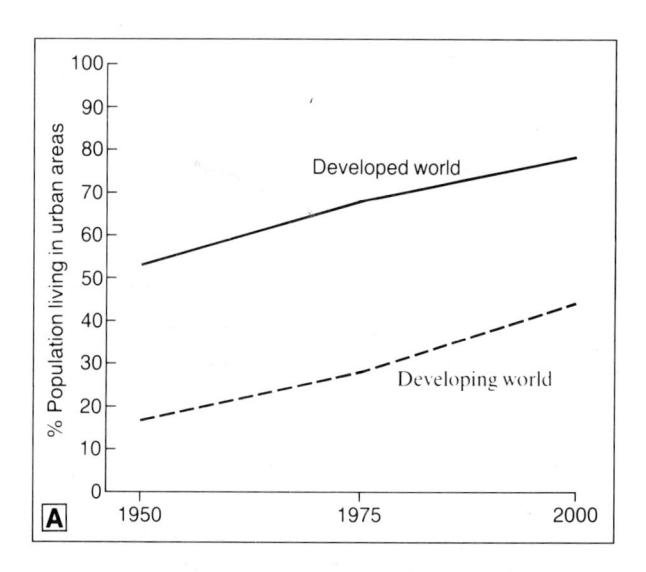

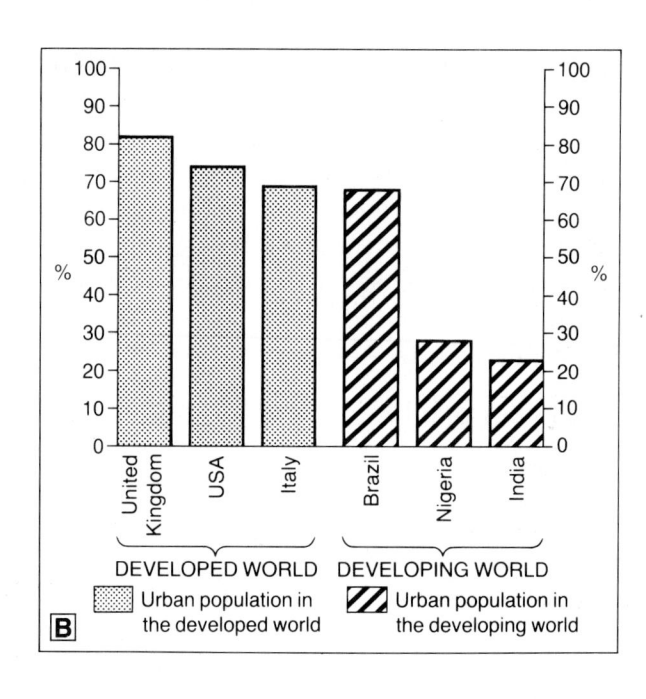

Newspapers, documentary programmes and textbooks tend to concentrate on the problems of urbanisation – poverty, squalor and ill-health. It is important to remember, however, that the process of urbanisation does not always involve problems. For many people, city growth can mean more employment, better job opportunities and an improved standard of living – ie better housing, health care and education.

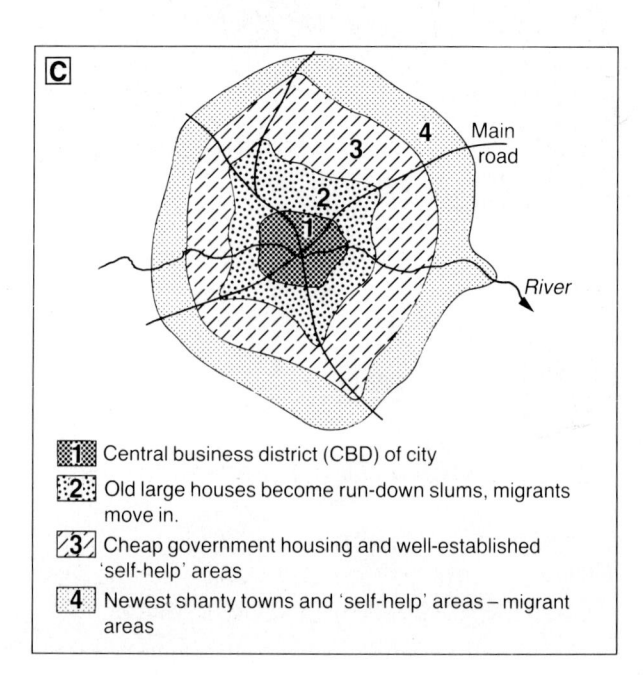

Urbanisation – the process of change

Urbanisation is perhaps the most important change taking place in the developing world today. People migrate from the countryside to the towns and cities because of different 'push' and 'pull' factors (see Unit 1.6). The built-up area of the city grows and people adopt an urban lifestyle – working in the service industries, living in flats and apartments, going to the cinema . . .

As population grows, cities expand outwards (**C**). But they spread more rapidly than their services. It takes much longer for piped water, sewerage systems, electricity supply and tarred roads to reach the city outskirts. New migrants to the city often live in very poor conditions (see **D**).

C
1. Central business district (CBD) of city
2. Old large houses become run-down slums, migrants move in.
3. Cheap government housing and well-established 'self-help' areas
4. Newest shanty towns and 'self-help' areas – migrant areas

Skills	interpreting graphs, empathy
Concepts	urbanisation, change, expansion
Issues	quality of life

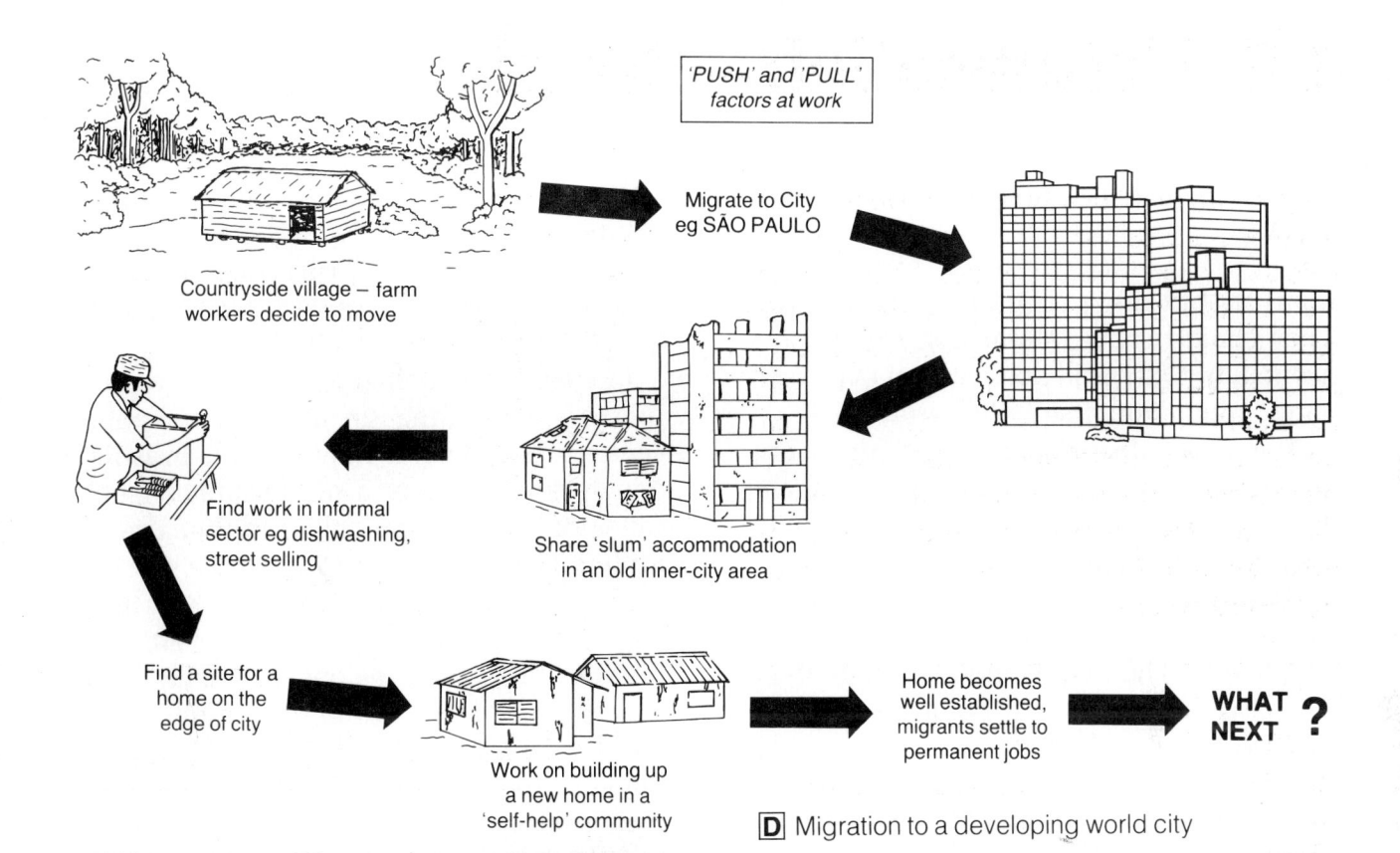

'PUSH' and 'PULL' factors at work

Countryside village – farm workers decide to move → Migrate to City eg SÃO PAULO → Share 'slum' accommodation in an old inner-city area → Find work in informal sector eg dishwashing, street selling → Find a site for a home on the edge of city → Work on building up a new home in a 'self-help' community → Home becomes well established, migrants settle to permanent jobs → **WHAT NEXT?**

D Migration to a developing world city

E

1. What do you understand by the term 'urbanisation'?
2. Study graph **A**. Describe the growth of urbanisation in
   ● the developing world; ● the developed world.
3. Study **C**. Write a short description of each zone or area of the city shown in the key (about three sentences for each zone).
4. Look back at what José said in Unit 1.6. Draw a picture story to show his move to São Paulo. You could write his comments in the form of 'speech bubbles'.
5. Quickly write down everything you can think of to do with:
   a possible problems of urbanisation in a developing country such as Brazil
   b advantages of urbanisation
   Go through your list of problems and advantages and underline the most outstanding ones. Do you think urbanisation is a 'good' or 'bad' process?

FURTHER WORK

● Newcomers to the cities of Brazil often follow the stages shown in diagram **D**. José's family (see Unit 1.6) are typical of such migrants.
Use Units 1.6, 1.7 and this unit to help you write a story of 'Everyday life in a Brazilian city'. Illustrate your work with simple line sketches.

23

POPULATION AND SETTLEMENT

1.9 Population Distribution in Brazil

Mapping population distribution in Brazil

Maps should give a good visual impression. They should show information clearly and accurately. How well does each map (**A – C**) show population distribution in Brazil?

A is a **dot distribution** map – the more dots it has in an area, the more people there are. It shows clearly that more people live on the coast.

B is a **density shading** or **choropleth** map. The denser the shading the more people live in the area. The map is more accurate than **A**; it also shows clearly that more people live on the coast than inland.

C simplifies the population distribution into three areas – the **core**, the **intermediate area** and the **periphery**. The core is the south east of Brazil. This area has dominated the economy of the country during the 20th century. It has grown at the expense of the rest of Brazil. People have moved to the core from surrounding rural areas and the poor, dry north east of the country. Many of the rural areas have suffered **rural depopulation**. People left the countryside for a variety of 'push' and 'pull' reasons (see Unit 1.6).

In 1960 the Brazilian government began a process of building up a new population centre. They built a new capital, **Brasilia**, which now has over a million inhabitants. Cities of this size are called **millionaire** or **million** cities.

New highways have been built. These make it easier for people to move into the **interior** (the inland regions of Brazil.) They also give people access to new farming and forestry areas, as well as to important mineral resources. The most famous new road is the Trans-Amazonian Highway (**D**). It is 5600 kilometres long. It provides a link between Amazonia and the densely-populated area of north-east Brazil.

E shows the main changes in Brazil's population distribution. This map simply

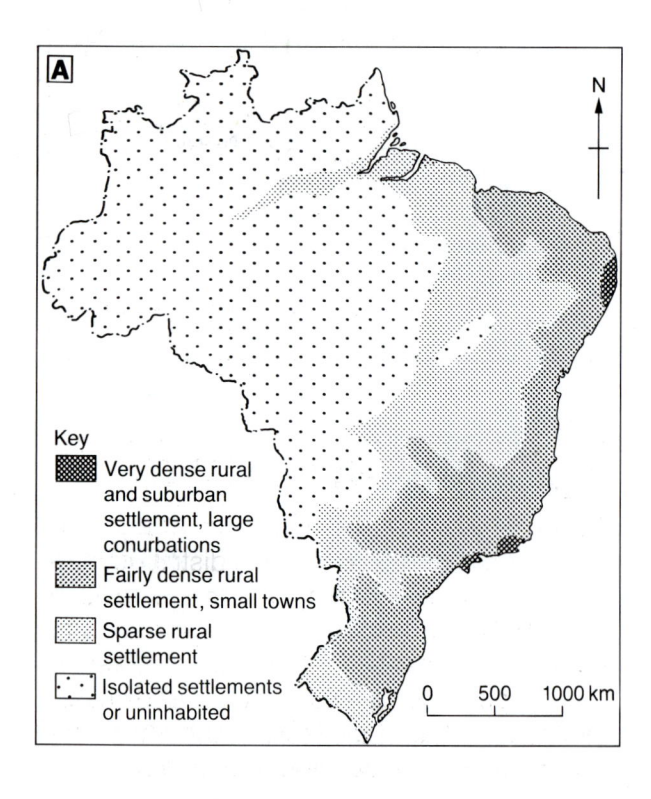

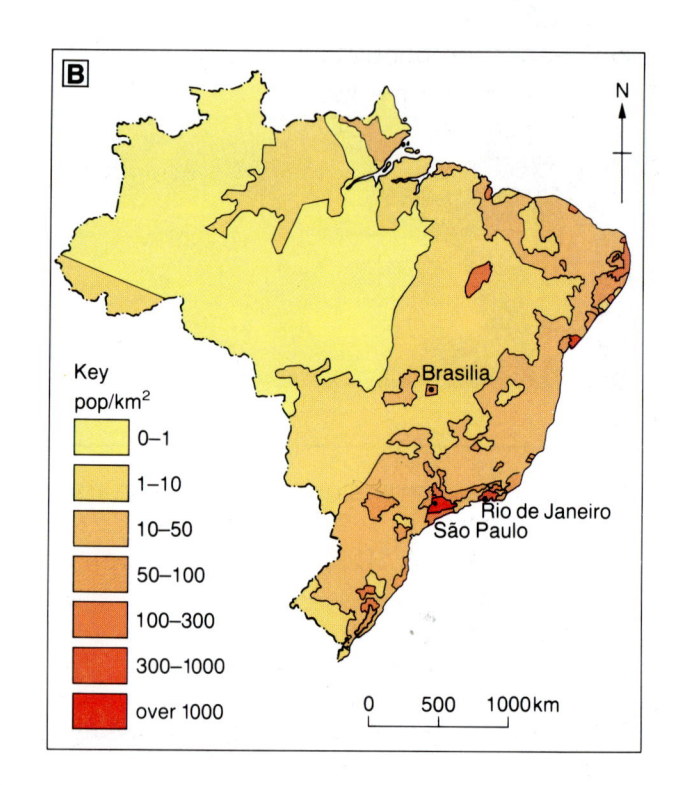

24

Skills	map work
Concepts	population distribution, millionaire cities

C THE INTERIOR

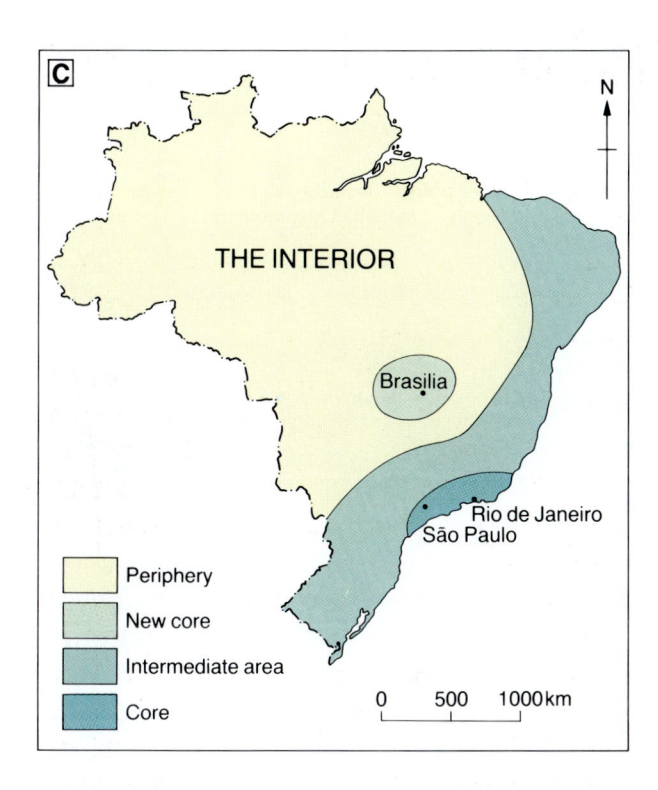

Brasília

Rio de Janeiro
São Paulo

- Periphery
- New core
- Intermediate area
- Core

0 500 1000 km

summarises the main movements of population; it does not give accurate statistical information.

---

1 Study maps **A** and **B**.
   a Which parts of Brazil are the most densely populated?
   b Where is the population density lowest?
2 Why do few people live in the central and south interior of Brazil?
3 Why do so many people live near the coast? (Clues: the colonisation of Brazil – the country was settled by Portuguese people who came by sea; Indian people lived in scattered groups throughout Brazil).
4 Study map **C**. What do you understand by
   ● a 'core' area; ● a 'periphery'?
5 a What problems do you think the core area of south east Brazil has?
   b Why do you think the Brazilian government wanted a new location for the capital city?
6 Study map **E**.
   a Why might people want to move to the urban areas?
   b Give reasons for people moving to the new capital, Brasília.
   c Explain the movement of people to the interior.

D

E

Trans-Amazonian Highway

from the poor North East

Brasília

from the core

Rio de Janeiro
São Paulo

→ Migration to Brasília
→ Migration to urban centres
→ Migration to the interior

0 500 1000 km

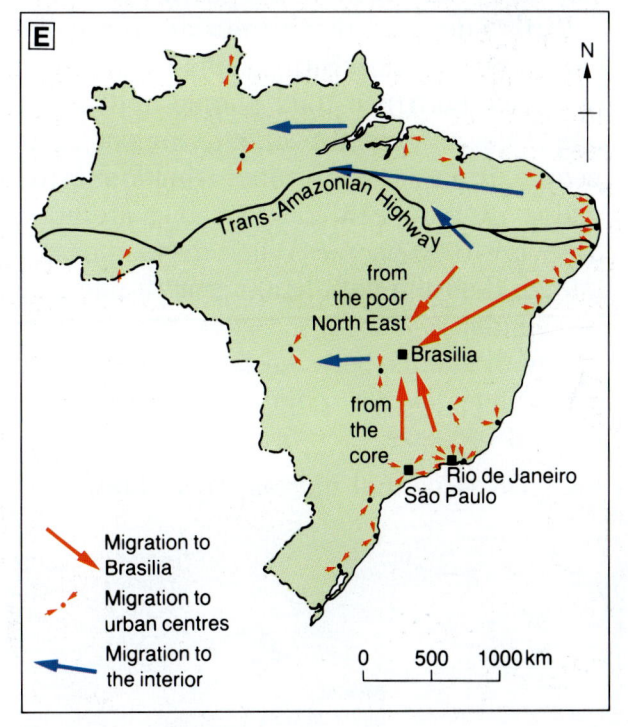

FURTHER WORK

● Choose another developing country and find a map of its population distribution in your atlas. Try to explain the population distribution in the country. (Link it with climate, vegetation and relief and the settlement patterns of Europeans and other settlers.) What other factors can affect the distribution of population in a country?

POPULATION AND SETTLEMENT

1.10 Population Change

The total population of any country constantly changes. There are two main reasons for this:

1 Natural population change
This depends on two factors:
- birth rate
- death rate

2 Change caused by movement of people
- immigration (moving into a country)
- emigration (moving away from a country)

This unit looks at **Natural population change**. You can find out about change caused by movement of people in Unit 1.12.

Birth rates and **death rates** are normally expressed as ratios. Birth rate is the number of babies born per 1000 people and death rate is the number of people dying per 1000 people. If we say the United Kingdom birth rate is 13, we mean that 13 babies are born for every 1000 people. When these rates are known then the population growth rate can be calculated.

The difference between the birth rate and death rate is the population change or **natural increase**.

BR − DR = natural increase (per 1000).

B
Families in Brazil are larger because:
More children mean... more hands to work for cash income and on the farms

...more help at home, especially with the elderly

...sons (sometimes daughters) to pass land and businesses on to.

Fewer reliable methods of family planning (contraception) are available. Brazil is a Roman Catholic country and the Church does not encourage contraception.

A gives population statistics for Brazil and the United Kingdom. Brazil has a higher birth rate than the United Kingdom. **B** gives some reasons for this. In the United Kingdom people do not want large families because their income is higher and there is a welfare state which looks after the sick and the very old. Children are not needed to work in the home or with relatives. Contraception is readily available.

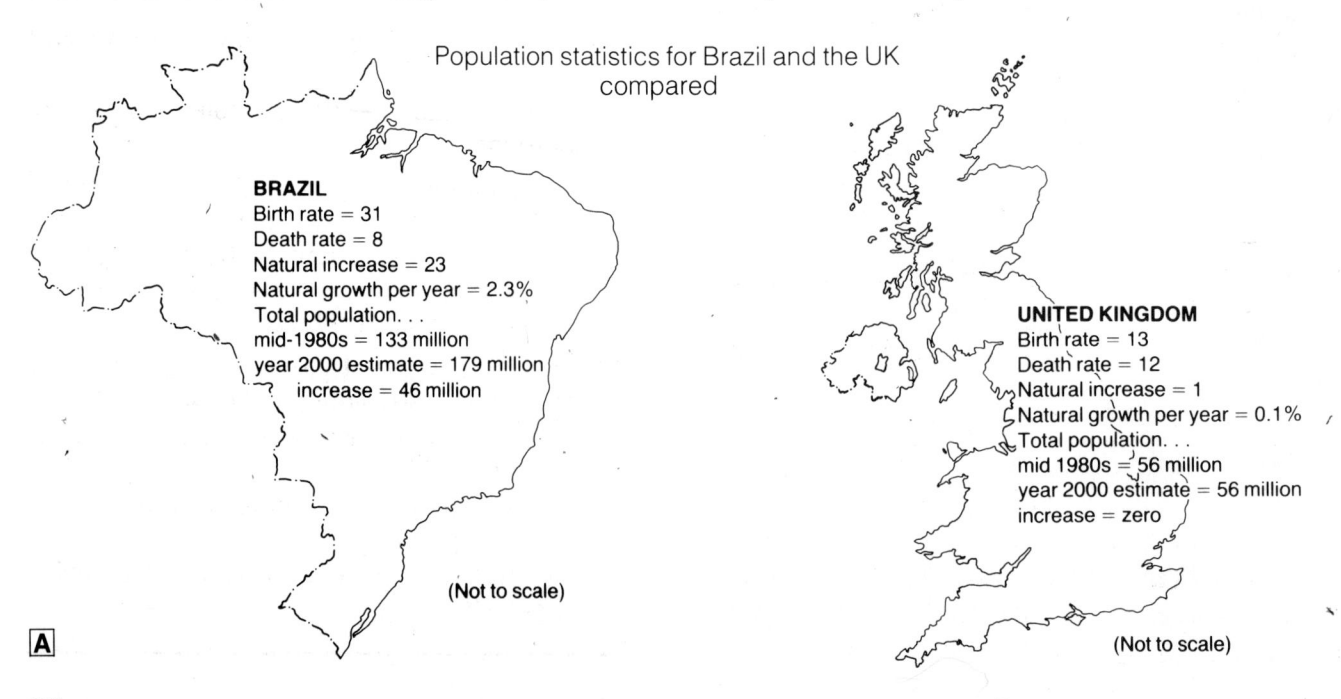

Population statistics for Brazil and the UK compared

BRAZIL
Birth rate = 31
Death rate = 8
Natural increase = 23
Natural growth per year = 2.3%
Total population...
mid-1980s = 133 million
year 2000 estimate = 179 million
increase = 46 million

(Not to scale)

UNITED KINGDOM
Birth rate = 13
Death rate = 12
Natural increase = 1
Natural growth per year = 0.1%
Total population...
mid 1980s = 56 million
year 2000 estimate = 56 million
increase = zero

(Not to scale)

A

Skills *Graph work*
Concepts *population change, birth/death rates*

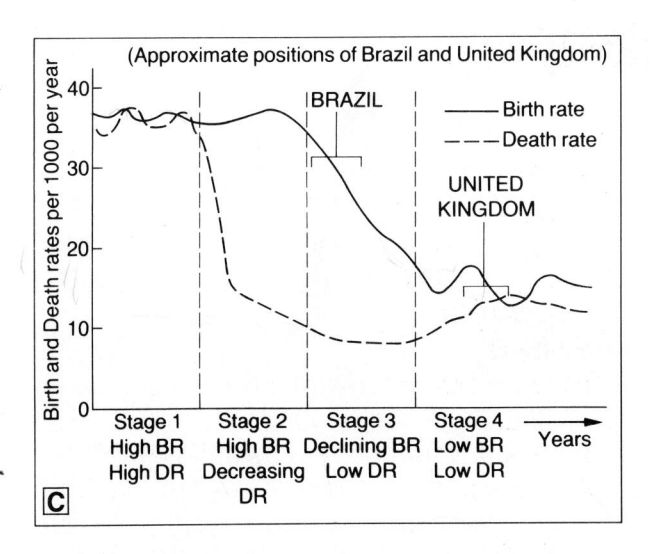

C (Approximate positions of Brazil and United Kingdom) — graph of Birth rate and Death rate per 1000 per year across Stage 1 (High BR, High DR), Stage 2 (High BR, Decreasing DR), Stage 3 (Declining BR, Low DR), Stage 4 (Low BR, Low DR). Brazil is positioned in Stage 3; United Kingdom in Stage 4.

Brazil's death rate is 8 per 1000. In the United Kingdom it is 12 per 1000. This does not mean that people live longer in Brazil; the population is younger so there are proportionately fewer old people. In the United Kingdom the death rate is slightly higher because there is a higher proportion of old people.

C shows the stages that the population of a country will go through. In a very undeveloped country the birth rate and the death rate are high. As the country develops the death rate falls but the birth rate remains high. At this time (Stage 2) there is a high natural increase. You can follow the next changes in birth rate and death rate on the graph. The changes are linked to the level of development of the country.

An Age-Sex pyramid exercise

Pyramid D shows the population of a developed country. It is really a double bar graph with two labelled axes. The vertical axis shows age groups; the horizontal axis shows either the total population or the percentage of the population. Age-sex pyramids contain evidence of the types of population change. They vary in shape, for example, the pyramid for a country with a high birth rate and a low death rate will have a wide base. This is because every year more children are born than in the previous year, so the base of the pyramid widens.

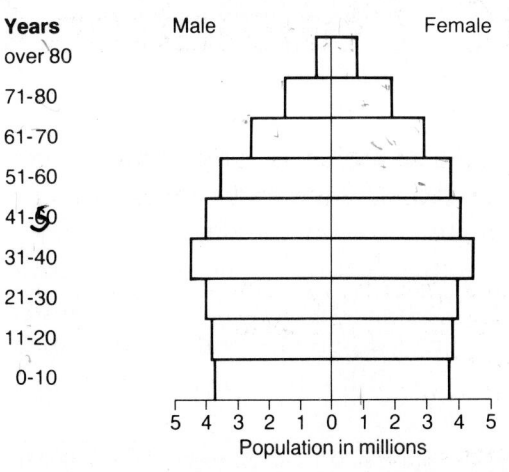

D Age-sex pyramid with age groups on vertical axis (0-10, 11-20, 21-30, 31-40, 41-50, 51-60, 61-70, 71-80, over 80) and Population in millions (0–5 each side) on horizontal axis.
Total males = 28 million Total females = 29.5 million
Total population = 57.5 million

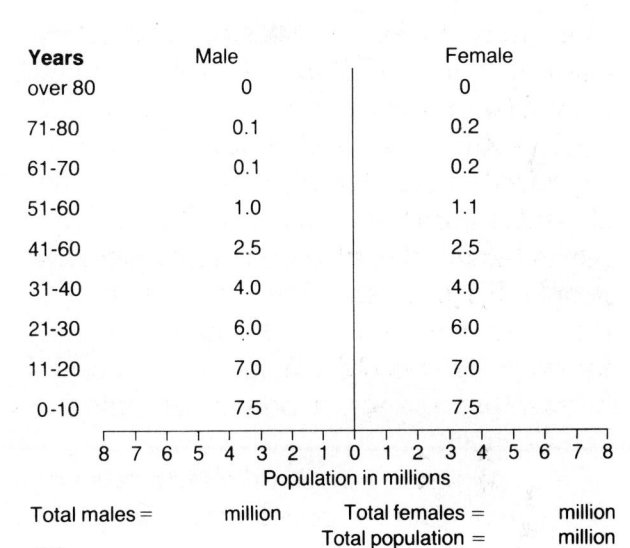

E

Years	Male	Female
over 80	0	0
71-80	0.1	0.2
61-70	0.1	0.2
51-60	1.0	1.1
41-60	2.5	2.5
31-40	4.0	4.0
21-30	6.0	6.0
11-20	7.0	7.0
0-10	7.5	7.5

Population in millions (scale 8 to 0 to 8)
Total males = ____ million Total females = ____ million
Total population = ____ million

---

1 In one sentence, state what you understand by:
● birth rate; ● death rate; ● natural increase.

2 Study all the details in **E** then use them to draw out the age-sex pyramid. Does the country it shows belong to the developed or developing world? (There is an outline of these questions in *Activity sheet 8*)

3 Use your developing world pyramid to answer the following questions:
a What evidence is there of a high population growth?
b What evidence is there of people not reaching old age?
c Is there any evidence that females outlive males?

POPULATION AND SETTLEMENT

1.11 Millionaire Cities

In Unit 1.8 you looked at the growth of cities in Brazil. Since 1800 the world's population has increased 30% but the number of people living in cities has increased 3000% in the same time. This has given rise to **Millionaire cities**: that is, settlements with a population of at least one million people.

1 What is a millionaire city?
2 a Study **A**. What was the first millionaire city?
  b Were the first three millionaire cities in the developed or developing world?
3 Study **B**.
  a How many millionaire cities were there in: 1860, 1940, 1960, 1980?
  b Present your answers as a bar graph.
  c How many millionaire cities are in Africa, Asia, Australasia, Europe, North America, South America?
4 Which cities have over six million people and are among the fastest growing in the world?
5 How many millionaire cities are there in the developing world? Is this more or less than in the developed world?

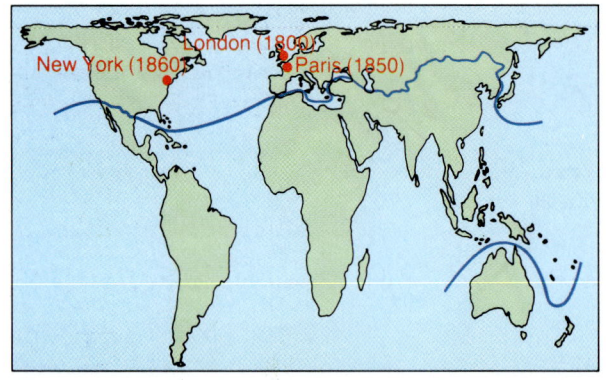

A The first millionaire cities

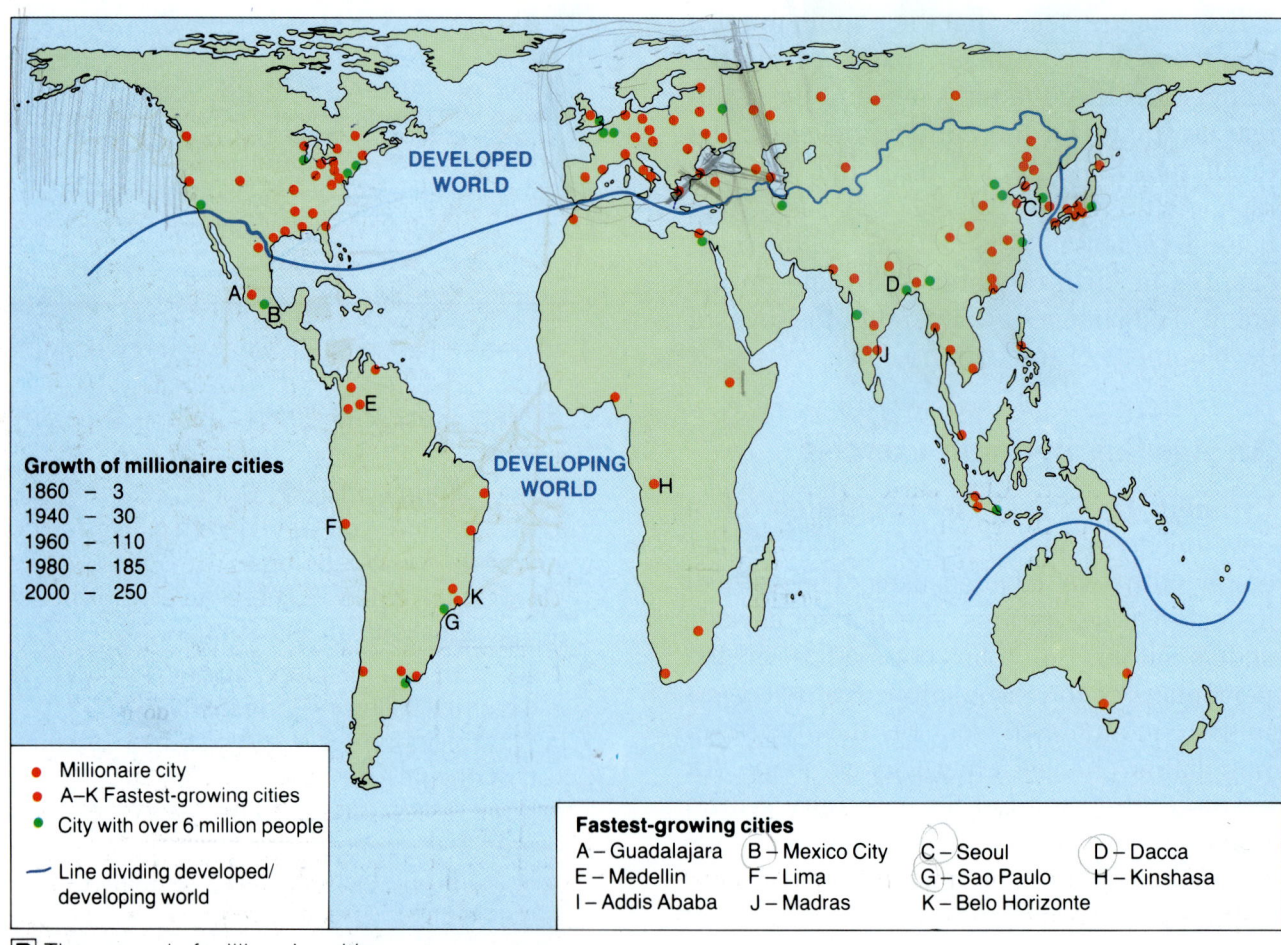

Growth of millionaire cities
1860 – 3
1940 – 30
1960 – 110
1980 – 185
2000 – 250

- Millionaire city
- A–K Fastest-growing cities
- City with over 6 million people
— Line dividing developed/developing world

Fastest-growing cities
A – Guadalajara B – Mexico City C – Seoul   D – Dacca
E – Medellin   F – Lima   G – Sao Paulo H – Kinshasa
I – Addis Ababa J – Madras   K – Belo Horizonte

B The spread of millionaire cities

Skills	map work, empathy
Concepts	millionaire cities, population growth
Issues	inner city problems

C

The future

By the year 2000 half the world's people will be living in cities. There are already problems in cities in the developed world. In Britain the government is trying to improve the **inner cities** where crime, unemployment, poor housing conditions and homelessness are problems. What will happen to cities in the developing world, where city growth is greatest?

A school pupil drew cartoon **C** to show the problems of living in a European city.

D describes what might happen in the fast growing cities of the developing world.

---

6 Look at **C** and **D**. Make a list of the problems faced by people in ● a European city ● a city in the developing world, in the future. Think about housing, jobs, overcrowding and services.

7 In what ways are the problems similar? How are they different?

As the sun beats down on this monster city of twenty five million people the homeless seek shelter. These are the unlucky ones. For the many who do have shelter home is in the 140 kilometre wide mass of smoky shanty town that surrounds the rich, powerful city centre. Many have no jobs. A cholera epidemic has swept the city but the victims are left to die for there is no medical help available. As in any other day, more hungry people from the countryside pour into the city hoping to make their life better, many will end up sleeping in doorways.

D

POPULATION AND SETTLEMENT

1.12 International Migration

Unit 1.10 looked at **natural population change**. Change in the total population of a country can also be the result of **international migration** (movement between countries):
- **migration** – people move into a country
- **emigration** – people move out of a country.

A summarises the ways in which a country's population can change.

B shows what can happen in one year to a **hypothetical** (imaginary) country with a population of 50 million.

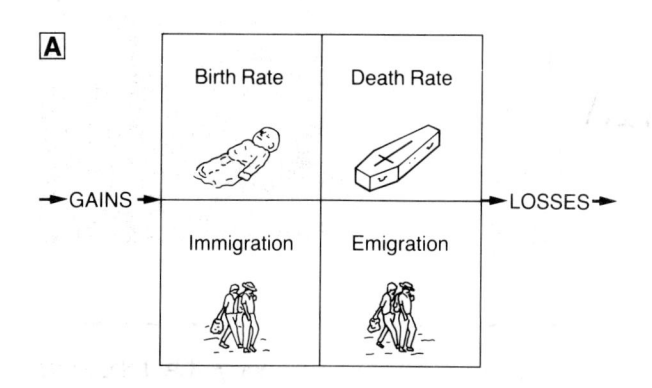

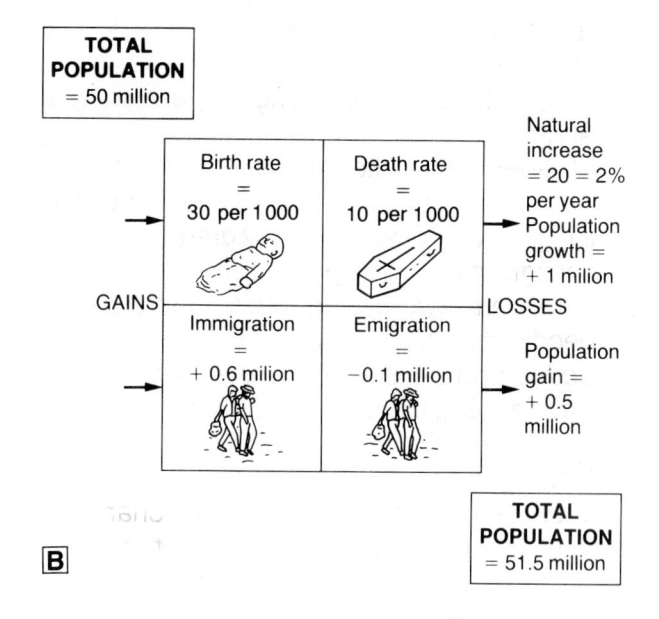

A

	Birth Rate	Death Rate	
→GAINS→			→LOSSES→
	Immigration	Emigration	

B

TOTAL POPULATION = 50 million

	Birth rate = 30 per 1000	Death rate = 10 per 1000	Natural increase = 20 = 2% per year Population growth = +1 million
GAINS			LOSSES
	Immigration = +0.6 million	Emigration = −0.1 million	Population gain = +0.5 million

TOTAL POPULATION = 51.5 million

The people of Brazil

If you walked along a street in the central business district of São Paulo (**C**) you would see a variety of different people.

They are part of the **multicultural** society that has grown up in the city of São Paulo.

If we look at the family histories of these people we begin to see how important international migration has been to Brazil.

Xali comes from an interior Indian tribe which has lived in the country for thousands of years. When the first **colonial** settlers arrived from Portugal in the 1500s the Indians were the only inhabitants.

Stan comes from a long-established Portuguese family. The early Portuguese brought black slaves from Africa to work on their sugar cane plantations.

Maria has descended from the old slave people who were brought to Brazil from Africa.

Julia is of mixed race; Portuguese and African people have inter-married in her family.

You can also meet recent **immigrants** in São Paulo. **Luigi** is an Italian who has come to work in the city. He had no job in his small Italian village.

Ellen is a divorced American woman who has come to be a doctor in a downtown hospital. She works for an American aid programme.

Some Brazilian emigrants

There are branches of Brazilian banks in London and there is a Brazilian embassy. Some Brazilian people have emigrated to Britain to work. At the Notting Hill Carnival held yearly in London, members of the Brazilian community parade their float through the streets, dancing the Samba and

Skills	group work, empathy
Concepts	migration/emigration, push and pull factors

C São Paulo

singing Brazilian songs. They wave their yellow and green flags bringing evidence of an immigrant community to the streets of London.

International migration can be explained by push and pull factors in the same way that migration to cities can be explained – see Unit 1.6.

	'Push' factor	'Pull' factor
Maria's ancestors	forced migration as slaves	Portuguese wanted labour for plantations
Stan's family	left Portugal because of poverty	new land and opportunity
Luigi	unemployment in Italy	promise of work, link up with family
Ellen	marriage break-up	working with the poor in São Paulo

1 In a group, list reasons why the following people emigrate from Brazil. Remember to list at least one push and one pull factor for each person.
Jimi, a Brazilian pop singer, goes to Los Angeles
Elisabeth, a solicitor, moves to London
Alfonso, a young man wanted by the Brazilian police, crosses into Paraguay (an illegal immigrant into Paraguay)

2 In the same way list reasons for the following people moving into Brazil.
Seth an American mining engineer
Bella an English nuclear scientist
Catherine a French aid worker

3 Make a summary chart listing reasons for international migration. Divide the chart into push and pull factors. Illustrate it with colourful arrows. Try to think of more reasons for international migration such as religious persecution, war, famine and medical reasons. There is an exercise based on this on Activity Sheet 10.

PEOPLE AND THE ENVIRONMENT

2.1 Natural Environments

Different parts of the world have different **climates**. **A** shows the variety of climates in the developing world. Where the climate is the same over a large area, geographers use the term **climatic region**. You can find details of climatic regions in your atlas.

Each climatic region has its own **natural vegetation**, for example, some regions have a lot of forest, others have mainly grassland or desert plants. (*Note* Trees or crops planted by people are not defined as natural vegetation.)

A The Developing World: Climate regions

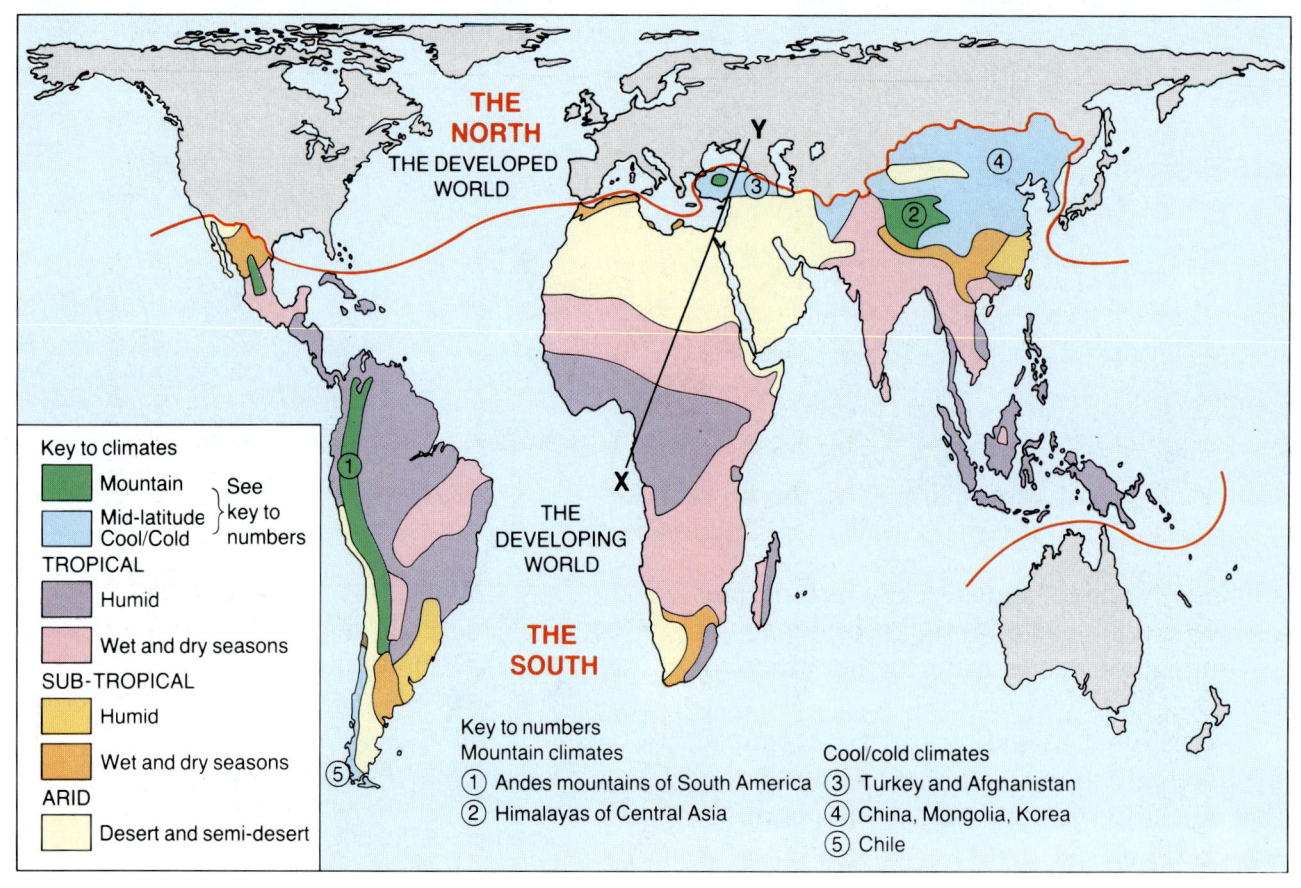

Key to climates
- Mountain } See key to numbers
- Mid-latitude Cool/Cold } See key to numbers

TROPICAL
- Humid
- Wet and dry seasons

SUB-TROPICAL
- Humid
- Wet and dry seasons

ARID
- Desert and semi-desert

Key to numbers
Mountain climates
① Andes mountains of South America
② Himalayas of Central Asia

Cool/cold climates
③ Turkey and Afghanistan
④ China, Mongolia, Korea
⑤ Chile

Cross-section **B** and the photographs show the main types of vegetation in the developing world.

1 Use **A**, **B** and your atlas.
   a Which African countries does the cross-section X – Y go through?
   b Which vegetation types does the cross-section go through?
2 Which countries in South America have the following types of climate:
   ● Tropical humid; ● Tropical wet and dry seasons; ● Arid desert; ● Mountain?

3 Draw up a table like the one below. Describe the type of natural vegetation shown in each photograph, and state how you think the natural vegetation in that region has affected people's lives.
(Use words such as: dense forest, sparse tree cover, no trees, bushes, grassland.)

Photograph	Type of vegetation	How it has affected people

32

Skills map work, cross section
Concepts climate, regions, vegetation

B

Natural vegetation	RAIN FOREST tall trees, continuous canopy	SAVANNA widely-spaced trees and grasses	DESERT shrubs and grasses — sometimes no vegetation	MEDITERRANEAN SCRUB small trees, evergreen shrubs	TEMPERATE DECIDUOUS FOREST trees lose leaves in autumn
Latitude	0° Equator		23½°N Tropic of Cancer		40°N
Countries	Gabon	Cameroon	Chad	Egypt	Lebanon	Turkey

Line of cross-section: X — Y

33

PEOPLE AND THE ENVIRONMENT
2.2 Brazil's Rain Forest

A shows an **ecosystem** – a set of links in the environment. These links can be described as energy flows between climate, vegetation, animals, people and soil. Ecosystems depend on the sun, which provides the energy plants need for **photosynthesis** (the process by which plants obtain nutrients from the air, soil and water).

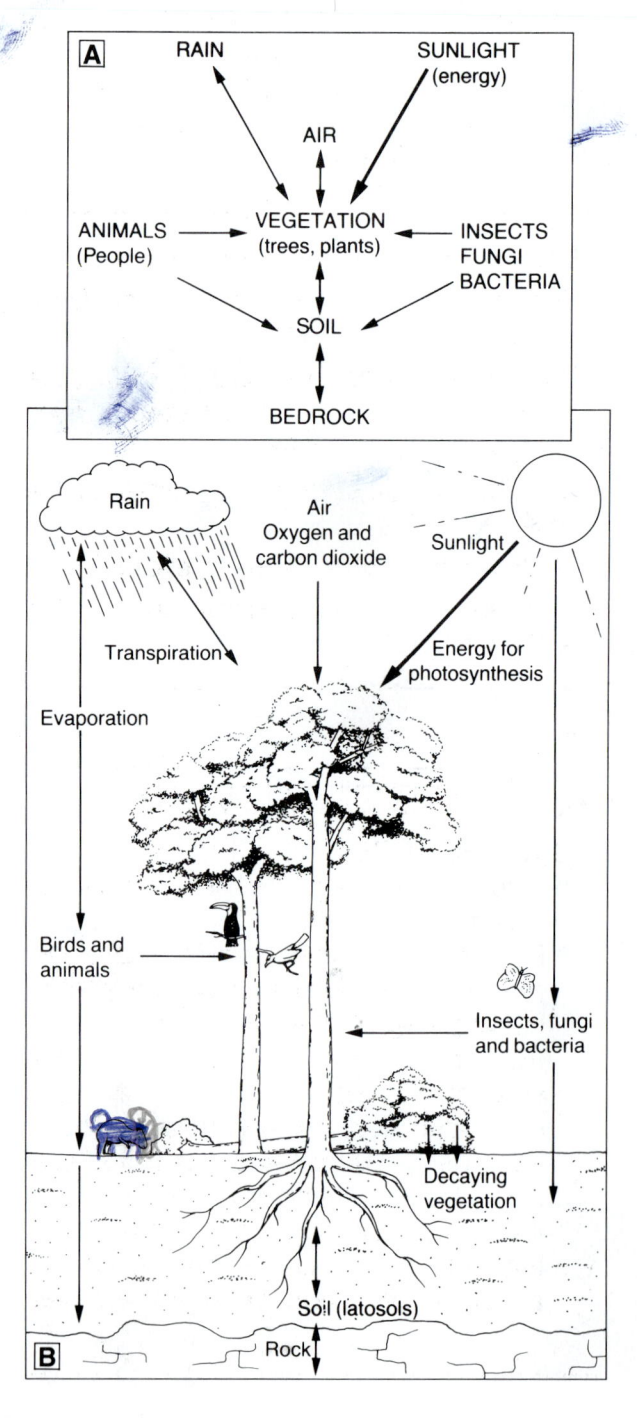

B shows the ecosystem of the rain forest, or **selva**. This dense forest (**C**) is the largest of its kind in the world. It spreads over the Amazon Basin, in Brazil (**D**). The climate of the region is constantly hot and humid; it has no distinct seasons.

Soil and bedrock play an important part in providing nutrients in most ecosystems. But this does not happen in the selva. The soils here are called **latosols**; this means that the minerals and nutrients have been washed (**leached**) out of them. Vegetation in the selva lives on the decaying mass of leaves, twigs, animals, plants and insects on the forest floor. This **organic material** is vital to the selva ecosystem. Without it, the land would not be fertile.

But the selva ecosystem is in danger. All over the world, 12 million hectares of forest (an area the size of England) are cleared each year. Most of this massive deforestation occurs in the tropics (**E**). The selva of the Amazon is severely threatened. **F** shows the effects of deforestation.

Deforestation in the selva

Why are the forests in danger? The Brazilians use raw material from the forest to

Skills	debating, writing report
Concepts	ecosystem, rain forest
Issues	deforestation

manufacture products for export. Brazil is deeply in debt. Export earnings help the country to pay off its huge loans. People chop down the trees in order to:

- clear land for crops and vast cattle ranches
- use the wood for fuel
- use the hardwoods for furniture making
- make pulp and paper from the wood
- clear land for highway building
- make way for mineral mining

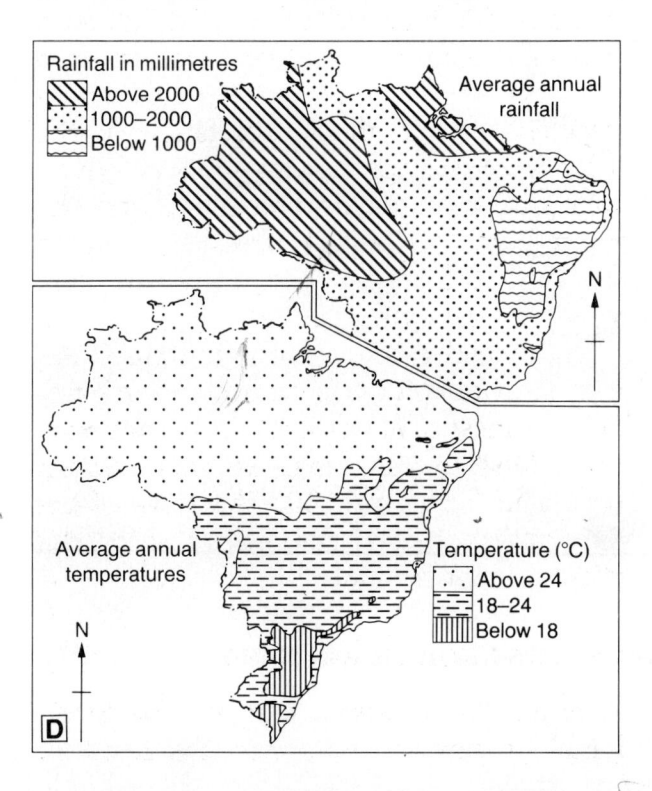

Severe soil erosion	– soils are easily washed away
Severe soil exhaustion	– minerals and nutrients are quickly washed out (leached)
Rainfall decreases	– less water in the ecosystem
Oxygen decreases	– fewer trees produce less oxygen
Carbon dioxide increases	– clearance by burning releases carbon dioxide into the atmosphere

F The effects of deforestation

1. Describe how an ecosystem like **A** works.
2. Study **B**. Describe how the tropical rain forest ecosystem works.
3. Describe the selva forest shown in **C**. (Use words and phrases such as tall trees, canopy layer, dense forest, luxuriant.)
4. Describe the temperature and rainfall in the forest region (**D**).
5. Why is the Brazilian forest being cleared?
6. What are the effects of deforestation in the Amazon region?

FURTHER WORK

- SAVE THE FOREST

  a Discuss in a group how the selva can be saved.

  b Prepare a document which you could present to the Brazilian government suggesting ways of saving the selva.
  (Remember, the responsibility for the survival of the forest lies with the developed world which demands cheap food, beef, minerals and wood products. It is also the developed countries that invest in developments in the forest region.) Some conflicting viewpoints about the forest appear on Activity Sheet 13.

PEOPLE AND THE ENVIRONMENT
2.3 West Africa's Savanna

A

Photograph **A** shows one of the world's most beautiful environments. Rolling plains of grassland stretch to the horizon, dotted with trees and shrubs. This open parkland is called **savanna**. Savanna stretches right across West Africa (**B**). To the south lies tropical rain forest (see Unit 2.2). To the north lie the wastes of the Sahara Desert.

The climate of the savanna has two seasons: a hot, wet season and a hot, dry season (**C**).

The vegetation of the savanna varies depending upon the total rainfall and the length of the dry season. The southernmost savanna, closest to the rain forest, has many trees and tall grasses. This area is called the Guinea Savanna. There are fewer trees further north. Nearer to the Sahara Desert

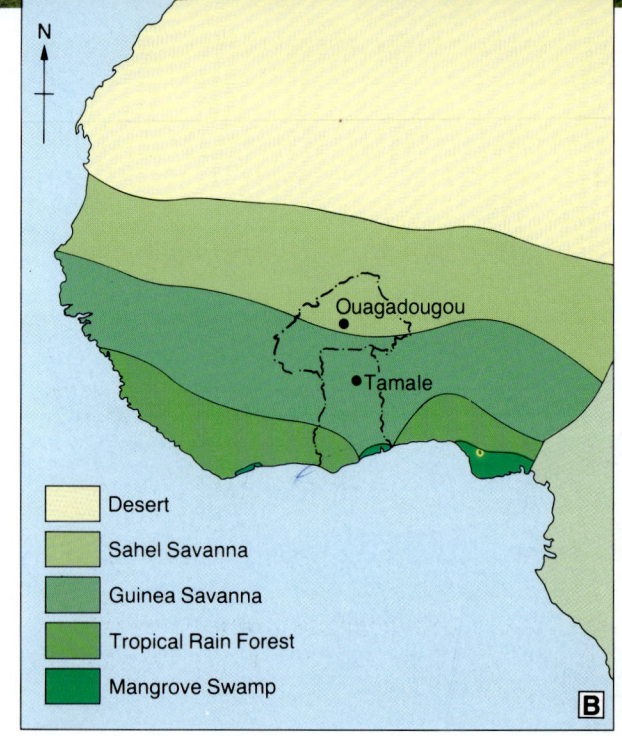

Desert
Sahel Savanna
Guinea Savanna
Tropical Rain Forest
Mangrove Swamp

B

Skills	interpreting graph
Concepts	savanna, seasonal change
Issues	people's effect on environment

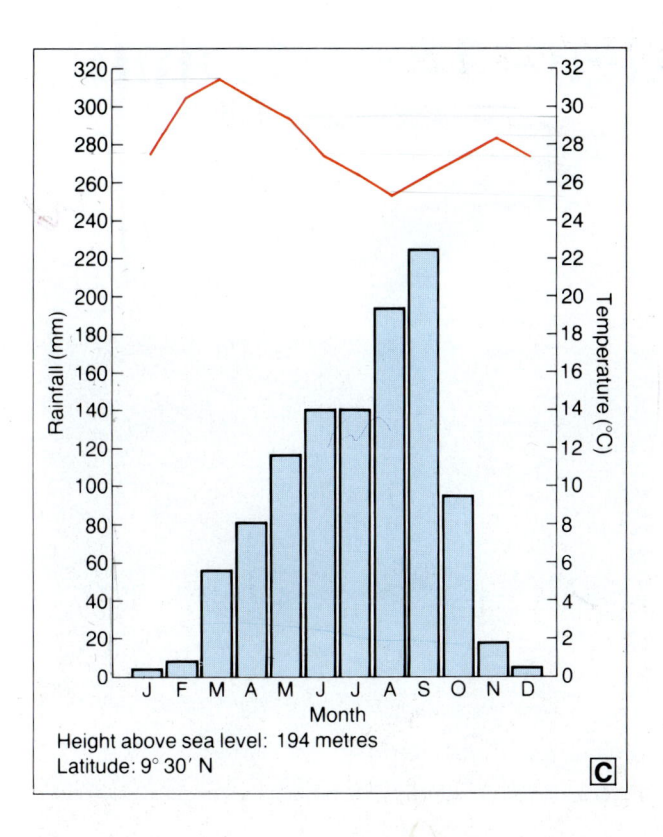

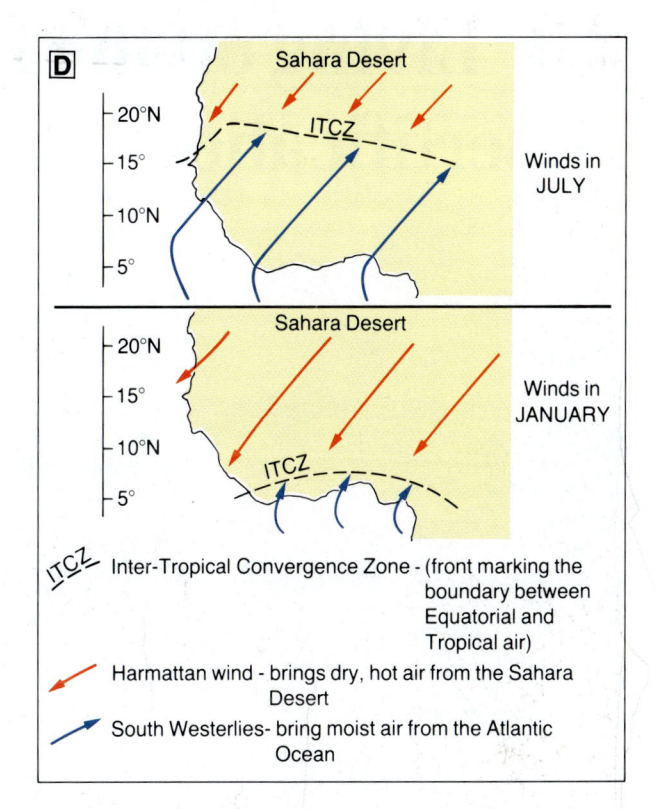

C Climate graph for Tamale, Northern Ghana
Height above sea level: 194 metres
Latitude: 9° 30' N

D Winds in JULY and JANUARY over West Africa

ITCZ — Inter-Tropical Convergence Zone - (front marking the boundary between Equatorial and Tropical air)

Harmattan wind - brings dry, hot air from the Sahara Desert

South Westerlies - bring moist air from the Atlantic Ocean

there are no trees, just thorny bushes such as the acacia and short, tussocky grass. The most northerly savanna area in West Africa is called the Sahel.

What causes the pronounced wet and dry seasons in the savanna lands? The answer is the wind direction. During the wet season the winds blow from the south west across the savanna. These winds come from the Atlantic Ocean and carry plenty of moisture. During the dry season the winds blow from the north east across the savanna. These winds come from the Sahara Desert. They carry little moisture, but plenty of sand and dust. The changing wind direction is due to the movement of atmospheric belts (**D**).

People have affected the West African savanna in many ways. Even the type of vegetation in the area may be the result of peoples' actions. Some geographers think that the grassland has developed because of repeated burning of woodland for farming.

1 **C** shows the climate of Tamale in Northern Ghana.
   a Name the six months of the hot, wet season.
   b Name the six months of the hot, dry season.
   c Name the wettest month, and give its total rainfall.
   d Name the driest month, and give its total rainfall.
   e Ghana is in the northern hemisphere. Why does the temperature fall between March and August?
   f Which is the correct figure for the total rainfall of Tamale:
      ● 750mm   ● 1100mm   ● 1400mm
      ● 1700mm?
   g What is the **temperature range** (the difference between the coolest and the hottest month)?

2 How do you think the savanna vegetation around Tamale differs from that further north around Ouagadougou?

3 What is the Sahel?

4 How may people have affected the vegetation in the savanna areas of West Africa?

5 Use **D** to help you explain why the savanna climate has such clear wet and dry seasons.

PEOPLE AND THE ENVIRONMENT

2.4 Living on the Edge – Deserts and Desertification

What does the word 'desert' make you think of? Sand? Camels? Heat? Photograph **A** probably represents your idea of a desert. But not all deserts are like this. Look at **B**.

Geographers define **deserts** and **semi-deserts** according to their rainfall and temperature. A desert has rainfall of less than 250mm a year, and temperature ranges between 50°C in the day and 0°C (freezing) at night. Semi-desert has a little more rain and slightly lower daytime temperatures.

Both deserts and semi-deserts have a wide range of **diurnal** (daily) temperatures and are very **arid** (dry). Because of this dryness and the **extremes** of temperature (from very hot to very cold), most living things find it difficult to survive in desert areas.

---

1 In your own words, explain how geographers define deserts and semi-deserts.
2 Describe what you can see in photograph **B**. Use about 100 words.
3 What do you understand by the words 'diurnal' and 'arid'?
4 Why are deserts hostile places for most living things?

Desertification

C shows areas of the world that are desert. Desert covers about 30% of the world's surface.

Around 700 million people live in desert regions. Most live in rural areas and support themselves by keeping livestock like cattle, goats and sheep. These animals can **overgraze** the land (eat away all the natural vegetation). In times of drought, overgrazing is a very serious problem. Natural vegetation protects the soil. The roots of trees and plants bind the soil together. When no trees, shrubs, bushes or grass are left, the soil is **eroded** by sudden, heavy rainfall, or by winds blowing it away. Overgrazing leads to erosion; the next stage can be desert. This process is called **desertification**.

As well as letting their animals overgraze the soil, there are other ways in which people can help cause desertification:

- cutting down trees for firewood
- clearing land for growing crops
- using poorly-designed irrigation
- overcultivation (often in an attempt to provide food for a growing population)

Skills	interpreting photographs, mapwork
Concepts	desert, climate
Issues	desertification

D shows the areas threatened by desertification. 250 million people live in these threatened areas.

---

5 a In your own words, describe what leads to overgrazing.
  b Describe the effects of overgrazing.
6 Draw up a keyword plan to show the causes of desertification.

What can be done?

There are no easy answers to the problem of advancing deserts. It is very difficult to change natural desert to productive soil, without using expensive irrigation projects (see Unit 2.5). In the semi-desert lands, people have stopped the advancing desert by simple measures like planting trees, bushes and other vegetation. These bind the soil, stop erosion and provide a barrier against the wind.

Trees also help to store water. In large numbers they can increase the moisture (humidity) in the atmosphere – which helps create the right conditions for rainfall. They also provide much-needed shade for people and animals. Mature trees provide fuel, fodder for animals and building materials. But they must be cared for while they are growing. It is difficult to change people's ways and stop them grazing their animals near the young trees, or cutting them down. People need educating in how to manage their land.

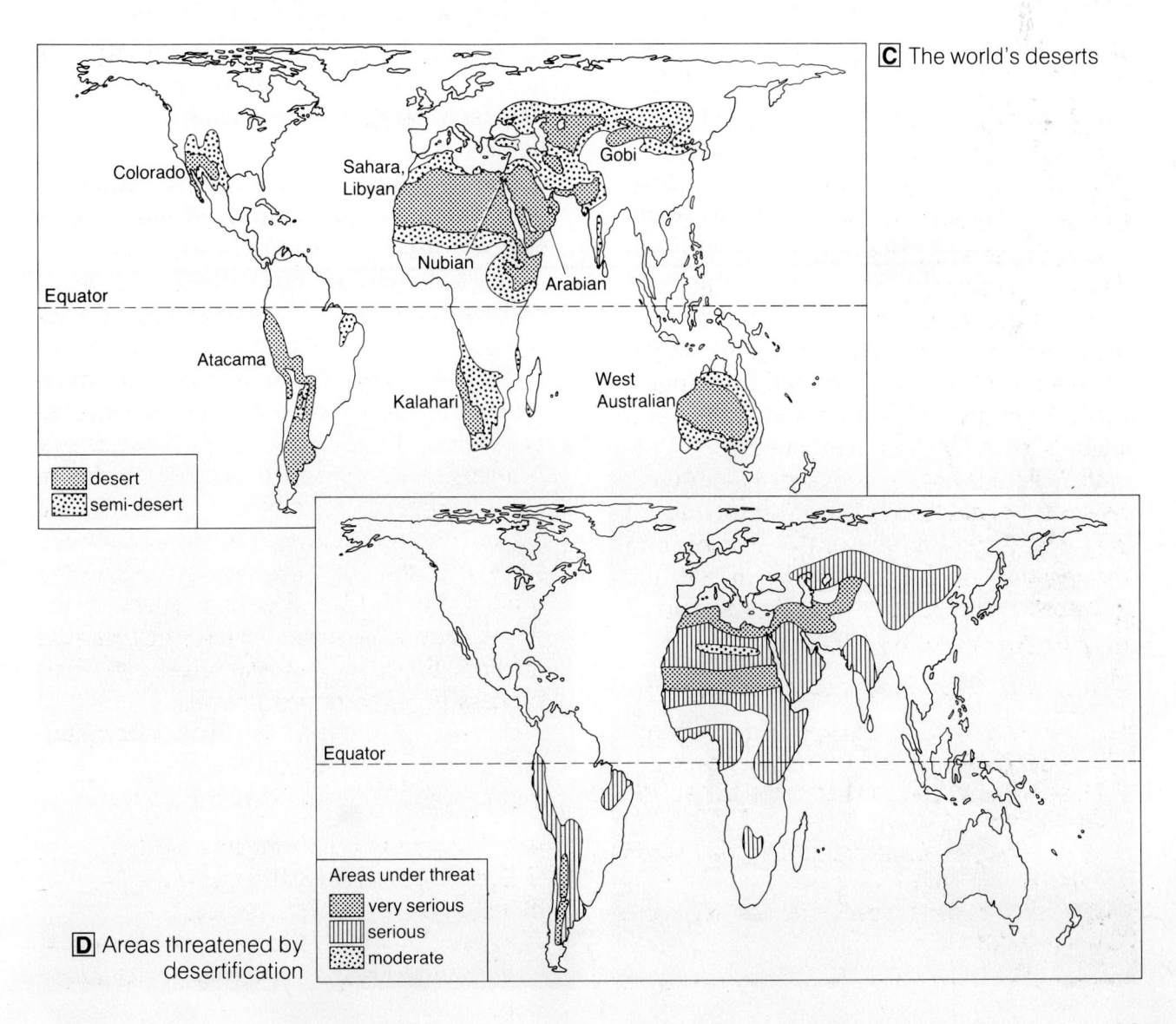

C The world's deserts

D Areas threatened by desertification

PEOPLE AND THE ENVIRONMENT

2.5 Irrigation

Farming in North Africa is difficult because of the hostile environment. Farmers cannot always get enough water for their crops. In some places, where the land is dry and rainfall is unreliable, people **irrigate** the land. This means they use artificial methods to control, store, raise and distribute water over the land. People in Egypt have irrigated their land for thousands of years.

12% of the world's cultivated land is irrigated. Farmers can often grow two crops a year on this land, and it produces 20% of the world's harvest.

The scale of irrigation varies. Small-scale, simple methods like the **shadouf** and the **sarkia** (**A**) are used to move water to the fields in remote areas. Such schemes are often set up by local people, working together and using what is around them.

B shows a large-scale irrigation project. The river has been **dammed** to create a large lake which holds water for irrigation. Developing countries often need help from developed countries for such large-scale projects – in the form of heavy machinery, and loans to pay for building and operating the dam.

1 What do you understand by the term irrigation?
2 Why do people need to irrigate the land?
3 Explain the differences between the irrigation systems shown in **A** and **B**.

The Gezira

One of the biggest **rural development schemes** in Africa is an irrigation scheme in an area of Sudan called the Gezira (**C**). The scheme started in 1925 when the **Sennar Dam** was completed. The **barrage** (dam) blocks the Blue Nile. **Sluice gates** control the flow of water through the dam into the main canal that takes the water to where it is needed. A small network of smaller channels feeds water from the main canal to the fields.

The soil of the Gezira is **impervious clay** (soil which does not let water through). This clay was used to line the irrigation channels; it was much cheaper than expensive imported concrete. The land of the Gezira slopes gently away from the river and the main canals, so the irrigation water runs

Skills	identifying problems
Concepts	irrigation, rural development, cash crops
Issues	small scale versus large scale

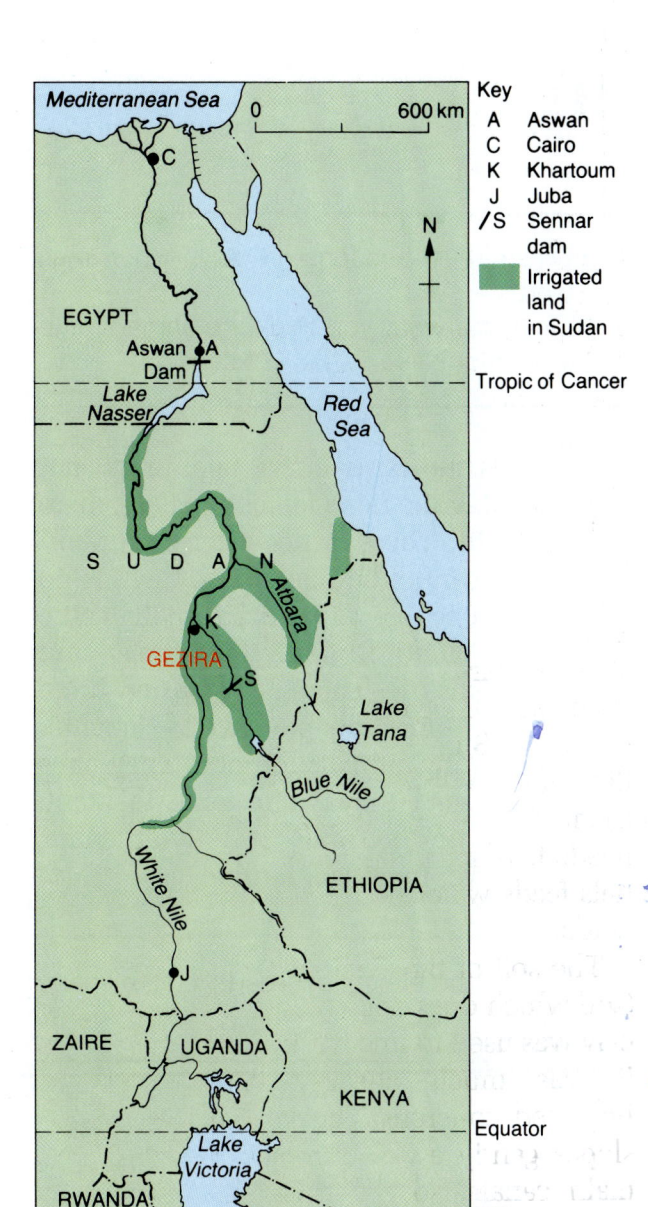

from the main canals to the fields without having to be pumped. The flow of water is controlled by sluice gates. This method of irrigation is called a **gravity flow system**.

Most farmers on the Gezira scheme are **tenants** who rent small plots of land from the Sudan Gezira Board. Inspectors and **cooperatives** (small groups of farmers) control the flow of water, distribute seed, fertiliser and pesticides, and organise the collection and sale of the **cash crop** (a crop which is mainly grown for export).

The main cash crop grown on the Gezira is cotton. This is sold and exported to other countries. Food crops are also grown. They include wheat, lubia beans, sorghum and vegetables.

The Gezira scheme was the first big project in Sudan for **agricultural development**. Over the years, it has expanded. It is a model for other schemes in the Sudan and elsewhere.

This unit has looked at the importance of irrigation for watering crops. Irrigation schemes also help **control** the flow of water in periods of heavy rainfall. Unfortunately, the dams and sluices cannot always cope. In August 1988 exceptionally heavy rains caused the White and Blue Niles to burst their banks. Khartoum (the capital of Sudan) and the Gezira area were flooded. In the short-term, people faced homelessness and disease. No-one yet knows the long-term consequences for Sudan.

4 What is the Gezira Scheme?
5 Why are pumps and expensive concrete-lined channels not needed?
6 How is use of the land organised?
7 Why was this scheme an important **agricultural development** for Sudan?

FURTHER WORK

- What problems could the scheme have caused for the nomads living in the area now flooded by the lake created by the Sennar Dam?
- What do you think might be the problems for a developing nation borrowing huge sums of money to build large irrigation schemes?

PEOPLE AND THE ENVIRONMENT

2.6 Where is the Rain?

Drought in Africa

In the semi-desert lands south of the Sahara most of the country looks like **A** during the **dry season**. The people wait for the rains to come – bringing water for their crops and their animals, and refilling the wells with drinking water. The rains usually come in April, and the **wet season** lasts until October (see Unit 2.3).

1 a Describe the scene in **A** in your own words.
 b Describe what you think the same scene would look like in the wet season.

Sometimes the rains arrive late, or do not come at all. If the rains fail completely, there is a **drought**. There is no water to support life. Crops cannot be planted, so there is no food for the people. Livestock (usually cattle and goats) cannot find any food to eat, and many animals die. There is a **disaster**. If the drought continues, people have to slaughter their remaining animals for food. They have to eat the seed they were going to plant. Eventually, if the rains still don't come, people starve; there is a **famine**.

2 Describe the effects of drought on the scene in **A**.

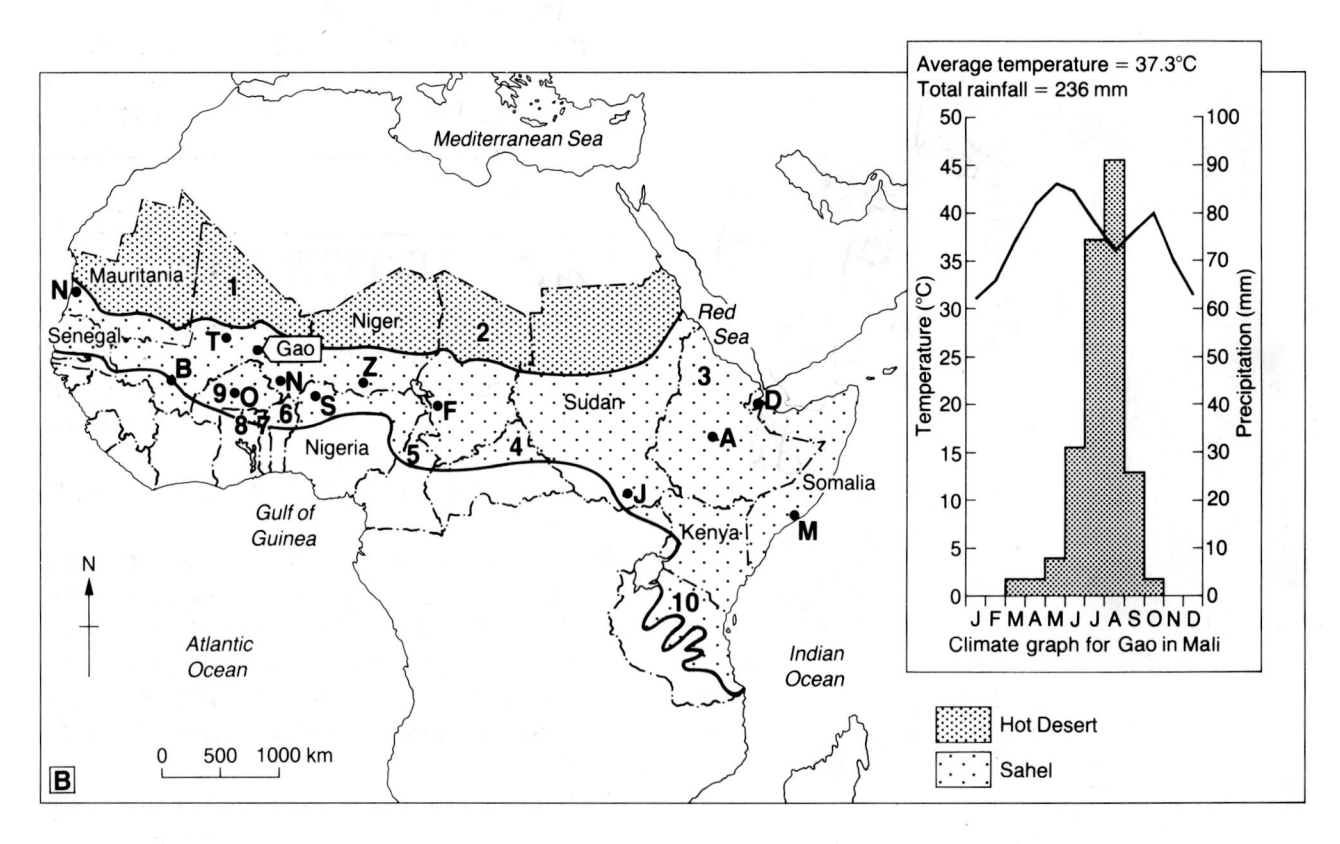

42

Skills	describing from photographs, empathy
Concepts	drought, seasons, famine
Issues	natural disaster

The semi-desert lands south of the Sahara are called the **Sahel** (**B**).

---

3 On a copy of map **B**
  a Use an atlas to help you name countries 1–9.
  b Name the cities located with a dot (the first letter of each name is given, to help you).
  c Name all the countries in the Sahel.
4 Look at the climate graph in **B**.
  a How many months have no rainfall in Gao?
  b What is the total rainfall?
  c What is the average monthly temperature?
  d When would people expect to grow crops?

Drought!

Between 1968 and 1974 there was a drought in the Sahel district of Ethiopia. The drought killed 250 thousand people and 20 million cattle, sheep and goats. Many people were forced to leave the Sahel region and head south to seek help in the nearest towns and cities. The rains failed again in 1980 and 1984 (**C**). Between 1984 and 1986 a further two million people died from drought in the Sahel.

Local people can do very little to avoid this type of disaster. The situation is caused partly by failure of the rains and partly by the action of people – for example, overgrazing (see Unit 2.4) and growing cash crops for export, rather than food crops (cash crops usually occupy the best, most fertile land). In Ethiopia the problems are made worse by **civil war**; rival groups attack relief lorries or prevent supplies of food getting through to the people who need it.

The government of a developing country may ask for help from aid agencies or foreign governments. Help for the countries of the Sahel includes long-term measures to combat drought, including:
● digging new wells
● irrigation projects
● growing more food and less cash crops

---

5 Look at **C**. Why are the two aid agencies appealing for help?
6 a Apart from money, how else do you think the developed world could help people in the drought areas?
  b What projects could Sahel governments set up to avoid their people waiting and asking 'Where is the rain?' each year?

FURTHER WORK

● Imagine you are a farmer living in the Sahel. Describe your feelings as you wait and hope for the rain. You have experienced drought before. You know it will happen again if the rain fails. You could present your answer in the form of a diary kept by the farmer.
● Ask members of your family, or your teachers, about their memories of the 1976 drought in Britain. Go to your local library to find out more about what happened. How was the effect of the drought in Britain different from the effect of drought in the Sahel?

PEOPLE AND THE ENVIRONMENT

2.7 Earthquake!

'There had been earthquakes before. We live with them. We're used to them. But this was different. It was dark, I heard what sounded like a clap of thunder rolling down the valley. There was a tremendous noise and the earth shook and heaved. It felt as if the earth was turning to water: waves surged through the ground. My house groaned and creaked. It was difficult to stand. I made a dash for the door. These were moments of madness. My house was collapsing around me. I can remember the sound of someone screaming, grating in my ears. It took me some time to realise that the screams were my own.'

A

On 5 March 1987, a series of earthquakes struck northern Ecuador, in South America. The worst hit areas were in the mountains east of Quito, the capital city. Over 2000 people died and 75 000 lost their homes. The earthquakes triggered off mudflows which cascaded down the river valleys, sweeping away bridges, roads, buildings, even complete villages.

The disaster area was cut off from the outside world by the destruction of roads and bridges. This made rescue operations very difficult. Farmers lost the access to markets which they depended upon for their livelihood. A vital pipeline carrying oil from the Lago Agrio oil field to the coast was shattered by the earthquake. Oil polluted the rivers and killed the fish on which the native Indians depended. The oil was Ecuador's main export and the economy of the whole country suffered a serious blow. The total cost of the earthquakes was over $1000 million: a crippling sum for a country which was already heavily in debt to banks in the developed countries.

The survivors of the earthquakes needed help immediately. Many had lost everything; they desperately needed blankets, tents, food and water. The victims camped

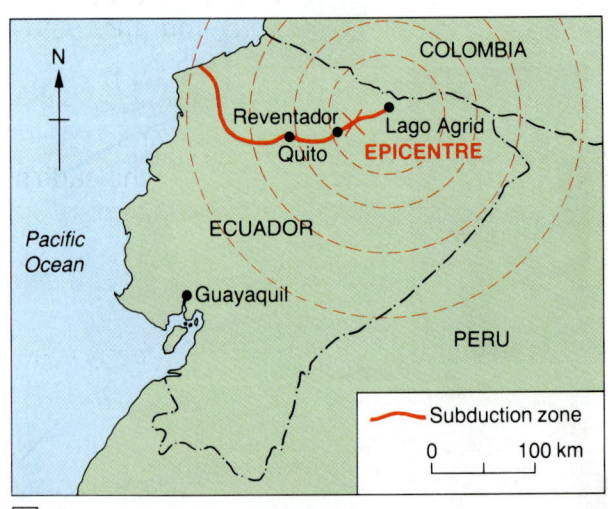

B The centre of the earthquake

Skills	writing report
Concepts	earthquake, volcanic activity
Issues	natural disaster

out in overcrowded, unhygienic conditions; water supplies were infected and diseases spread rapidly. The destruction of the roads meant that only aircraft could reach the area. Helicopters brought supplies, but they did not always reach the people who needed help most. Work on rebuilding the roads began, but it was a long, slow process.

What caused the earthquake? Ecuador lies above a **subduction zone** (**B, C**). This is where great earth movements occur. Each movement is an earthquake. Shock waves pass through the earth from the **focus**, the point where the earthquake started. The point on the surface above the focus is called the **epicentre**.

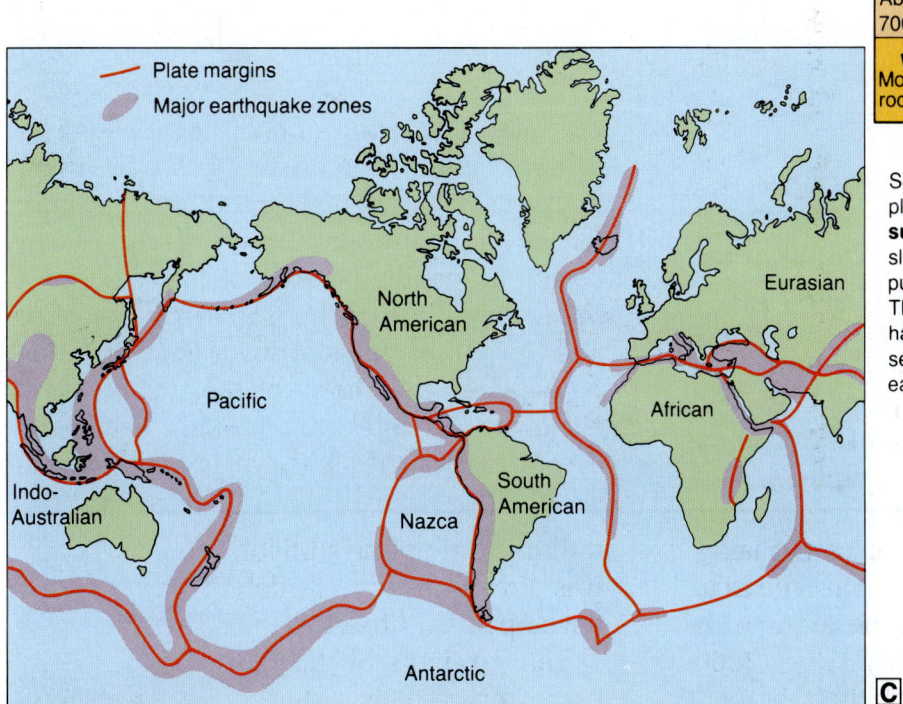

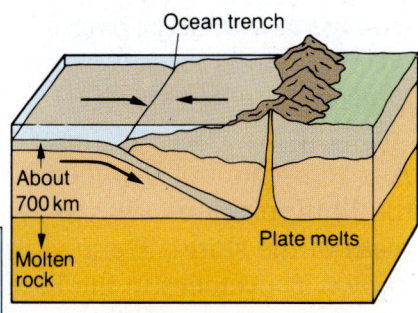

Scientists have discovered that the earth's crust is divided up into a number of different sections called **plates**. The plates move slowly across the surface of the planet. Earthquakes happen at the **margins** (edges) of the plates.

A Subduction Zone

Some plates slide past one another. Some plates move apart. Some plates collide. A **subduction zone** occurs where one plate slides beneath another. The sea floor is pulled down to create a deep ocean trench. The movements are not continuous. They happen in a series of jerks which may be separated by many years. Each jerk is an earthquake.

1 Copy and complete the following sentences choosing the correct word from the wordbank below

  a The .... of an earthquake is the point where the earthquake starts.
  b Scientists have discovered that the earth's .... is divided up into a number of different sections called ....
  c The epicentre is the point on the .... above the focus.
  d Where one crustal plate slides beneath another a .... zone occurs.

  Wordbank: surface subduction epicentre focus plate earthquake crust

2 What caused the Ecuador earthquake?
3 What dangers face survivors in the days following an earthquake?
4 You are a reporter for a television company. On 8 March 1987 you are flown into the earthquake area in Ecuador. You have to prepare a five-minute report for the television news.
  a Work out ten scenes to film and write the script to go with them. Try to make your report informative and interesting. For example, will you include any aerial views, diagrams or interviews?
  b If possible, record your commentary using a cassette recorder or a video camera.

45

PEOPLE AND THE ENVIRONMENT

2.8 Typhoons and hurricanes

On 16 October 1987 a strong storm hit southern England. The English newspapers called it a hurricane, but wind speeds only reached above 120 km per hour in short gusts. 18 people died and there was much damage to buildings; over four million trees were blown down. It was the worst storm in England for over 280 years. Yet in the tropics such a storm would be thought unimportant. **A** is an account of Typhoon Nina, which hit the Philippines in 1987. **B** shows the aftermath of the storm. These violent storms are known as **cyclones** in the Indian Ocean and **hurricanes** in the Caribbean.

One of the strongest hurricanes this century in the western hemisphere was Hurricane Gilbert in 1988. It started in the Eastern Caribbean and swept across Cuba, Jamaica and part of Mexico (**C**). Wind speeds reached 175 km per hour, and the hurricane caused widespread destruction. Over 250 people died and many more lost their homes.

What causes typhoons? A typhoon is a swirling mass of air about 300 km across (**D**). The air over tropical seas becomes very warm and starts to rise. As it does so it sucks up water. The rising air cools and condenses to form clouds which can reach over 15km high. Air rushes at high speed into the space left by the rising air currents. The typhoon begins to revolve because of the rotation of the earth. Winds of up to 250 km per hour and torrential rainstorms accompany the typhoon. In the centre of the typhoon is a small area of calm, dry weather called the **eye** of the storm. The eye is caused by a strong downdraught of air.

Why do tropical storms kill so many more people than storms in developed countries? Northern Australia and the southern USA

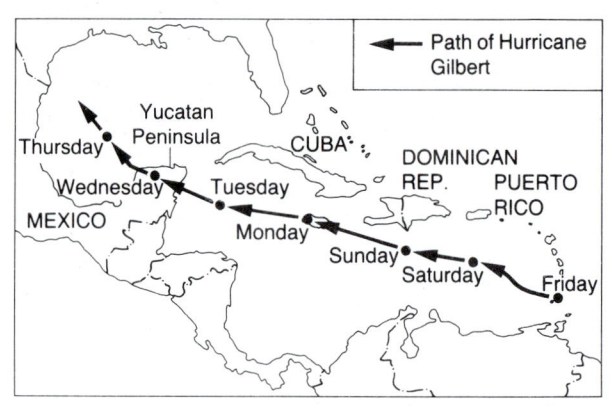

C The path of Hurricane Gilbert

TYPHOON NINA KILLS AT LEAST 380 PEOPLE

MANILA, PHILIPPINES (Reuter) – the death toll from a typhoon that tore through the central Philippines reached 380 yesterday, a military commander said.

Brigadier-General San Andres said that more than 100,000 people had been made homeless when Typhoon Nina lashed the Bicol region on Wednesday with winds of over 200 km per hour. Many of the casualties were in coastal areas smashed by giant waves.

Rescue workers battled through flooded areas yesterday, searching for survivors in deserted villages, damaged rice fields and coconut plantations.

President Aquino declared a State of Calamity in eleven provinces in the central part of the country. Nina was the 15th typhoon to hit the Philippines this year.

(Based on an article in The Independent newspaper 28.11.87)   **A**

Skills	interpreting diagrams
Concepts	hurricane/typhoon
Issues	natural disaster

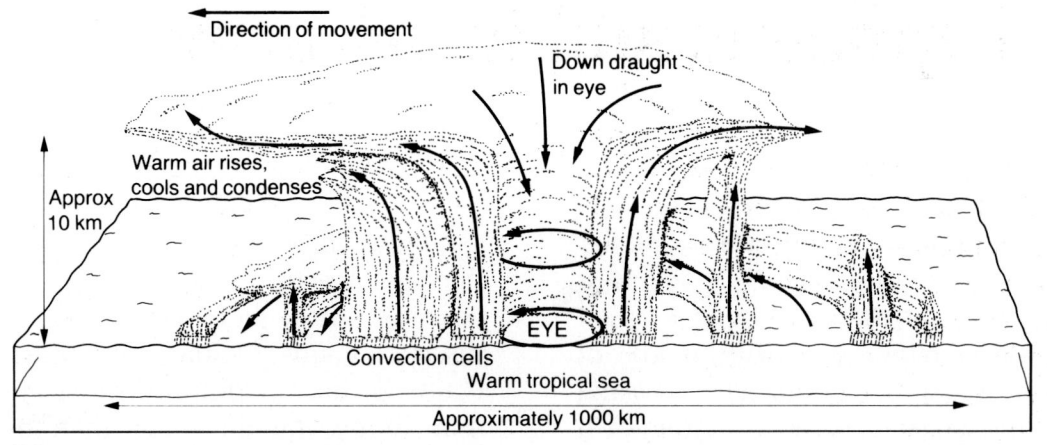

D Cross-section of a typhoon

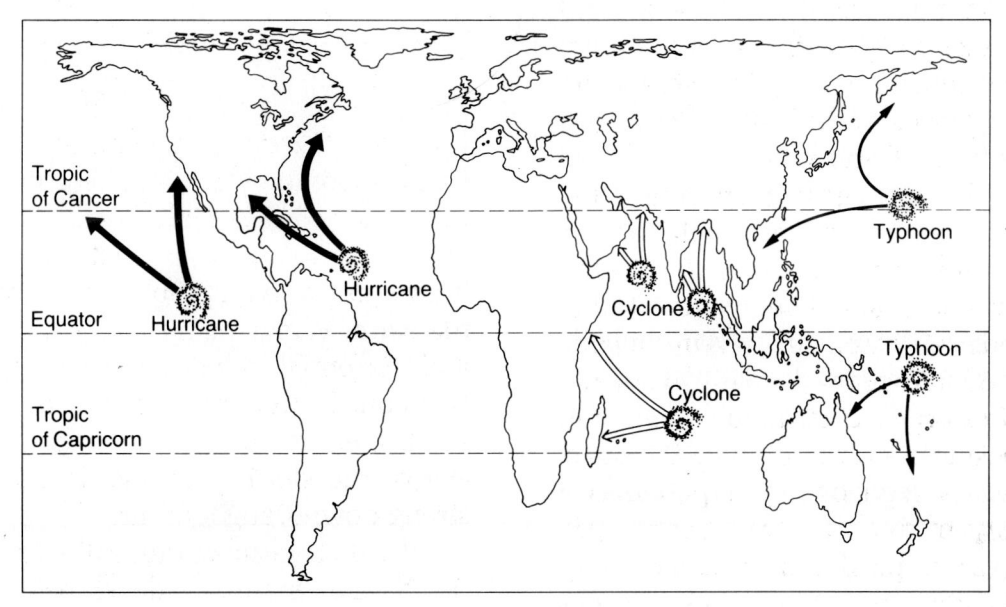

E Source areas of tropical storms

suffer from tropical storms, but far fewer people die in developed countries than in developing countries. One reason is that there are better warning systems in developed countries: satellites monitor the tracks of storms, television and radio channels broadcast warnings. A second reason is that buildings tend to be better built and able to withstand strong winds. Better road and rail networks also make it easier for people to escape when there is a storm warning.

1 Read **A**
  a Where did Typhoon Nina occur?
  b How many people were killed?
  c What speeds did the typhoon achieve?
  d What damage did the typhoon cause?

2 How did the effects of Typhoon Nina compare with the effects of the storm which hit southern England in the previous month?

3 Describe the appearance of a typhoon. Use **D** to help you. Mention the shape, size and structure of the storm.

4 How is a typhoon formed?

5 **E** shows the source areas of tropical storms.
  a Name the tropical storms formed in: ● the Caribbean ● the Indian Ocean ● the Pacific Ocean.
  b Name four countries threatened by ● typhoons ● hurricanes ● cyclones

6 In your own words, explain why the effects of tropical storms in developed countries are usually less severe than in developing countries.

47

PEOPLE AND THE ENVIRONMENT
2.9 People Upset the Environment

It is night time on 3 December, 1984. Most of the population of Bhopal, in the Indian state of Madhya Pradesh (**A**) are asleep. At the Union Carbide chemical factory on the edge of the city (**B**) a container has burst. Carried on the gentle wind, a deadly cloud of cyanide gas wafts across the city, passing through the homes of over a quarter of a million people...

Over 2000 men, women and children died within seconds of inhaling the cyanide (methyl isocyanate – MIC). Over 200 000 others suffered injury to their lungs and eyes. Many of them suffered terrible pain. Many will never recover their health or their eyesight. **C** shows some of the victims of the Bhopal disaster.

Bhopal, a city of 300 000 people, was the scene of one of the world's worst environmental disasters caused by human action. The effects of the disaster are all too plain to see, but the causes are less clear. The tragedy made many people ask serious questions about the involvement of multinational companies in the developing world.

Union Carbide is a US-owned multinational company with factories in many countries throughout the world. After the disaster many people in India accused Union Carbide of taking fewer safety precautions in their Indian factory than they did in their American and European factories.

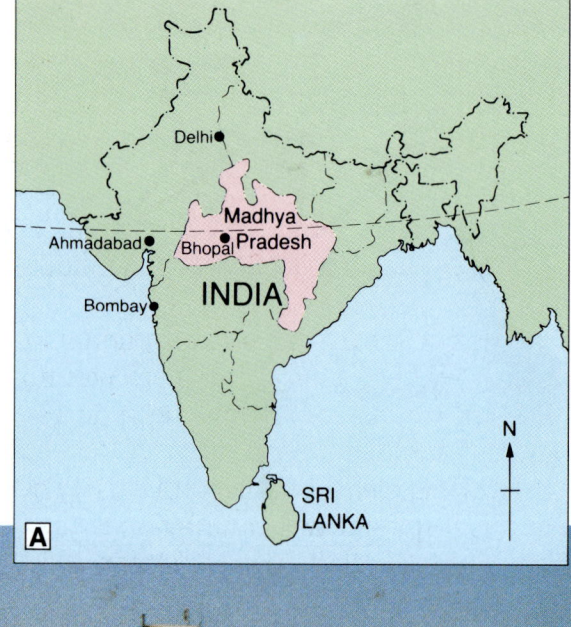

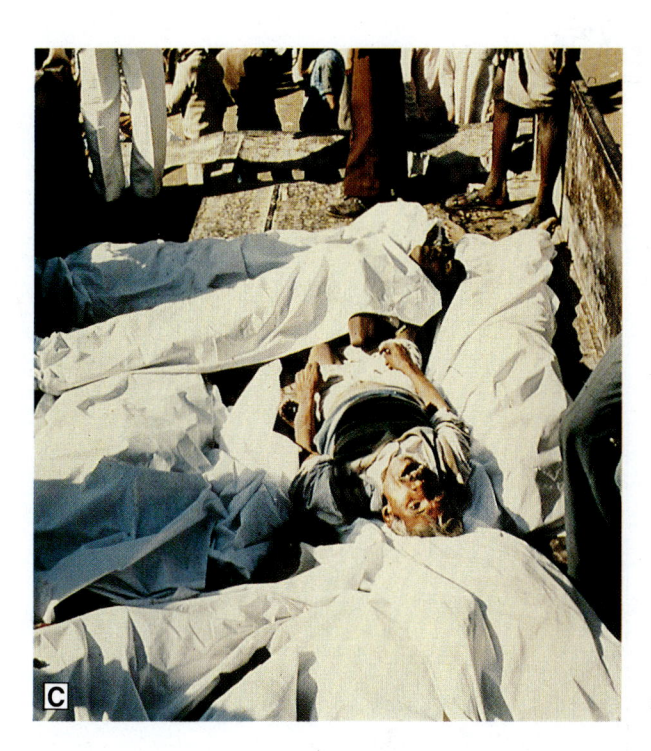

They gave many examples to support their case. Among their claims were the following:
- Poor design meant that a large amount of deadly MIC was stored, but there was no effective means of neutralising it in the event of a leak.
- Cost-cutting measures meant that rusty or faulty equipment was not repaired.
- The plant regularly broke Union Carbide's own safety rules. There had been several fatal accidents in the past, but workers who protested were fined or sacked.

Union Carbide claimed that the leak had been caused by an employee with a grudge against the company. They refused to accept responsibility for the disaster. Opponents of Union Carbide say that even after the disaster at Bhopal the company did not take proper safety precautions (**D**). The Indian authorities have also been criticised for being so desperate for modern industrial employment, plus the fertiliser which Bhopal produced, that they were prepared to ignore Union Carbide's unsafe procedures. The authorities also did little to prevent poor people's housing being built near the chemical plant.

The legal battle for compensation for the victims dragged on for years. Most of them were poor and illiterate, unable to fight for their rights. Many of the victims died while the discussions continued.

UNION CARBIDE THREATEN TO CLOSE DANGER PLANT IN BOMBAY

US multi-national Union Carbide, the company whose Bhopal plant killed 2500 people and injured hundreds of thousands more, has threatened to close its Bombay polyethylene factory. The closure threat follows a request from the government of Maharashtra state to carry out safety improvements and give an assurance that the plant would be run safely. Opponents of Union Carbide claim that this is further evidence of the company's unwillingness to pay for safety measures in its Indian plants.

D

---

1. **a** Where is Bhopal?
   b What is its population?
2. What is a multinational company?
3. **a** What happened on 3rd December 1984 at Bhopal?
   b What were the effects of the disaster?
4. Study the Heads and Tails below and write out the correct sentences:

Heads	Tails
Union Carbide claimed that . . .	for ignoring Union Carbide's unsafe procedures.
The Indian authorities have been criticised . . .	than similar factories in the developed world, claimed Indian opponents of Union Carbide.
The Bhopal factory had fewer safety precautions . . .	an employee with a grudge caused the leak. . .

5. Who do you think was responsible for the Bhopal disaster? Who should pay for the damage and the injuries?

PEOPLE AND THE ENVIRONMENT

2.10 Costs and Benefits

The Aswan High Dam

The Aswan High Dam is a marvel of modern engineering. It is 100 metres high and its **reservoir**, Lake Nasser, extends for 560 kilometres behind the dam (**A**). The dam provides **hydro-electric power, irrigation water** and **fresh water** for Egypt's growing population. It also controls **flooding** in the Nile Valley.

The amount of farmland in Egypt has doubled since 1900. This is mainly a result of irrigation projects. The Aswan Dam has played an important part in this since its completion in 1970. Financial and technical help for building the dam came originally from the former USSR, and later from Britain and the USA.

This **multi-purpose** water project has brought many benefits to Egypt (**B**). But it has also meant new problems or 'costs' (**C**):

1 Much of the Nile Delta is made up of **silt**. This is the eroded material carried by the river. In times of flood, the Nile would pick up a heavy load of silt and deposit it at the mouth of the river (the Delta). The Aswan Dam now controls flooding, so no new silt is deposited. Parts of the Nile Delta are being eroded at the rate of 40 metres per year.

2 Egyptian fishermen are no longer able to catch sardines off the Nile Delta. The nutrients the fish lived on were once

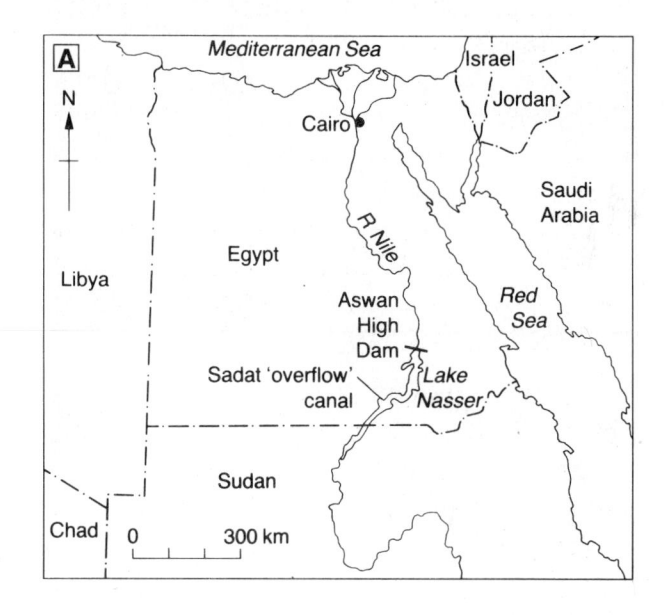

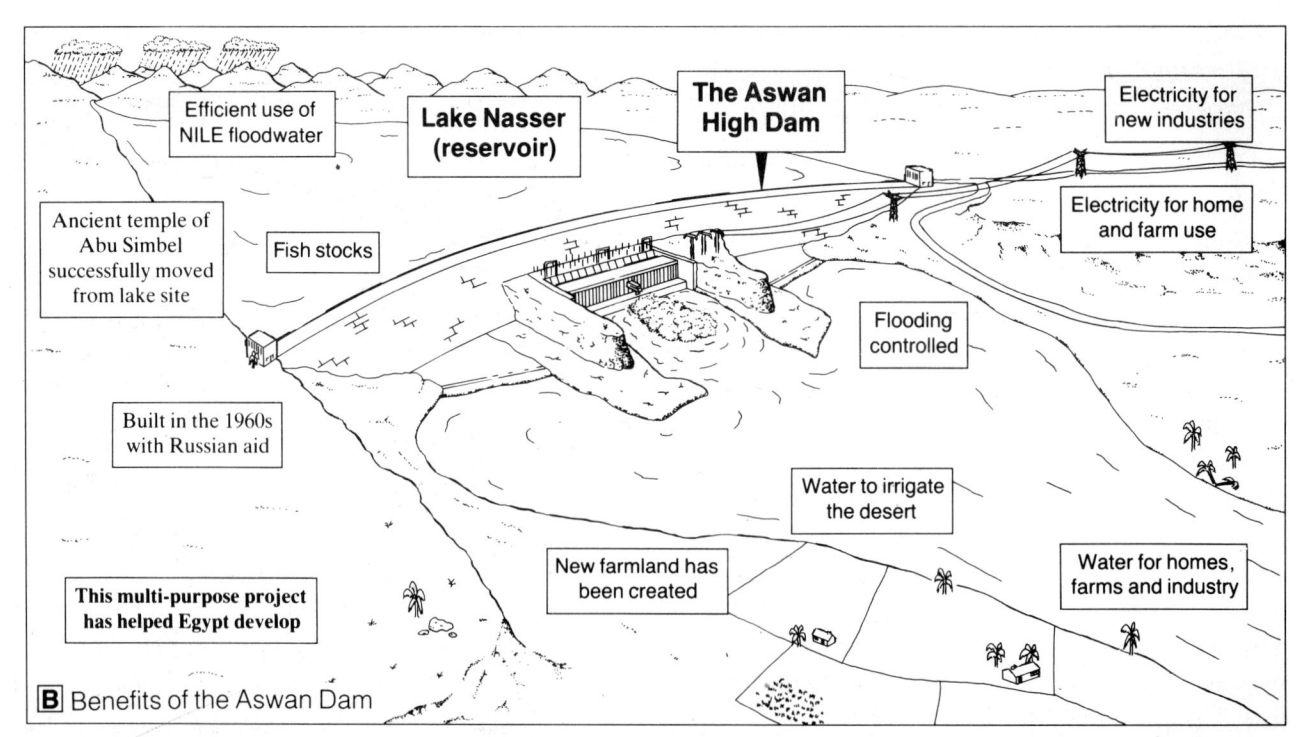

B Benefits of the Aswan Dam

Skills	problem solving, role play
Concepts	HEP, irrigation, multi-purpose project
Issues	resources, human interference

brought down by the Nile floods. Now the floods are held back, and the nutrients remain in Lake Nasser.

3 Cairo brickmakers no longer have new silt deposits to make their bricks.
4 Peasant farmers relied on natural floodwater to water their land. Now those who do not have channelled irrigation water suffer.
5 There has been an increase in water-borne diseases such as **bilharzia**, which is carried by water snails which breed in irrigation channels.

The Aswan High Dam is an example of a scheme which has both 'costs' and benefits (disadvantages and advantages). Many people in Egypt have benefited from the Aswan project. When it was built there was no other way for Egypt to produce the food and electricity it needed. But some people had to suffer.

Throughout the developing world there are examples of Western technology being used in places where it is not **appropriate**. Big projects often have problems; there are always extra, hidden 'costs'. Sometimes these disadvantages outweigh the advantages of the new technology.

1 The Aswan High Dam was built during the 1960s. What alternative schemes can you now suggest which would help Egypt produce food and electricity?
2 What is a 'multi-purpose' scheme?

FURTHER WORK

● **Aswan Dam – role play**

In a small group (preferably 4), or on your own, decide on the following roles:
  1 An Egyptian Government Minister
  2 A local peasant farmer who has not received Aswan irrigation water
  3 A peasant farmer who has received irrigation water from the scheme
  4 A city dweller in Cairo

● Each of you work out your arguments for or against the Aswan multi-purpose scheme.
● Discuss your point of view with the others in the group.
● One person should briefly note down the viewpoints of all the people. Then divide them into viewpoints *in favour* of the Dam and those *against* the water scheme.

(You can find more help for this role play in the *Activity pack*.)

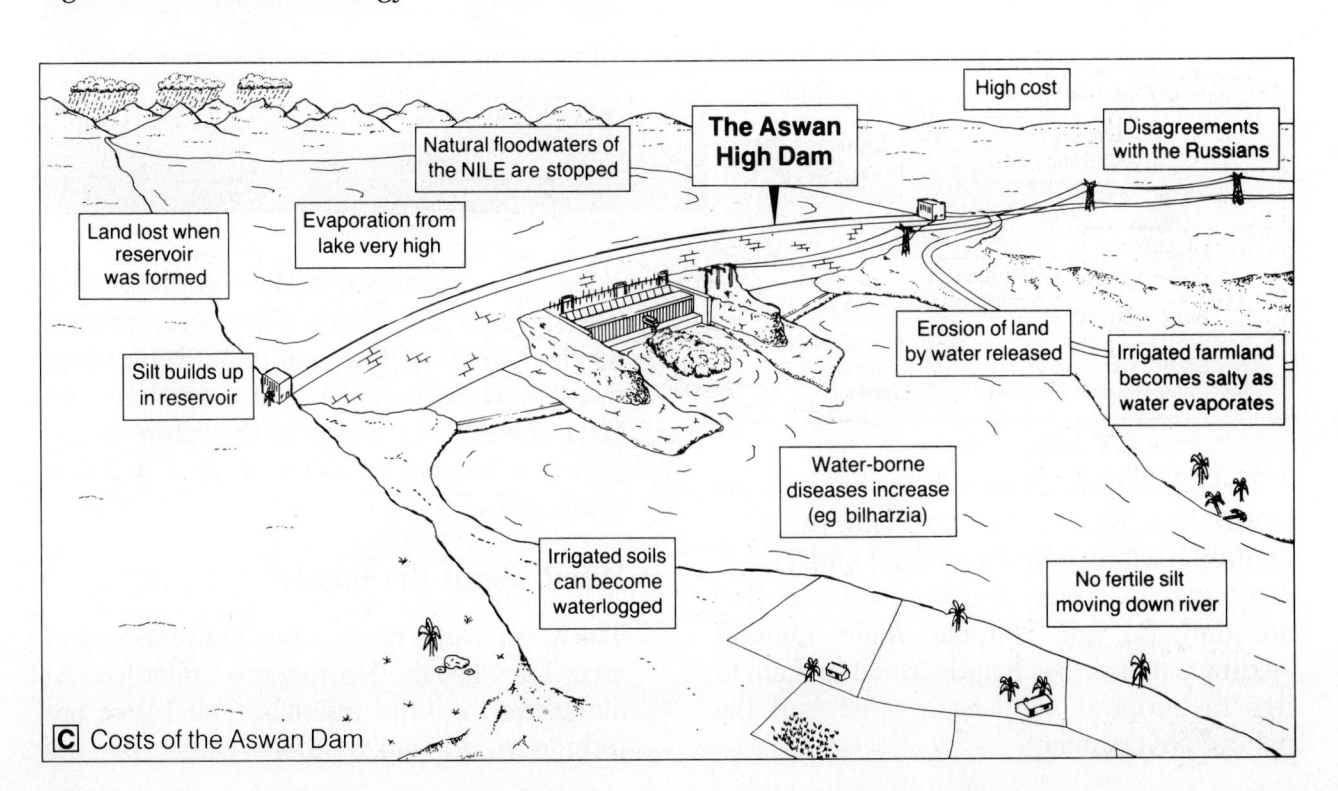

C Costs of the Aswan Dam

PEOPLE AND THE ENVIRONMENT

2.11 Conservation: African Game Parks

Game parks are special reserves set up to safeguard wildlife and natural environments. A number of game parks have been established in Africa. **A** shows the game parks in Kenya and Tanzania. These areas **conserve** the grass-eating animals of the savanna grasslands.

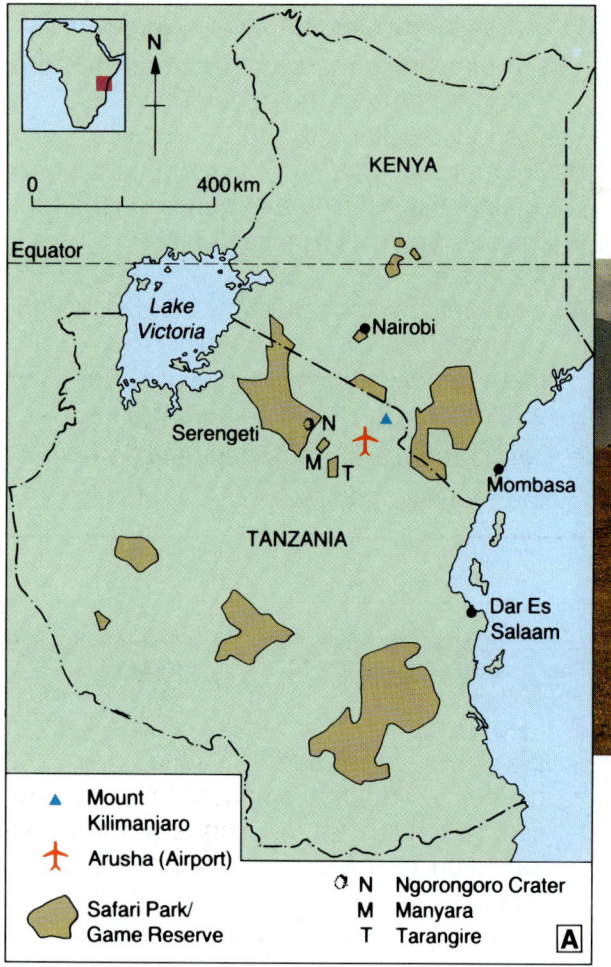

The Serengeti National Park supports more than half a million wild animals, including zebra, wildebeest, topi and Thomson's gazelle. These species feed together, but they do not compete; their different feeding patterns (see **B** and **C**) enable them to live in harmony with each other and the natural environment.

Why conserve?

Africa is a large continent with millions of wild animals. So why must special parks be established?
- The population of Africa is increasing; all these people need food.
- People are becoming increasingly mobile; many people from the developed world can travel by air and reach Africa in a few hours.
- Many people in the developed world are becoming wealthier; they want souvenirs and luxury goods such as leather bags and coats, skins and furs.

B and **C** show some of the complexities of the savanna ecosystem. The environment needs careful conservation, and development must be controlled. If animals are to graze the African plains in the future, game parks must be established and wildlife preserved.

What about the locals?

The Masai cattle herders live in the Serengeti area. They use the Ngorongoro Crater (see **A**) alongside the wild animals. The Masai are forbidden to graze their cattle in the

Skills	research
Concepts	ecosystem, conservation
Issues	conservation

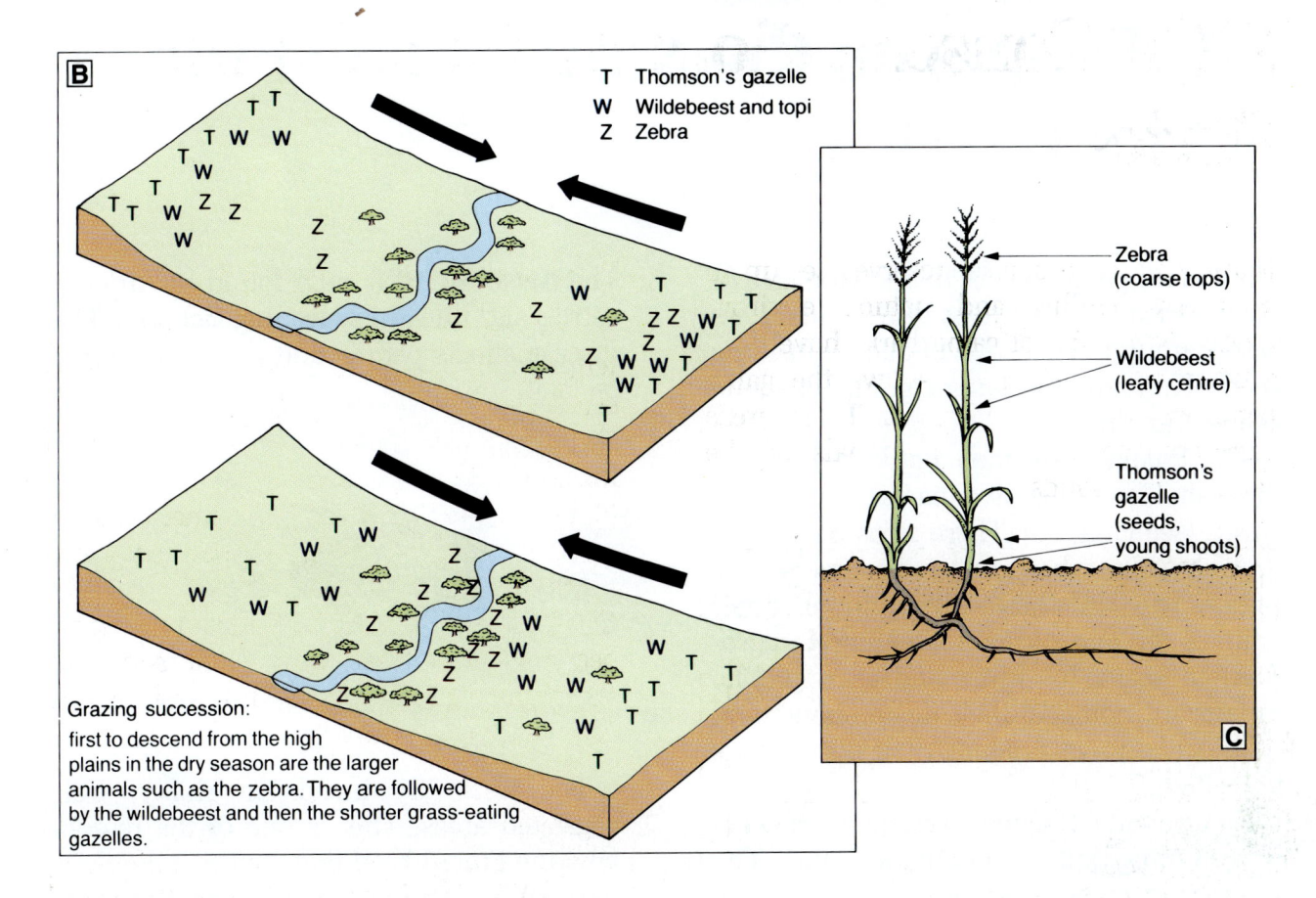

B

T Thomson's gazelle
W Wildebeest and topi
Z Zebra

Grazing succession: first to descend from the high plains in the dry season are the larger animals such as the zebra. They are followed by the wildebeest and then the shorter grass-eating gazelles.

C

- Zebra (coarse tops)
- Wildebeest (leafy centre)
- Thomson's gazelle (seeds, young shoots)

Serengeti Park itself, because they would eat the vegetation the wild animals need. **D** shows the benefits and the costs of conservation.

1. What does 'conservation' mean?
2. Why do you think conservation has been necessary in Africa?
3. a What do you understand by a 'grazing succession' (**B**)?
   b Explain how different species of wild animals use the grasslands
   c What could happen to the natural grazing succession if the local cattle herders were allowed to graze their cattle everywhere?
4. Study **D**. Draw up two columns headed **Costs** and **Benefits** of conservation. Try to add another cost and benefit not shown.

FURTHER WORK

- Find out about other wild animals that live in the savanna grasslands of Africa. Design a cover for a tourist brochure which advertises a touring safari. Emphasise the conservation of the animals and the environment.

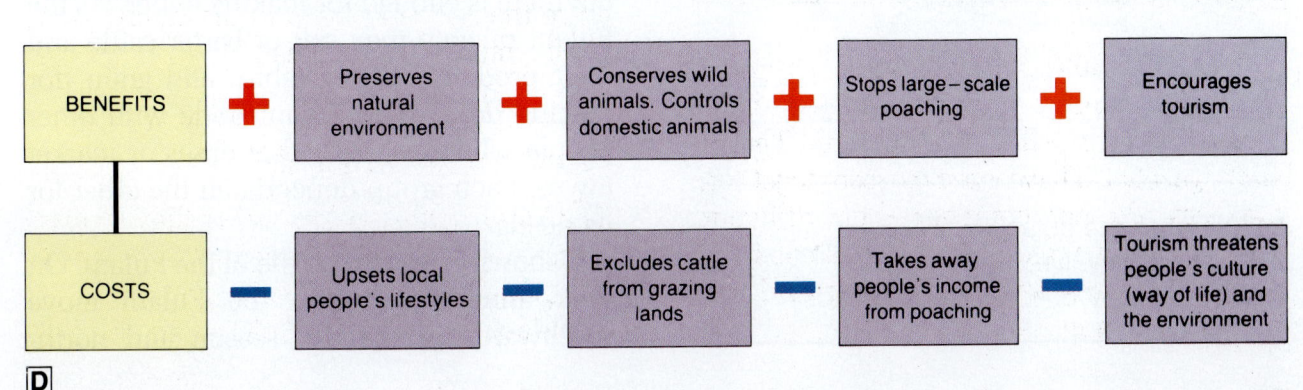

D

BENEFITS	+ Preserves natural environment	+ Conserves wild animals. Controls domestic animals	+ Stops large-scale poaching	+ Encourages tourism
COSTS	− Upsets local people's lifestyles	− Excludes cattle from grazing lands	− Takes away people's income from poaching	− Tourism threatens people's culture (way of life) and the environment

PEOPLE'S NEEDS

3.1 People on the Move – The Fulani of West Africa

The **Fulani** people live across a wide area of West Africa (**A**). The lives of the Fulani are based around the needs of the cattle they keep. They are the largest group of cattle keepers in Africa.

The Fulani graze their herds throughout the Sahel and the savanna lands of West Africa (see Unit 2.6). These areas have long, dry seasons when water becomes very scarce. The cattle herders have to take their animals on long journeys (an **annual migration**) in search of water and grazing. The Fulani are **nomads**: they move about with their cattle all year, taking their possessions with them.

Cattle are the Fulani's livelihood. They are also an important part of Fulani culture. The number of cows a person has is a sign of **social status** (the more cows you have, the more important you are).

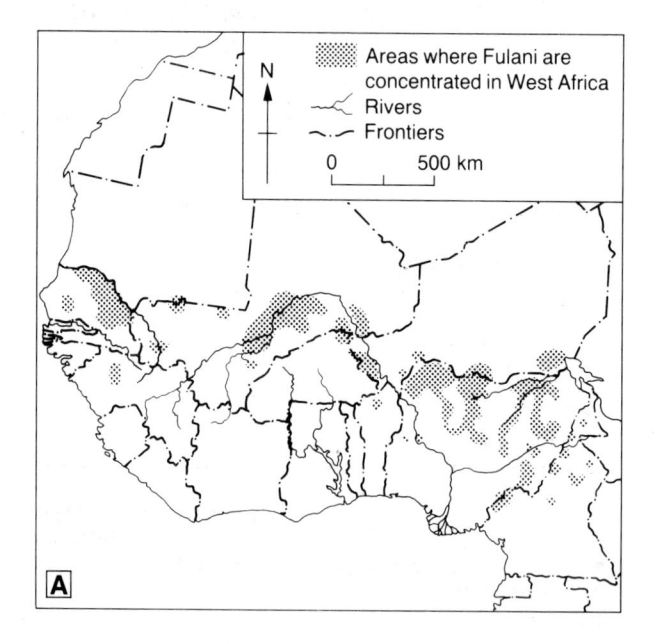

A

1 Where do the Fulani live?
2 What do they live on?
3 Why are they described as nomads?

The **tsetse fly** (**B**) is only found in Africa. It carries and transmits **sleeping sickness**. This disease affects people and cattle, and it can be fatal.

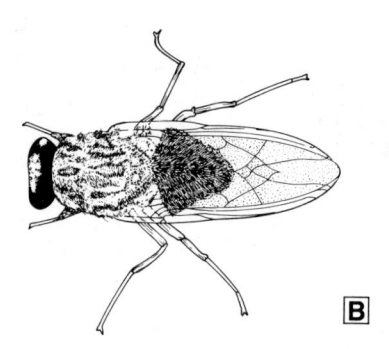

B

The tsetse fly breeds in shady, well-vegetated areas. This is one of the reasons why the Fulani keep their cattle in the drier, more difficult environment of the Sahel and northern savanna lands. Even there, the flies can be a problem in the short, wet season. This is another reason why the Fulani are always on the move, keeping to higher areas as far as possible.

4 What is happening in **C** and **D**? What season do you think this is?
5 How does the tsetse fly affect the lives of the Fulani?

The Fulani live on the produce of their cattle. The cattle do not provide a lot of milk, but there is enough for making butter. As the Fulani migrate they sell or barter cattle and their produce for vegetables and grain (for making flour). The Fulani trade with other people who have settled at oases or market towns. Each group depends on the other for its needs.

E shows a year in the life of the Fulani. On their annual migration the Fulani move southwards in the dry season and north-

Skills	empathy
Concepts	annual migration, transhumance

wards in the wet season. This pattern of movement is known as **transhumance**. Similar patterns take place in many other parts of the world. For example, in the Alps of Europe cattle are moved to lowland pasture in winter and back to highland pasture in summer.

---

6 a What is 'transhumance'?
  b How and why do the Fulani practise transhumance?
  c Why do you think people in the Alps practise transhumance?
7 Use **E** and the base map in the *Activity pack* to plot the yearly cycle of movement of the Fulani.

FURTHER WORK

● Imagine you are a Fulani cattle herder. You are telling the children about one eventful year in your life. Events you could describe include: the rain failing/coming late; attacks from hyenas; sleeping sickness; an adventure while searching for new grazing land; bartering for things you need in a village. Write down the story of your year and do some drawings to accompany it.

E The Fulani year

SEPTEMBER
Back near home village. Build enclosures for cattle; Feasts to celebrate reunion. Receive visit from chief of village.

Late JULY/AUGUST
Move slowly north to drier ground, grazing cattle.

JULY
Join up again as a large group; cattle graze on new grass.

JUNE
Rains arrive. Herders follow dark clouds in hope of finding grass when they arrive. Only leave wells when sure there will be pasture in the north.

FEBRUARY – MARCH – APRIL – MAY
Stay near wells. Water animals in early morning then travel further each day to find new pasture but return to wells in late afternoon. Heat becomes unbearable, cattle lose weight, the dry season is at its peak.

NOVEMBER
Wet season ends – time to move from 'Home' village.

Divide into small groups and move south.

Camp near water (up to six days at each site)

DECEMBER
News of good grazing in north-east so move in that direction

FEBRUARY
Move westwards to wells near friendly village

Groups wander looking for grass and water until **JANUARY**

Move to a river in the south west

PEOPLE'S NEEDS

3.2 Water for Everyone

How long could you survive without water? Water is essential for all living things on earth. Without it everything dies.

A shows where water comes from. 73% of this water is used for agriculture, 22% goes to industry, and 5% is used for domestic purposes.

In the developing world only 40% of people have easy access to clean water. 90% of people in the developed world enjoy such access. Most people in the developed world take clean water and **sanitation** (the removal of sewage) for granted. But in developing countries providing clean supplies of fresh water and sanitation poses serious problems.

B shows percentages of people with clean water in rural and urban areas in some developing world countries. Most people in the developing world live in rural areas and survive by working on the land.

There are other problems connected with a lack of clean water:

Disease The World Health Organisation (WHO) has estimated that 80% of all disease is caused by infected water supplies. Diseases related to water include cholera, typhoid, bilharzia, malaria, sleeping sickness and hookworm.

Transport In many developing world countries it is the women's job to get water. This often means walking several kilometres to the nearest river, pond, waterhole or well, and then carrying the water home (**C, D**). The water is often polluted and dirty.

In 1978 the United Nations recognised the problem of the inequality of world water supplies. They started a campaign to provide 'Clean water and sanitation for all by the year 1990'. The campaign faced major problems.

A The water cycle

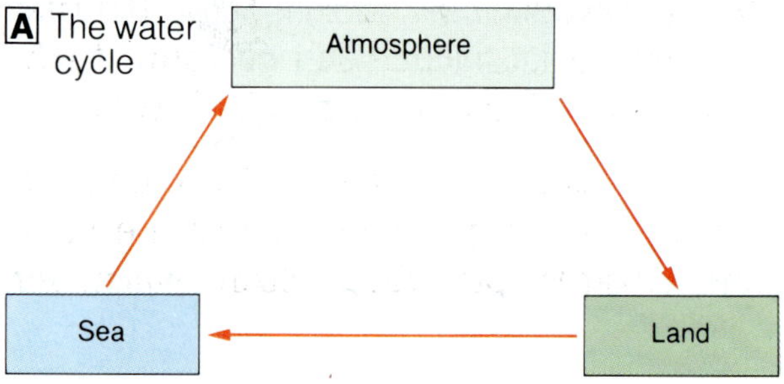

Water evaporates from the **sea** and rises in the **atmosphere** to form clouds. Water returns to the **land** as precipitation (rain, snow, sleet, ice). Most flows back to the **sea** as rivers. Some is stored as fresh water in lakes and reservoirs, or underground.

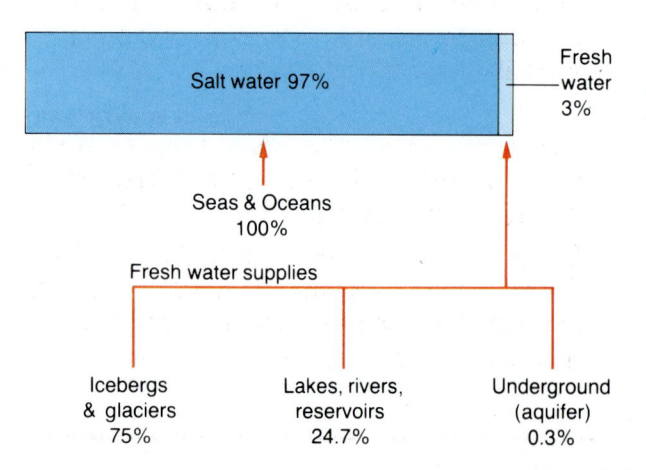

Salt water 97% — Fresh water 3%

Seas & Oceans 100%

Fresh water supplies:
- Icebergs & glaciers 75%
- Lakes, rivers, reservoirs 24.7%
- Underground (aquifer) 0.3%

	Urban (%)	Rural (%)	
Africa	81	25	Sample Regions
Latin America	75	23	
Asia & Pacific	70	30	
Bangladesh	43	71	Sample Countries
Brazil	75	5	
Ethiopia	82	4	
Ghana	94	30	
India	82	30	
Kenya	100	13	
Malawi	70	37	
Mexico	62	42	
Papua New Guinea	53	10	
Saudi Arabia	65	20	
Sudan	49	45	
Tunisia	96	29	
Zaire	43	5	

B Percentages of population with clean water in some developing countries

Skills	keyword plan, designing poster
Concepts	water supply, world water decade
Issues	use of resources

Problems

- difficulty in raising the $300 billion needed. Investments were less than expected.
- dealing with drought emergencies (for example, in the Sahel in the 1980s) set back the target
- the need to develop appropriate technology (big schemes might work in cities but are not suitable for country areas)
- the need to educate people in public health as well as supplying them with clean water
- helping people develop the skills to construct and manage water supply projects
- persuading governments in developing countries that water supply projects are as important as big industrial developments
- maintaining equipment (in one project, 60% of pumps did not work. Spare parts had to come from Europe.)

After 1990 many of the projects were scaled down. What did the World Water Decade achieve?

Successes

- Malawi will have achieved 100% safe water by the year 2000, mainly as a result of small, self-help projects in the countryside.
- The Greater Cairo Wastewater Project, in Egypt, will replace Cairo's original sewage system, at a cost of $5 billion.
- The River Ganges is being cleaned up, at a cost of $170 million.
- The development of the Mark II water pump means that much of Tamil Nadu (Southern India) now has fresh water.

The successes may seem small, compared with such a huge problem, but they are a first step towards providing clean water for everyone.

---

1 How is most of the world's water used?
2 Draw up a keyword plan on 'Clean water and sanitation for all'. Add your ideas about:
   a Sources of water in the developing world
   b Health hazards from water
   c Difficulty of collecting water
3 Describe what you can see in photographs **C** and **D**. What is the environment like? What are the people doing?
4 Design a fund-raising poster for a Water Supply and Sanitation Campaign. In it, highlight the problems the campaign faces and what it aims to achieve.

PEOPLE'S NEEDS

3.3 Primary Products

Where are the world's resources? **A** shows where oil, copper and bauxite, three of the most important mineral resources, can be found. As you can see, developing countries have more of these resources.

1 a Use **A** and an atlas to name five countries with oil; copper; and bauxite reserves (15 different countries).
b Bauxite is a rock used in the production of a vital metal. Which metal?
2 B shows the world's leading producers of tin.
a How many of these nations are in the developing world?
b Use an atlas to help you locate the countries in **B**. Name the countries on an outline map of the world and draw symbols representing tin on them (there is an outline map in the *Activity pack*).

Country	**Tin production** (thousand tonnes)
Malaysia	43
Indonesia	23
Thailand	22
Brazil	20
Bolivia	20
China	18
The former USSR	17
Australia	8
UK	5
Peru	3

B World tin production

As well as large reserves of minerals, the developing world also supplies many other **primary products** (**C**). These include timber, food crops such as bananas, sugar cane and

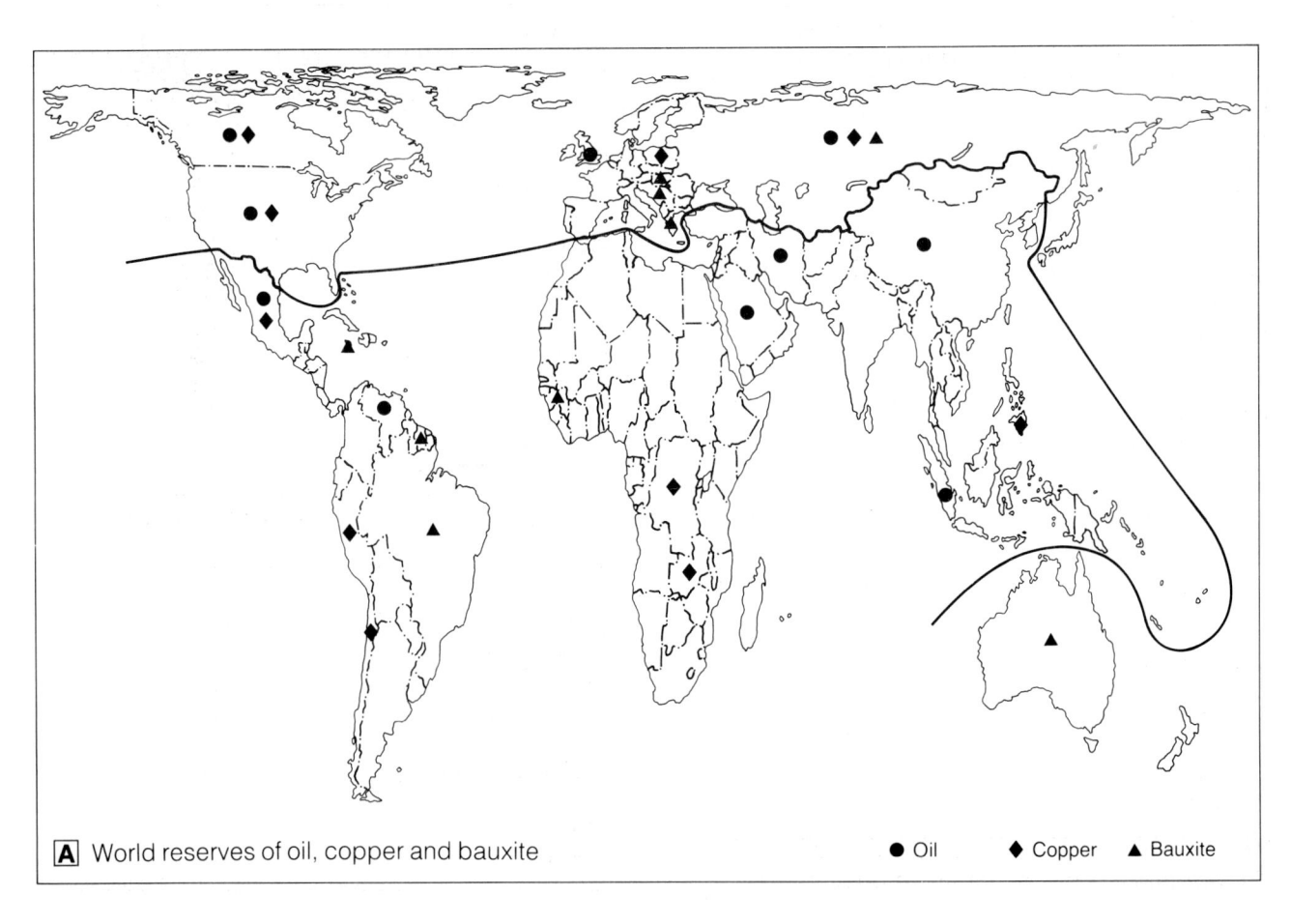

A World reserves of oil, copper and bauxite ● Oil ◆ Copper ▲ Bauxite

58

rice, beverage crops such as cocoa, coffee and tea, and other cash crops such as cotton and sisal.

The developed countries have a high demand for primary products from the developing countries. Developing countries export primary products to supply this demand. This trade shows how much the developed world depends upon the developing world.

---

3 The tables in **C** show the world's leading producers of five primary products.
   a On an outline map of the world, name the countries and draw symbols representing the primary products.
   b Describe the patterns revealed by your map, and try to explain why these non-mineral primary products are found mainly in the developing world.

RICE

Country	Rice production (million tonnes)
China	182
India	95
Indonesia	40
Bangladesh	22
Burma	15
Vietnam	15
Japan	14
Brazil	9
Philippines	9
South Korea	8

BANANAS

Country	Banana production (million tonnes)
Brazil	7
India	5
Philippines	5
Thailand	2
Indonesia	2
Ecuador	2
Mexico	2
Honduras	1
Colombia	1
Vietnam	1

C World producers of primary products

Skills	mapwork, atlas work, using statistics
Concepts	primary products, world trade
Issues	resource distribution, interdependence

FURTHER WORK

- Keep a record of the food you eat in a week. Try to find out the countries it comes from. (If it is tinned or packaged food, the label might help.) How much of your food comes from the developing world? How much from the developed world?
- Try the same research for your clothes, and for items in your classroom. What are they made of? Where might the raw materials have come from?

COFFEE

Country	Coffee production (thousand tonnes)
Brazil	1 350
Colombia	800
Indonesia	330
Mexico	270
Ethiopia	240
Uganda	205
El Salvador	170
Ivory Coast	150
Philippines	150
Guatemala	140

COTTON

Country	Cotton production (thousand tonnes)
China	12 150
The former USSR	5 300
USA	4 800
India	2 550
Pakistan	2 000
Brazil	1 200
Turkey	1 000
Egypt	680
Sudan	420
Mexico	400

HARDWOOD TIMBER

Country	Hardwood timber (mill. cubic m.)
India	214
USA	158
Brazil	153
China	121
Indonesia	121
Nigeria	80
The former USSR	60
Malaysia	40
Tanzania	39
Thailand	37

PEOPLE'S NEEDS

3.4 Remote Sensing

A

How can the advanced technology of the developed world help the developing world? One way is by **remote sensing**. **Satellites** in space have the best possible view of the earth. The data they send to earth gives geographers and scientists vital information.

The satellite **METEOSAT** hovers 36 000 km above the earth, over the coast of West Africa. It sends back pictures like **A**. These help **meteorologists** forecast the weather. You can see images like this on breakfast time television and on TV weather reports.

1 What is remote sensing?
2 What collects the data?
3 How is meteosat useful to people?
4 What part of the world does **A** show?

Uses of remote sensing

Satellites can scan huge areas. They repeat the process frequently, so any changes show up. Information gathered includes locations of forest fires, iceberg spread, ocean currents, geology, land use, soil erosion, crop development, pollution, urban growth and vegetation cover. Remote sensing provides more reliable and cheaper information than surveying on the ground can do.

5 What types of information can remote sensing provide?
6 What advantages has remote sensing over traditional ways of collecting data?
7 How does the satellite 'see'?
8 What do computers back on earth do with the data?

Problems

Remote sensing provides information. Information gives power. **Multinational** oil companies (see Unit 3.7) can afford to use remote sensing for exploration. But how can a country like Zambia find money for **river**

Skills	designing poster
Concepts	remote sensing
Issues	uses of technology

How does it see?
Sensors on the satellite record the very small changes in heat or light that happen when the surface of the earth changes. For example, roads reflect more heat than grass, so the sensor can 'see' roads as lines of heat. All the data is set back to earth where it is processed by computers. The data is converted into an image of what the sensor saw. The computer colours in the image. But it does not always use the colours you might see in a photograph. **B** is a satellite photograph of London. The built-up areas are light blue, vegetation is red.

What can it do for the developing world?
Information can help people understand what is happening now and plan for what may happen in the future. For example,
- images of vegetation in the dry and wet seasons can show up areas where people are allowing their animals to overgraze the land. This is very important for areas like the Sahel.
- remote sensing can help people monitor changes in cultivation. Land use schemes in Sudan are monitored in this way (**C**).
- areas of forest clearance (eg in the Amazon rainforest) can be spotted – this helps prevent illegal tree felling.
- rainfall can be predicted, so that farmers in the African Savanna do not plant their crops too early, before the main rains arrive
- the best sites for irrigation can be spotted.
- warnings of hurricanes and other weather hazards can be given well in advance.

flow sensing (using remote sensing to find out how much water there is in rivers and check where it goes)? The technology is very complicated and expensive and interpreting the images is a skilled job. Developed nations control most of the technology and the information. It is up to them to share this information freely, for the good of the developing world.

---

9 Design a poster to show what remote sensing can do for developing countries.
10 Why might the cost of remote sensing be a problem for developing countries?

FURTHER WORK
- Collect examples of remote sensing at work from papers, magazines and t.v.
- Can you think of other uses governments could make of remote sensing?

PEOPLE'S NEEDS

3.5 World Trade

A shows the pattern of world trade:

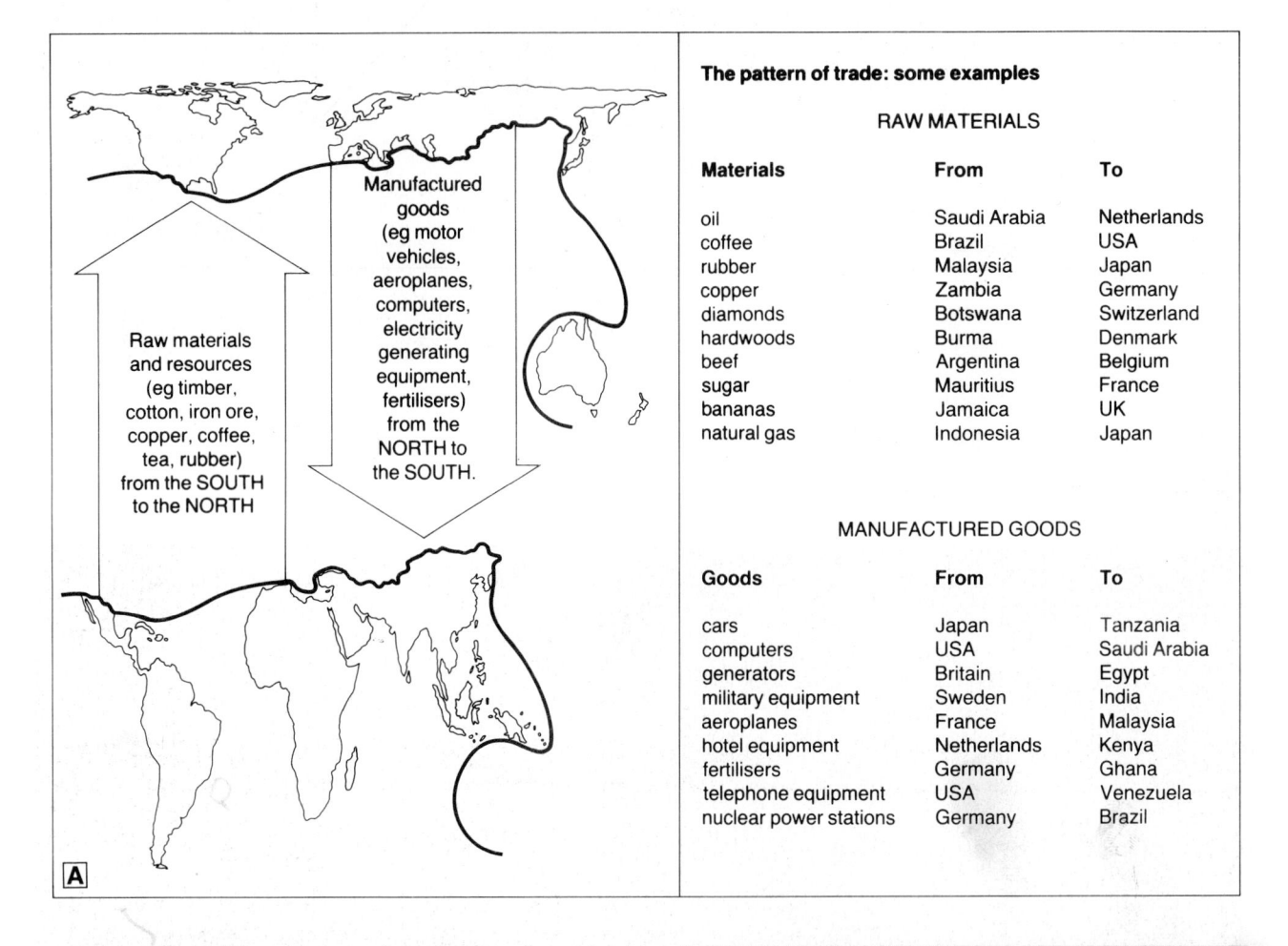

The pattern of trade: some examples

RAW MATERIALS

Materials	From	To
oil	Saudi Arabia	Netherlands
coffee	Brazil	USA
rubber	Malaysia	Japan
copper	Zambia	Germany
diamonds	Botswana	Switzerland
hardwoods	Burma	Denmark
beef	Argentina	Belgium
sugar	Mauritius	France
bananas	Jamaica	UK
natural gas	Indonesia	Japan

MANUFACTURED GOODS

Goods	From	To
cars	Japan	Tanzania
computers	USA	Saudi Arabia
generators	Britain	Egypt
military equipment	Sweden	India
aeroplanes	France	Malaysia
hotel equipment	Netherlands	Kenya
fertilisers	Germany	Ghana
telephone equipment	USA	Venezuela
nuclear power stations	Germany	Brazil

Map shows: Raw materials and resources (eg timber, cotton, iron ore, copper, coffee, tea, rubber) from the SOUTH to the NORTH. Manufactured goods (eg motor vehicles, aeroplanes, computers, electricity generating equipment, fertilisers) from the NORTH to the SOUTH.

A North-South pattern of trade developed during the 19th century. It was based on the colonial system. Developed countries took resources from the colonies and sold manufactured goods back to the colonies. This unfair system has continued despite the break-up of the colonial empires during the 20th century.

1 What is the general pattern of world trade (**A**)?
2 How did this pattern of trade develop?
3 B compares the export trade of Botswana in Africa with the export trade of the UK.
   a For each country, list its exports under the headings 'raw materials' (minerals and farm products) and 'manufactured goods'.
   b What percentage of Botswana's exports consist of ● raw materials? ● manufactured goods?
   c What percentage of the UK's exports consist of ● raw materials? ● manufactured goods?
4 What problems will Botswana face if:
   a the price of diamonds on the world market falls?
   b a cheaper subsitute is found to replace copper for many of its uses?
   c foot and mouth disease affects Botswana's beef cattle?
   d the prices of manufactured goods rise considerably?
   e its diamond mines become exhausted?

Skills	graph work
Concepts	world trade
Issues	unfair pattern of trade

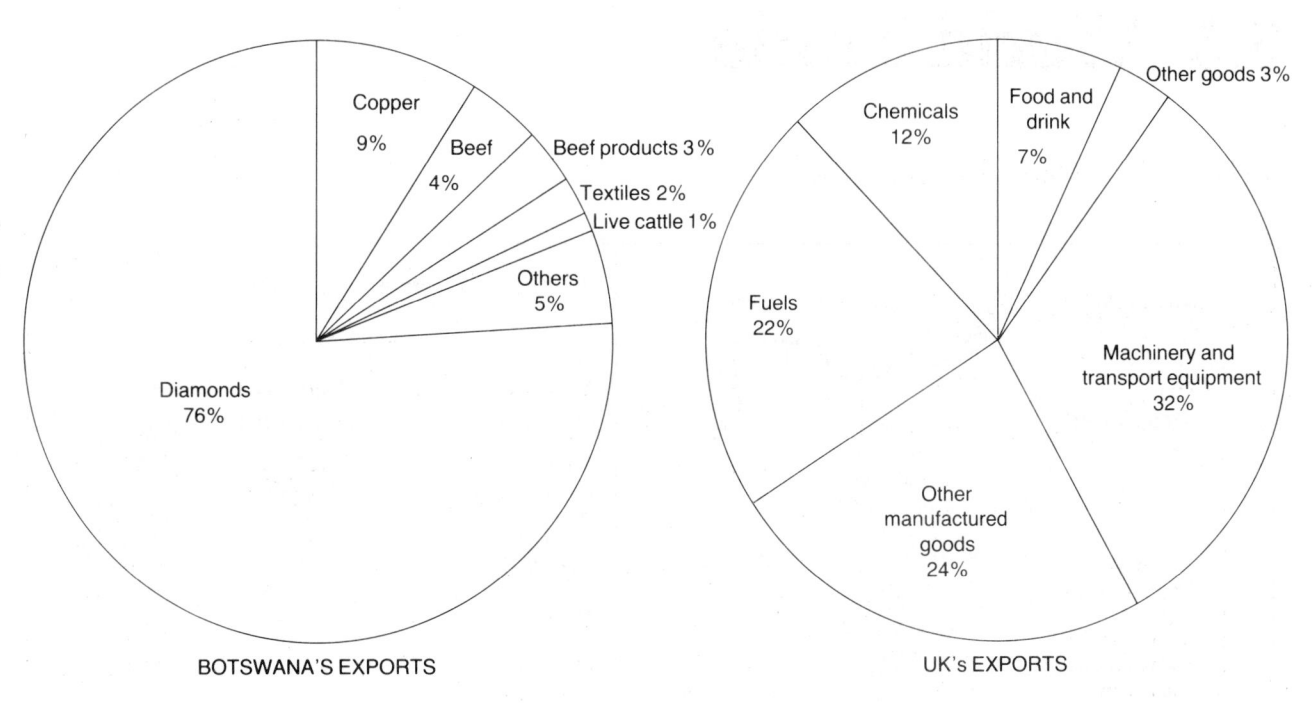

BOTSWANA'S EXPORTS
- Diamonds 76%
- Copper 9%
- Beef 4%
- Beef products 3%
- Textiles 2%
- Live cattle 1%
- Others 5%

UK's EXPORTS
- Machinery and transport equipment 32%
- Other manufactured goods 24%
- Fuels 22%
- Chemicals 12%
- Food and drink 7%
- Other goods 3%

B Exports from UK and Botswana compared

C A diamond mine in Botswana

63

PEOPLE'S NEEDS

3.6 Changing Needs after Colonialism

Unit 3.5 looked at the pattern of world trade. This pattern creates a difficult problem for developing countries. Prices of resources are low compared with the prices of manufactured goods, and the gap is steadily widening.

The trade trap

Many developing countries do not get enough money for the resources they export to enable them to buy the manufactured goods they need to import. **A** shows how the amount of rubber needed to buy a tractor (that is, the amount of rubber a developing country would need to sell to obtain the money for a tractor) changed between 1965 and 1988. This widening gap between the price of resources such as rubber and the price of manufactured goods such as tractors is known as the **trade trap**.

Developing countries are keen to set up their own manufacturing industries in order to escape from the trade trap. Brazil has made great progress in establishing manufacturing industries. **B** shows how Brazil's exports have changed since 1965. But industrialisation has plunged Brazil deeply into debt. Repayments amounted to a third of the country's export earnings! In order to earn more money, Brazil has increased its exports of minerals and cash crops. It has also cut spending on social services such as health and education.

Export commodity	% of total exports 1965	1987
Coffee	41	12
Sugar	5	3
Iron ore	6	8
Cocoa	3	4
Soya beans	1	10
Motor vehicles	–	5
Aircraft and ships	–	4
Machinery	4	10
Other manufactured goods	9	30
Others	31	14

B Brazil's exports in 1965 and 1987

A (bar chart: Tonnes of rubber needed to buy a tractor — 1960: 4, 1970: 6, 1980: 14, 1988: 18)

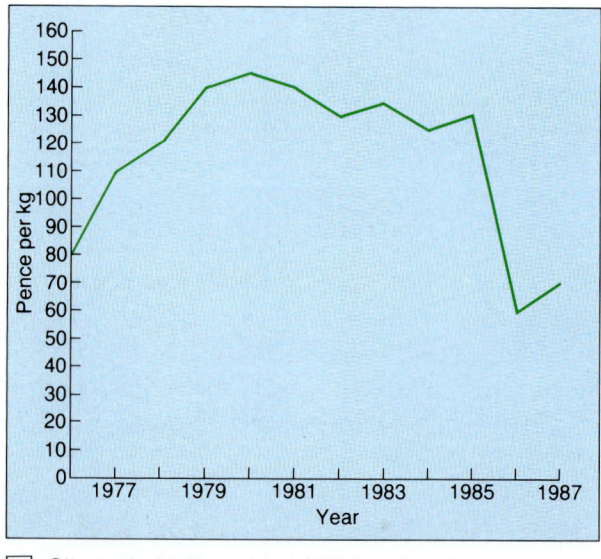

C Changes in the price of Malaysian tin

Map D labels:

- DEVELOPED WORLD
- Developing countries need manufactured goods
- Developed countries fix prices
- Industrialising countries may get into debt
- Supply and demand
- TRADE
- Changing technology
- Widening gap between resource prices and cost of manufactured goods
- Unfair pattern
- DEVELOPING WORLD

Skills: interpreting graphs, keyword plan
Concepts: resources, supply and demand
Issues: 'trade trap'

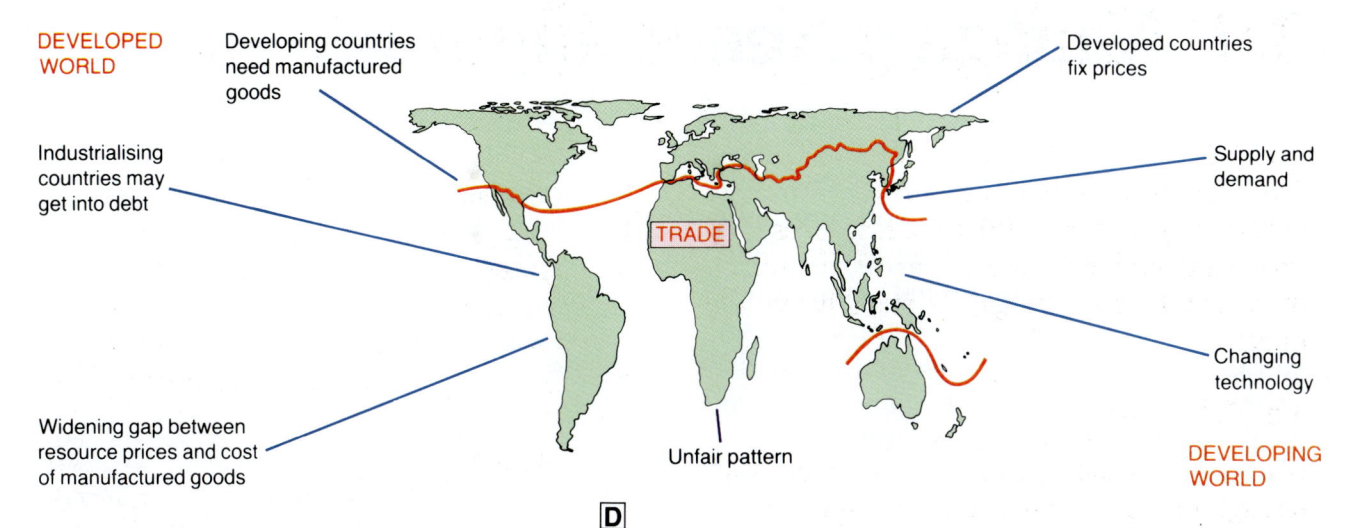

Resources

Prices of manufactured goods have increased steadily. But the prices of resources go up and down according to demand (**C**). Some developing countries depend on the export of only a few resources. If resource prices fall, such developing countries are in serious trouble. They can only afford to progress by borrowing money from the rich nations.

Why do resource prices vary so much?

- Prices may fall because of **changes in technology**. For example, aluminium has replaced copper for some purposes, such as electrical connections. Less copper is needed (there is a drop in demand) so the price falls.
- **Supply and demand** affect prices. Harvests may be affected by drought and disease. This makes the resource scarce and the price rises. A glut (too much of a product) will lead to a fall in prices.
- Prices for many resources are **fixed** by the consuming nations in the developed world. The developing countries depend on the richer nations to buy their resources, and have to agree to the fixed prices.

D shows some of the factors affecting trade between the developed and the developing world.

The pattern of trade is unfair. It is also short-sighted. If developing countries remain poor, they will be unable to buy manufactured goods from developed countries. Manufacturing industry in the developed countries will decline, jobs will be lost, and the economies of rich countries will suffer.

---

1. What problems are created by the pattern of world trade?
2. How is the pattern of world trade 'short-sighted'?
3. Why are developing countries keen to establish their own manufacturing industries?
4. Study **B**.
   a Draw two divided bars to illustrate these statistics.
   b How did the export trade of Brazil change between 1965 and 1987?
5. Study **A**.
   a How many tonnes of rubber were needed to buy one tractor in 1960?
   b How many tonnes were needed to buy one tractor in 1988?
   c What has happened to the prices of rubber and tractors between 1960 and 1988?
6. Study **C**.
   a What was the price of Malaysian tin in 1976?
   b How has the price changed since 1976?
   c What problems would the changing price cause for Malaysia?
7. Why do prices of resources, such as tin, vary so much?
8. Copy keyword plan **D** and add any other factors you can think of that affect the pattern of world trade.

PEOPLE'S NEEDS

3.7 Multinational Companies

What do BP, Esso, Gulf, Mobil, Shell and Texaco have in common? You probably know that they are all oil companies. They are also huge **multinational companies** (MNCs) which operate in several parts of the world. Companies like this control world markets for raw materials, manufactured goods, technology and information.

Most of the multinational companies originate in the developed world (**A**). They control 30% of the world's production of goods and services. The world's top ten MNCs have an annual turnover equal to the **Gross National Product** (GNP) of 150 nations. A country's GNP is the total value of all the goods and services that country produces in a year. Some people are concerned about the power and influence of MNCs. They feel that these big companies contribute to an unequal balance of trade, production and wealth between the developed world (the North) and the developing world (the South).

MNCs are international (see **A**) and have a variety of interests. For example, Unilever employs about 300 000 people and provides some 75 countries with a wide range of products and services (**B**).

Cheap primary products, a good supply of labour and low production costs attract MNCs to the developing world. The developing world has welcomed MNCs that have helped with big prestige developments,

Rank	Company	HQ	Sales $000s	A
1	General Motors (motor vehicles)	USA	102 813 700	
2	Exxon (oil)	USA	69 888 000	
3	Royal Dutch/Shell (oil)	Neths/UK	64 843 217	
4	Ford Motor (motor vehicles)	USA	62 715 800	
5	IBM (computers)	USA	51 250 000	
6	Mobil (oil)	USA	44 866 000	
7	British Petroleum (oil)	UK	39 855 564	
8	General Electric (electronics)	USA	35 211 000	
9	American Tel & Tel (electronics)	USA	34 087 000	
10	Texaco (oil)	USA	31 613 000	
11	IRI (metals)	Italy	31 561 709	
12	Toyota Motor (motor vehicles)	Japan	31 553 827	
13	Daimler-Benz (motor vehicles)	Germany	30 168 550	
14	EI du Pont de Nemours (chemicals)	USA	27 148 000	
15	Matsushita Electric (electronics)	Japan	26 459 539	
16	Unilever (food)	Neths/UK	25 141 672	
17	Chevron (oil)	USA	24 351 000	
18	Volkswagen (motor vehicles)	Germany	24 317 154	
19	Hitachi (electronics)	Japan	22 668 085	
20	ENI (oil)	Italy	22 549 921	
21	Chrysler (motor vehicles)	USA	22 513 500	
22	Philips (electronics)	Neths	22 471 263	
23	Nestle (food)	Switzerland	21 153 285	
24	Philip Morris (tobacco)	USA	20 681 000	
25	Siemens (electronics)	Germany	20 307 037	
26	Nissan Motor (motor vehicles)	Japan	20 141 237	
27	Fiat (motor vehicles)	Italy	19 669 581	
28	Bayer (chemicals)	Germany	18 768 914	
29	BASF (chemicals)	Germany	18 640 985	
30	Amoco (oil)	USA	18 281 000	

---

1 Where do most of the multinational companies in **A** originate from?

2 a Work out the total annual sales of the top 30 MNCs (use a calculator).
  b What does GNP mean?
  c How does the total turnover of the top 30 MNCs compare with the GNP of the USA – the wealthiest country in the world (GNP – $4258.7 billion)?

3 Why are people worried about MNCs?

| Skills | group work, writing report |
| Concepts | GNP, multinationals |

for example building dams, developing rain forest for agriculture, building roads and airports. **C** looks at the profits and losses for the developing countries who deal with MNCs.

FURTHER WORK

- Work in pairs (or two small groups). One of you is a minister in a small developing country that wants to develop industry. The other represents a multinational company that wants to start manufacturing in that country.
- The company representative has to prepare a report explaining the benefits of the project to the company.
  The government minister has to prepare a statement of the possible benefits and disadvantages to the people of the developing country.
- Prepare your reports and present them to each other. Then make an agreement about what will happen and how both sides can benefit from the arrangements.
- This exercise illustrates what might happen in the future, if developing countries begin to set conditions for MNCs. MNCs will have to think about the special needs of their host countries, and be more willing to share their information and technology.

Unilever's turnover = £16 693 million
The break-down between activities (£ million)

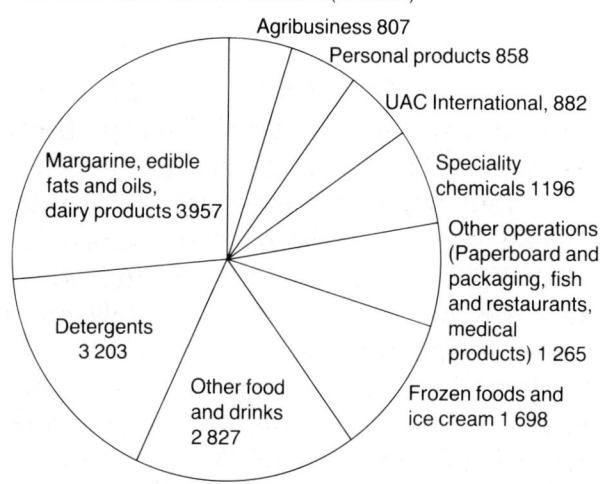

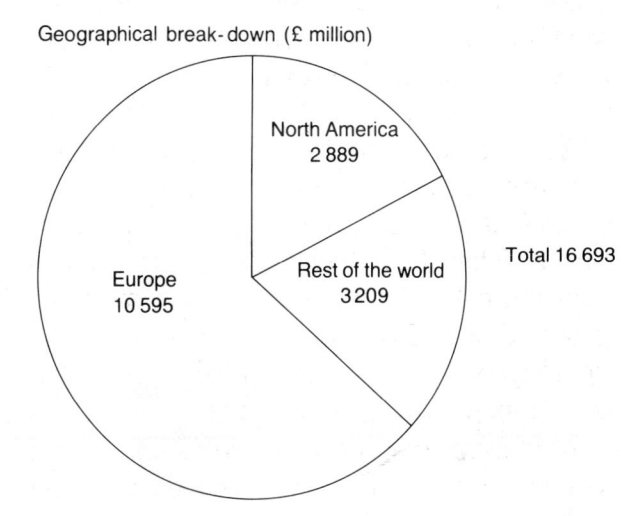

- Agribusiness 807
- Personal products 858
- UAC International, 882
- Speciality chemicals 1196
- Other operations (Paperboard and packaging, fish and restaurants, medical products) 1 265
- Frozen foods and ice cream 1 698
- Other food and drinks 2 827
- Detergents 3 203
- Margarine, edible fats and oils, dairy products 3957

Geographical break-down (£ million)

- North America 2 889
- Europe 10 595
- Rest of the world 3 209
- Total 16 693

B Unilever's operations worldwide

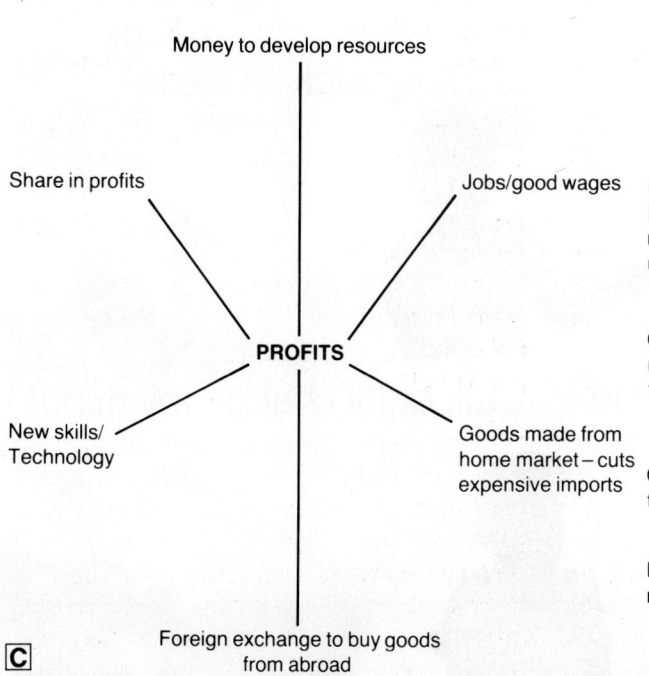

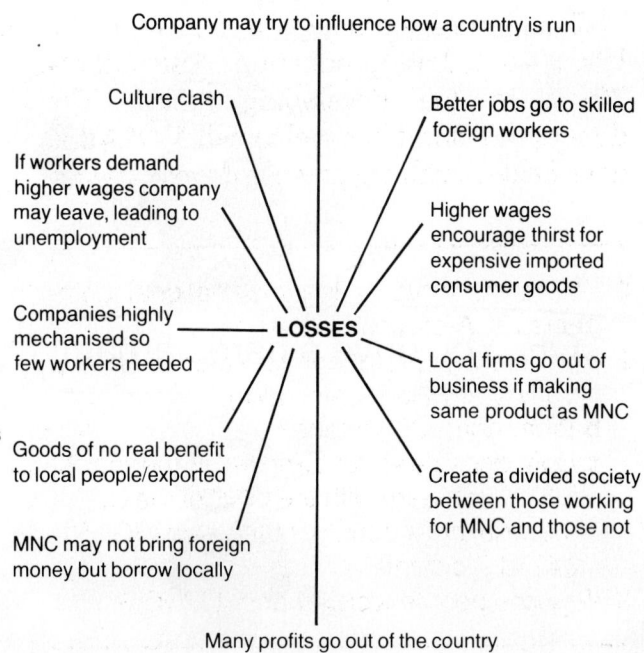

PROFITS
- Money to develop resources
- Share in profits
- Jobs/good wages
- New skills/Technology
- Goods made from home market – cuts expensive imports
- Foreign exchange to buy goods from abroad

LOSSES
- Company may try to influence how a country is run
- Culture clash
- Better jobs go to skilled foreign workers
- If workers demand higher wages company may leave, leading to unemployment
- Higher wages encourage thirst for expensive imported consumer goods
- Companies highly mechanised so few workers needed
- Local firms go out of business if making same product as MNC
- Goods of no real benefit to local people/exported
- Create a divided society between those working for MNC and those not
- MNC may not bring foreign money but borrow locally
- Many profits go out of the country

C

PEOPLE'S NEEDS

3.8 Countertrade

A simple swap, rather than a cash deal, is a good way of doing business between friends (**A**). Cash is normally involved when countries trade goods. Finding cash is easy enough for a developed country with its large reserves of money. But it is not so easy for a developing country which may well have little money available. The answer may be to engage in a swap. The term used when countries swap goods, rather than buy and sell them, is **countertrade**. Countertrade has become increasingly popular during the 1980s. Many developing countries are deeply in debt and lack money to pay for imports. By exchanging goods they can still manage to import the things they need (**B**).

Countertrade has several advantages for developing countries (**C**). Developed countries are not so keen on the arrangement but they often have little choice if they want to gain access to certain markets. Over 20 developing countries now regularly engage in countertrade. It offers a chance for the developing world to break free from the unfair pattern of trade and obtain a fair deal.

I've been trying to buy that record for ages. I'll give you £4 for it.

No thanks, I don't want money.

Well, if you give me the record I'll let you have this solar calculator.

Yes, I'd like that. You can have the record for the calculator provided you give me that paperback as well.

...OK. You drive a hard bargain!

Be careful, or I'll change my mind!

A

68

Skills	empathy
Concepts	countertrade

B

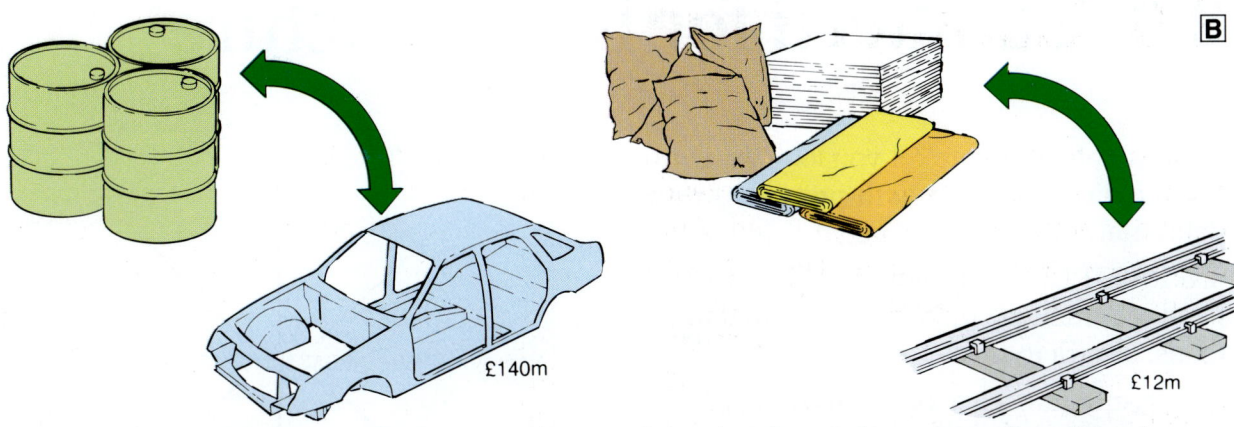

- Iran exchanged crude oil for £140 million worth of car parts with a British firm.
- Indonesia exchanged rubber, cocoa, textiles and paper for £12 million worth of railway equipment from Canada.
- Saudi Arabia exchanged crude oil for £600 million worth of aircraft from the USA.
- Brazil exchanged steel, oil drilling platforms and food for £450 million worth of crude oil from the former USSR. 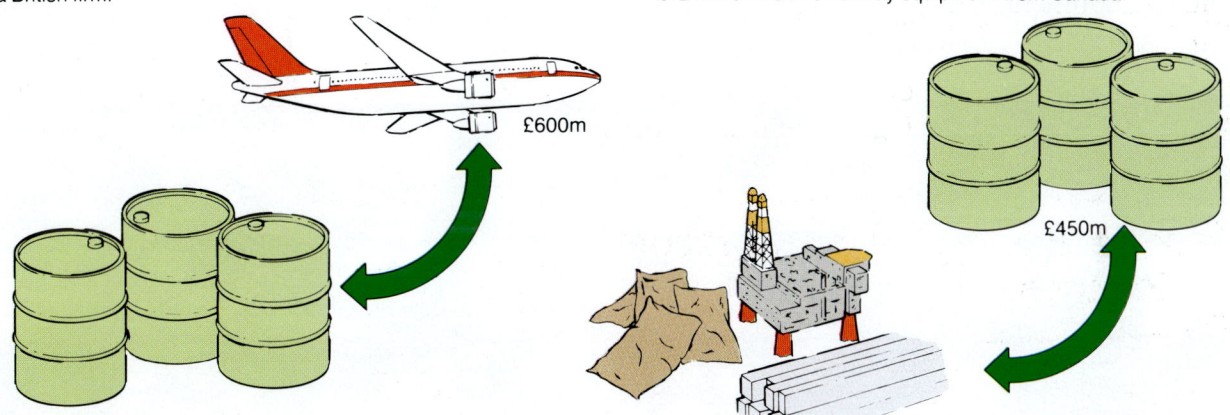

1 Copy and complete the paragraph below, choosing the correct words from the wordbank:

Countertrade means to …… goods rather than to buy and …… them. Developing countries like to set up countertrade deals because they allow them to continue to …… goods even if they do not have enough …… to pay for them. They may also be able to dispose of goods which may be in small …… Developed countries are not keen on countertrade because the goods may be …… to sell and may be of …… quality.

Wordbank: difficult swap money sell import lower demand

2 One of the disadvantages of countertrade in **C** is that: 'Countertrade deals threaten the world system of free trade'. Why might developing countries describe this as an advantage rather than a disadvantage?

C	Advantages	Disadvantages
	* it allows poor developing countries to continue to import goods	* It is not always easy for a company to find markets for the goods it has received in countertrade deals.
	* it allows developing countries to find markets for goods which may be in small demand	* The quality of goods in countertrade may be lower than those which have to be paid for in cash.
	* it allows developing countries to find markets in developed countries which might otherwise be closed to them.	* Countertrade deals threaten the world system of free trade, where goods are bought and sold without restrictions.

PEOPLE'S NEEDS
3.9 The Need for Infrastructure

What is 'infrastructure'? If you look the word up in a dictionary, you will probably find a definition like this:

'INFRASTRUCTURE (noun) . . . the stock of fixed equipment in a country, including roads, electricity, water supplies, etc . . .'

Infrastructure is a basic need of people and society; the foundation on which economic development is based.

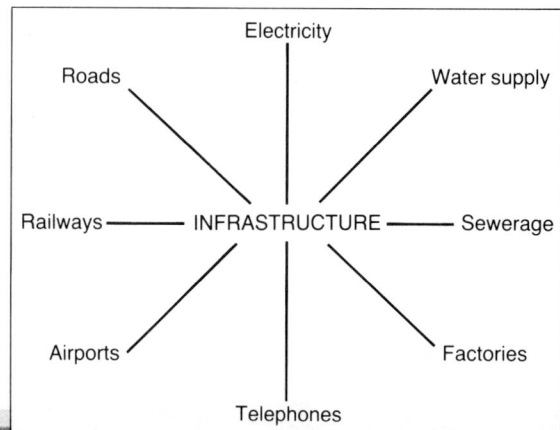

1 Study carefully the photograph of a street in Nairobi (**A**). Make a list of all the features of the infrastructure which you can see.

Building up an infrastructure like that in **A** takes time and costs much money. Many developing countries lack both. The population of many cities is growing very rapidly. Often, population increase happens so quickly that the construction of the infrastructure cannot keep up with it, and problems arise:
- the lack of roads creates problems of access and congestion.
- the lack of electricity means that oil lamps and candles have to be used and there is a higher risk of fire.
- perhaps most serious of all is the lack of water and sanitation, because this encourages disease.

Skills	interpreting photographs, keyword plan
Concepts	infrastructure, self-help
Issues	problems & development

The governments of developing countries often choose to spend money on large, impressive infrastructure projects such as airports and new roads (**B**). Sometimes developed countries pay for these projects but only on condition that the project is built by engineering companies from the developed countries concerned!

What is really needed is simpler infrastructure: improved local roads, sewerage systems, clean water supplies, and so on. Developed countries are not so keen to help with such projects because they do not involve such high technology engineering or look so impressive. The answer in some countries has been **self-help**: local people doing all they can to improve their own local infrastructure (**C**).

---

2 What effects do the following have on a country and its people: ● lack of roads; ● lack of electricity; ● lack of water and sanitation?

3 Why do the governments of developing countries spend money on impressive infrastructure projects?

4 a What is 'self-help'?
  b Why is self-help a useful method for developing countries to adopt?

PEOPLE'S NEEDS

3.10 Transport Development in West Africa – Rail and Road

Agriculture and industry need transport to move food, raw materials and finished goods around quickly and efficiently. A good **transport system**, involving road, rail, air and sea/rivers is very important for a country's development. A good network will also help with the spread of health care, education and new ideas.

A **transport system** is made of **nodes** (places) and **links** (types of transport which join places together). Many nodes are major cities or central places. All the links and nodes combine to make a transport system or **network** pattern. The more links there are, the denser the network pattern, and so the more developed the transport system. **A** shows Africa's railway network. **B** focuses on a particular part of that network: West Africa.

---

1 Why is transport development important to developing countries
2 Look at **A**.
  a Use an atlas map of Africa to help you name any countries or regions where the railway pattern is dense.
  b Why do you think a large part of North West Africa has no railway?
  c Why do you think not many railways cross Africa from coast to coast?

West Africa

During the 19th century many European countries, including Britain, relied on their **colonies** to supply raw materials for their developing industries. They developed good transport links between the inland sources of raw materials and the seaports from which these raw materials were exported to the **colonial powers**. West Africa was rich in tropical crops (cocoa, cotton, palm oil) and minerals (copper, oil, tin). Colonial powers such as Britain built railways to carry the raw materials they needed to the coast (see **B**).

A Africa's railway network

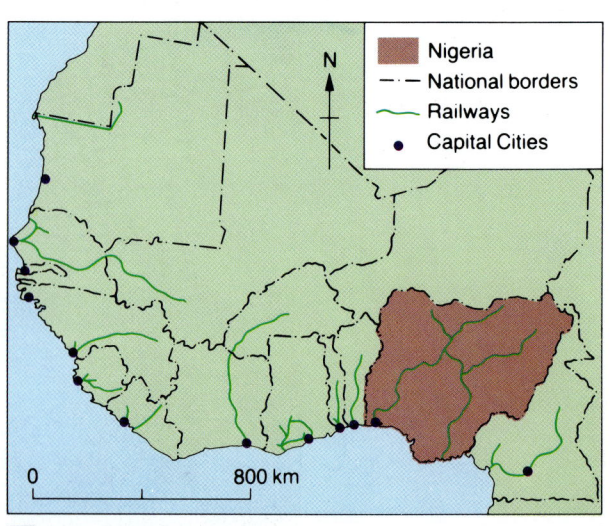

B Railways in West Africa

Skills	atlas work, interpreting photograph
Concepts	transport systems, network, colony
Issues	colonialism/independence

Nigeria

Railways in Nigeria were first constructed by the British (using local labour) beween 1890 and 1930. The system set up was to exploit Nigeria's cash crops and minerals (**C**). The rail **links** end at the **nodes** of Port Harcourt and Lagos, both deep-water ports. In the 1920s roads were developed so that export crops could be assembled at railway stations along the Kano – Lagos rail link. These roads also allowed colonial officers to administer and control the economy of the colony.

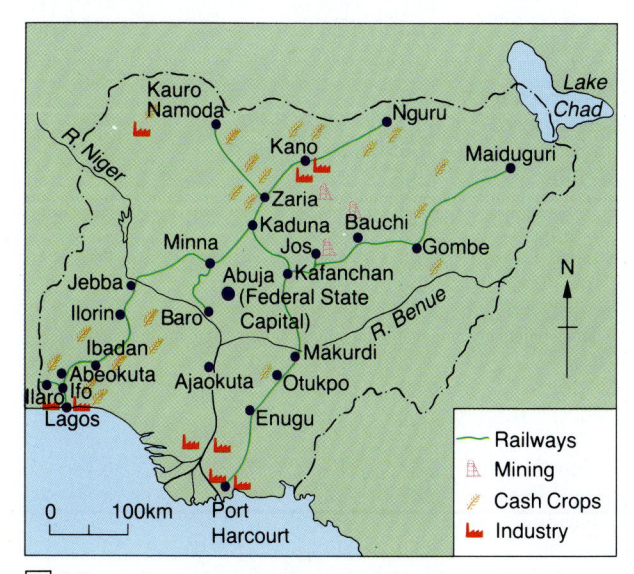

C Minerals and cash crops in Nigeria

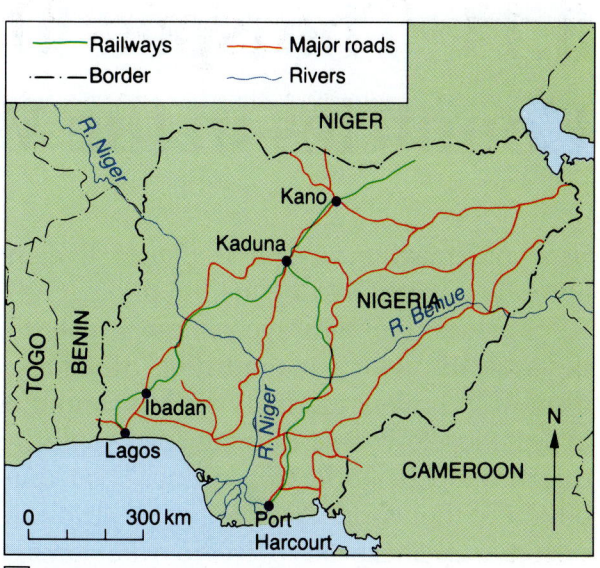

D Nigeria's modern transport network

Today Nigeria is **independent** and roads provide the main form of transport. 95% of internal movement of people and goods and 60% of all traffic to the seaports goes by road. Recently road links have been developed with other West African countries (**D**). For example the Lagos-Shagame-Benin City-Enugu-Manfe road has been built as part of the **Trans-African Highway**. Another new link is the Kaduna-Kano-Daura-Kongalam – Niger border. These road links encourage trade between Nigeria and other members of **ECOWAS** (Economic Community of West African States).

As road traffic increases the city streets become more congested.

3 Look at **B**. Copy and complete the following sentences.

Most railways link the _____ areas where ___ _____ were produced, to the ___ . Raw materials were _____ to the _____ countries for processing. Many of the ports are also _____ cities.

Wordbank: sea, raw materials, inland, sea, exported, capital, developed

4 Why do you think the **network** pattern of railways shown in **B** is found in West Africa?

5 Look at **C**.
  a Name the two nodes that are ports.
  b How many links has Kaduna (an old colonial centre)?
  c Does the pattern of railways follow the pattern of distribution of products? Give reasons for your answer.

6 Look at **D**. What has happened to transport development since independence in Nigeria?

FURTHER WORK

- Apart from resource exploitation what other reasons could there be for areas being poorly linked by rail? Look at **A, B** and **C**, and at political, physical and vegetation maps in your atlas. What might be barriers to building railways (eg highland, hostile environments and frontiers of countries . . .)

PEOPLE'S NEEDS

3.11 The Need for Aid – The Poorest Countries in the World

Can you imagine what it is like to live in **absolute poverty** like the man in photograph **A**? That is the term geographers use to describe life where malnutrition, illiteracy, disease and infant mortality are high and life expectancy low. It is difficult for people in the developed world to imagine – yet one billion of the world's people live in absolute poverty. Of these 90% live in rural areas. They tend to live in **fragile environments** which are easily upset by changes, for example population growth, or natural disasters such as drought and flood. Many do not have access to medical care, education and state benefits. They need help!

Many people are concerned about the plight of the very poor and the increasing gap between rich and poor – both within countries and between countries.

Where are the poorest countries of the world? The United Nations has identified 36 of these **Least Developed Countries** (LDCs). **B** lists some statistics about these countries.

Country	GDP ($) per capita	Adult literacy rate (%)	Urban dwellers (%)	Manufacturing share of GDP (%)
Afghanistan	209	24	15	10
Bangladesh	112	33	10	7
Benin	265	26	31	5
Bhutan	102	22	4	5
Botswana	908	71	30	8
Burkina Faso	171	13	8	11
Burundi	300	34	2	9
Cape Verde	250	47	20	5
Central African Republic	247	40	41	6
Chad	133	15	18	7
Comoros	224	N/A	12	5
Democratic Yemen	510	41	37	9
Djibouti	654	N/A	74	6
Equatorial Guinea	188	37	54	5
Ethiopia	140	55	13	10
Gambia	313	25	18	5
Guinea	419	20	19	3
Guinea-Bissau	192	31	24	2
Haiti	333	38	25	17
Laos	140	44	13	8
Lesotho	260	52	5	6
Malawi	206	25	10	12
Maldives	393	82	11	5
Mali	157	17	17	7
Nepal	155	26	5	4
Niger	317	10	13	5
Rwanda	268	47	4	14
Samoa	425	N/A	21	7
Sao Tome and Principe	306	N/A	33	5
Sierra Leone	443	N/A	25	4
Somalia	291	12	30	6
Sudan	376	N/A	25	7
Togo	262	41	17	7
Uganda	211	N/A	12	4
Tanzania	238	N/A	12	6
Yemen	430	14	10	7
Average of All LDCs	$203	32%	19%	7%

N/A = data not available

B The world's LDCs

A

Skills	graph work, keyword plan, empathy
Concepts	absolute poverty, aid, LDCs
Issues	underdevelopment, world poverty

1 Copy and complete the keyword plan:

```
              ?
  ?    PROBLEMS FACED BY    ?
          ABSOLUTE POOR

no medical care    ?    malnutrition
```

2 Describe the living conditions of the man in **A**.

3 How would you feel if you had to live in conditions like this?

4 Look at **B**. What factors have been used to identify LDCs?

5 On an outline map of the world, shade in the LDCs. Put a title and key on your map (There is an outline map in the *Activity pack*).

6 There are two **poverty belts**. One is in Africa, the other in Asia. They contain the LDCs. Use your world map to find out how many LDCs are in Africa.

7 Look at **C**. Put the causes of underdevelopment in rank order (with the main cause as Rank 1...) Compare rank orders with another member of your group. Discuss the similarities and differences between your rank orders.

8 Give reasons for your choice of the top ranked cause of underdevelopment

FURTHER WORK

- Draw two scatter graphs: one for GDP/adult literacy and one for GDP/manufacturing as a share of GDP (see Unit 1.3). Does the country with the highest GDP have the highest literacy % and manufacturing as a share of the GDP?
- Do you think that LDCs can be included in the term 'developing world'? Think about change in the developing world and why it might be difficult for LDCs.
- In what ways might the developed world have helped cause absolute poverty in the poorest countries of the world?
- Can you think of any examples of absolute poverty in the developed world (eg in Britain or the USA)?

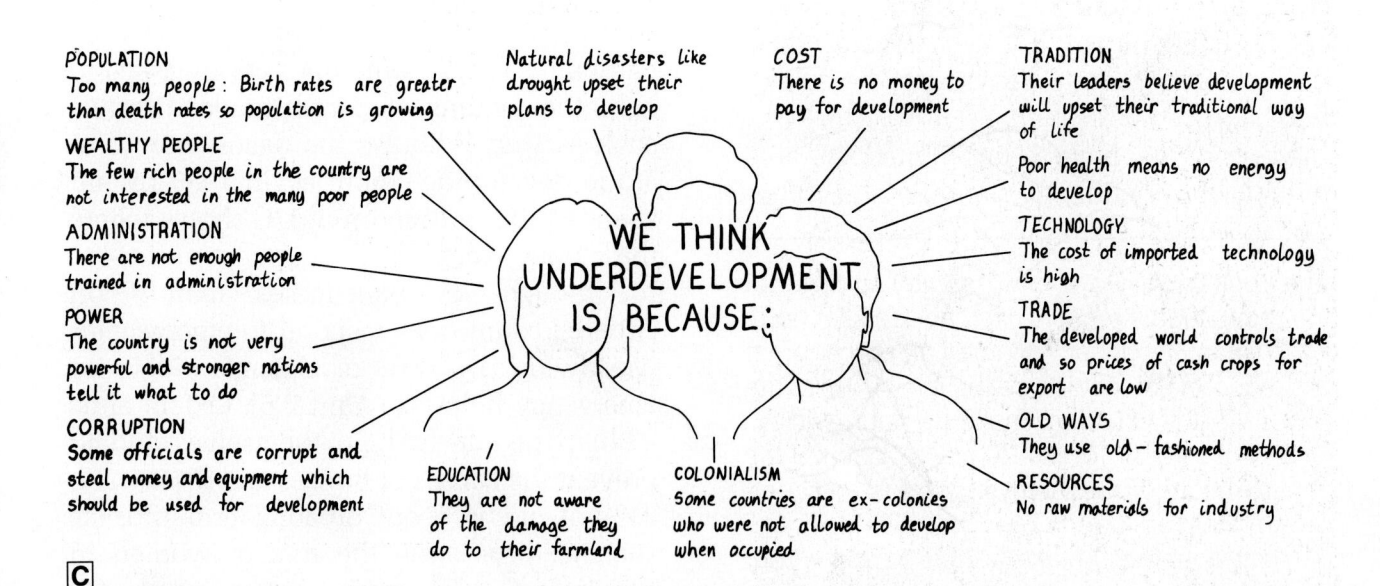

Many people in the world's poorest countries are frustrated by their poverty. But it is very difficult to improve conditions in these countries. They are caught in a trap of **underdevelopment**. **C** shows some people's ideas of what causes underdevelopment.

WE THINK UNDERDEVELOPMENT IS BECAUSE:

POPULATION
Too many people: Birth rates are greater than death rates so population is growing

WEALTHY PEOPLE
The few rich people in the country are not interested in the many poor people

ADMINISTRATION
There are not enough people trained in administration

POWER
The country is not very powerful and stronger nations tell it what to do

CORRUPTION
Some officials are corrupt and steal money and equipment which should be used for development

Natural disasters like drought upset their plans to develop

EDUCATION
They are not aware of the damage they do to their farmland

COLONIALISM
Some countries are ex-colonies who were not allowed to develop when occupied

COST
There is no money to pay for development

TRADITION
Their leaders believe development will upset their traditional way of life

Poor health means no energy to develop

TECHNOLOGY
The cost of imported technology is high

TRADE
The developed world controls trade and so prices of cash crops for export are low

OLD WAYS
They use old-fashioned methods

RESOURCES
No raw materials for industry

C

PEOPLE'S NEEDS

3.12 Raising the Money

A

[Muslim Aid poster: HELP OUR WORLD — Sudan... Afghanistan... Palestine... Bangladesh... India... Indonesia... Mozambique... Lebanon... Philippines. Fill in this form now and send your Zakah/Sadaqah to: MUSLIM AID, FREE POST, LONDON N7 8BR]

How do you feel when someone asks you to give money to help people in developing countries? Do you: Say no? Give automatically? Think about the request and then decide? Offer to help them with the collection?

Most of us have been invited to give money for victims of famine and other natural disasters. Sometimes we are asked to help the victims of people-made disasters such as war. **B** shows the major sources of aid to developing countries. In 1985 Britain spent £1292 million on aid. **C** shows where the money went.

Although it concentrates mainly on Africa, Oxfam does respond to emergencies worldwide (**D**). 69% of Oxfam's aid is for emergency help (see Unit 2.6). Oxfam aims to help people to help themselves and to prevent the causes of hunger and disease. So 31% of aid is spent on long-term projects such as promoting the role of women in development, improving water supply (eg well digging in Ethiopia), education, health and promoting self-help (ie small community work in Gujarat, India).

Governments – 70%
- respond to plans put forward by advisers
- respond to other countries' requests for aid
- give aid in return for certain conditions, for example that the country being helped must buy goods from the donor country

International agencies – 24%
- funded by many countries
- organise projects
- examples include United Nations Development Programme, World Bank

Charities – 6%
- mostly voluntary organisations
- tend to be non-political
- operate on a smaller scale
- promote self-help schemes (see Unit 4.6)
- examples include Oxfam, Christian Aid, Cafod, Help the Aged, Save the Children Fund

B Sources of aid to the developing world

---

1 a Look at **A**. Do a small survey to find out how people react to such appeals for help. Ask at least ten people, at home or at school. You could use the questions at the start of this unit, or make up your own.
 b In a group (or as a class) collect the results of your surveys. What is the commonest attitude to giving help to developing countries? Make a table to show your group's survey results and present them as a bar chart.
2 What is the major source of aid in **B**?

Skills	survey work, graph work
Concepts	aid, aid agencies

C

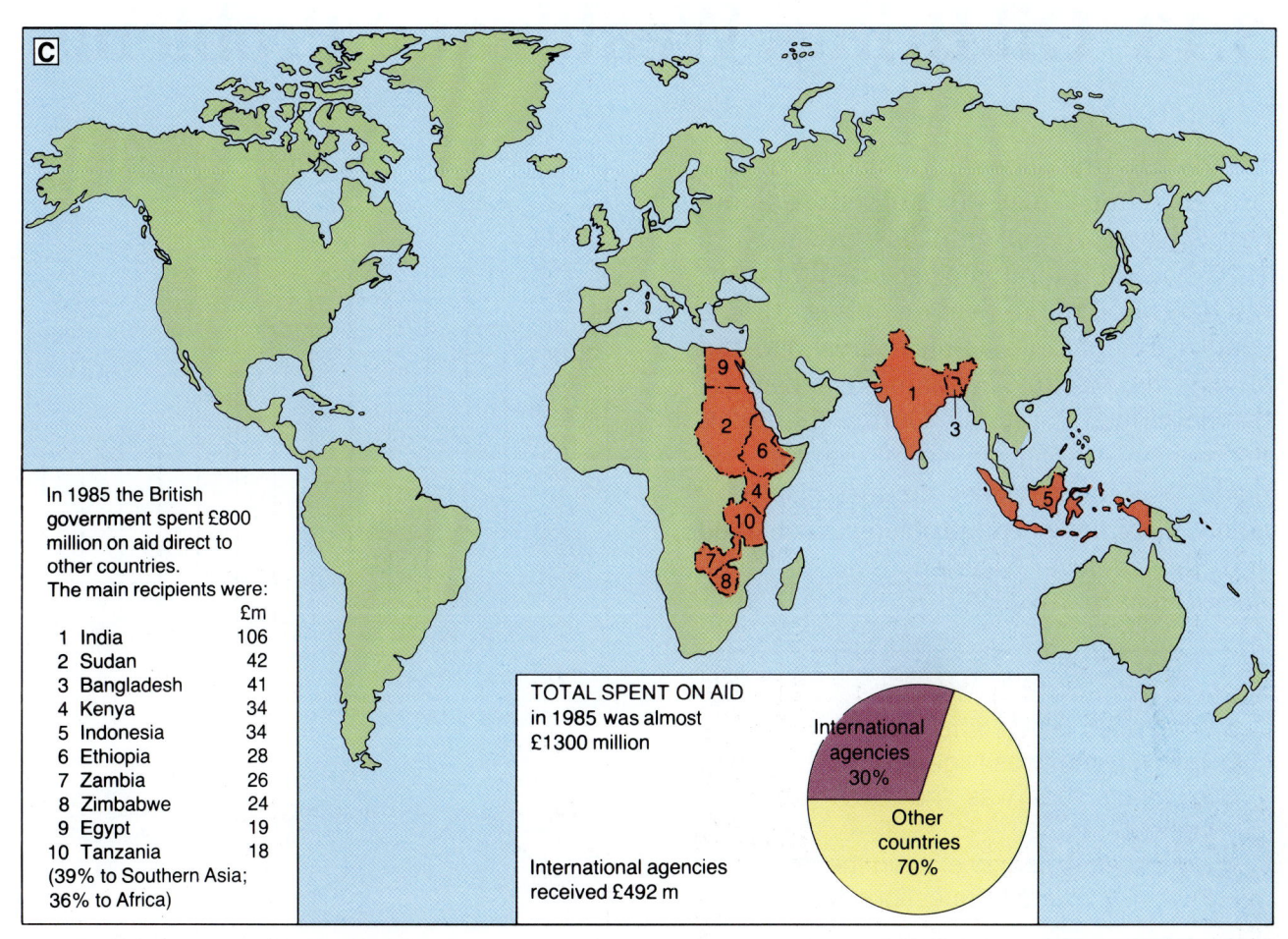

In 1985 the British government spent £800 million on aid direct to other countries.
The main recipients were:

		£m
1	India	106
2	Sudan	42
3	Bangladesh	41
4	Kenya	34
5	Indonesia	34
6	Ethiopia	28
7	Zambia	26
8	Zimbabwe	24
9	Egypt	19
10	Tanzania	18

(39% to Southern Asia; 36% to Africa)

TOTAL SPENT ON AID in 1985 was almost £1300 million

International agencies received £492 m

- International agencies 30%
- Other countries 70%

D How Oxfam allocated its funds overseas:

- Emergency 69% (includes £22.3m for African famine appeals)
- Social development 17%
- Health 8%
- Agriculture 6%

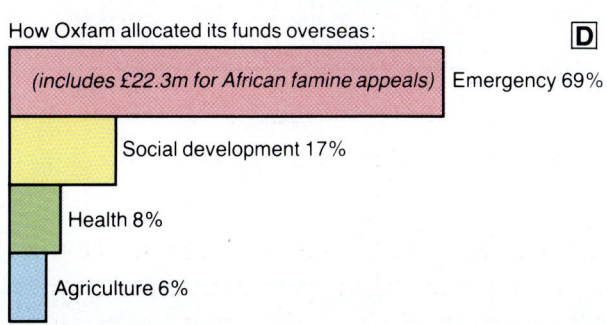

Destination	%
Horn of Africa	61
East Africa	6
Indian Subcontinent	6
Andean countries	4
Middle East and Egypt	4
Central America	3
Central and Southern Africa	3
Indonesia and Far East	3
Caribbean	2
Brazil	2
West Africa	2
Equatorial Africa	2
World general/UK	2

3 What are the similarities and differences between aid from governments, international agencies and charities?

4 Look at **C**.
  a How much does Britain spend on aid?
  b How many countries receive aid from Britain?
  c Where does most aid go?

5 Look at **D**.
  a Where does Oxfam spend most of its money?
  b What is the money spent on?

6 What are Oxfam's main aims?

7 Collect advertisements from newspapers that ask for people to help with problems in the developing world. Draw up a table to show who needs help, where and why, and the sort of help they are given.

8 How can people help the developing world, apart from giving money?

PEOPLE'S NEEDS

3.13 Oil Brings Wealth and Problems

Nigeria has the largest population of any African country, over 105 million. **A** shows how Nigeria's population has grown since 1970. Nigeria is fortunate because it has vast reserves of oil, more than any other African country except Libya. Oil is in great demand all over the world. The main customers are the developed countries. During the 1970s the money Nigeria received for exports of oil made it a much richer country. Unfortunately there have been problems since 1980 and the average Nigerian is now much poorer than in 1980 (**B**).

---

1 Study **B**.
  a What does GDP stand for?
  b In which year was Nigeria's GDP highest?
  c In which year was the GDP per head highest?
  d How does **A** help to explain the difference in your answers to questions **b** and **c**?

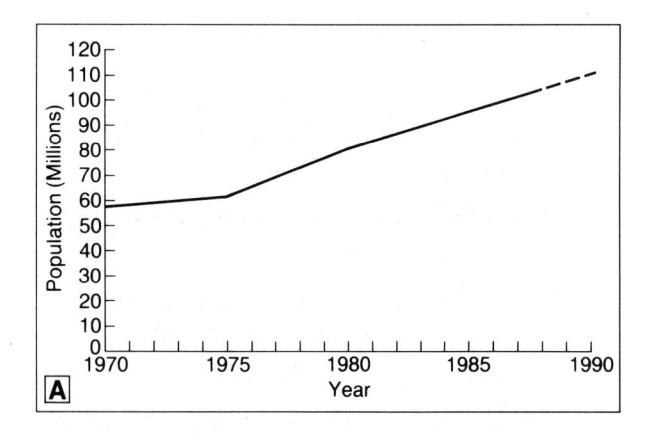

Oil was first discovered under the delta of the River Niger in the 1950s. There are now over 60 oilfields (**C**). Much of the oil is exported by tanker to the USA, Europe and Japan. By 1974 Nigeria was almost totally dependent upon oil exports. 98% of Nigeria's export earnings and 85% of the government's revenue came from oil. **D** and **E** show oil production and prices, 1975–1987.

Nigeria spent much of its oil money on developing manufacturing industry: oil

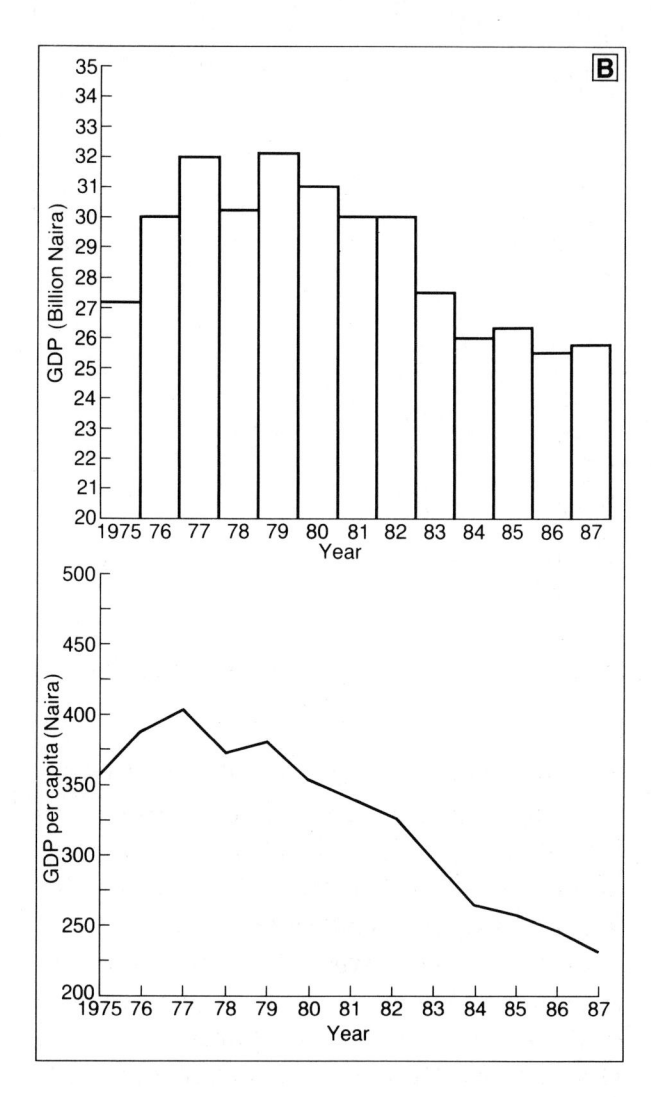

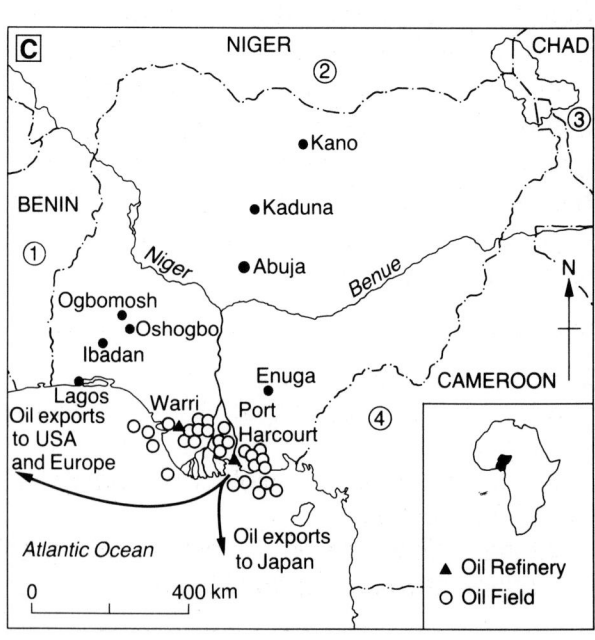

Skills	interpreting maps and graphs
Concepts	import substitution, industries
Issues	dependence on resources, importance of oil

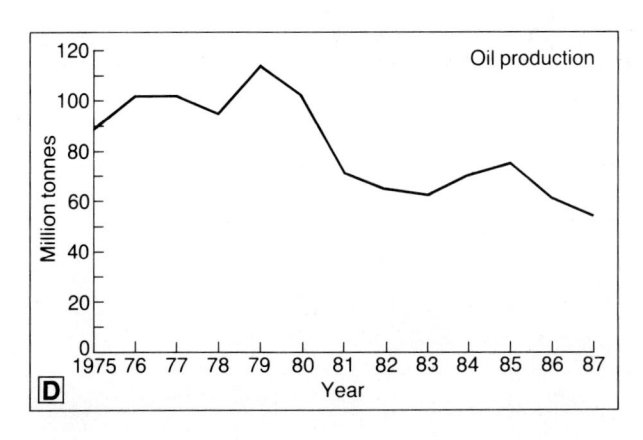

D Oil production (Million tonnes, 1975–87)

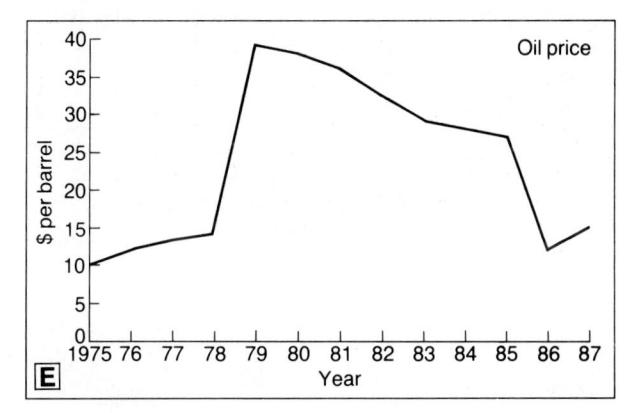

E Oil price ($ per barrel, 1975–87)

refining, paper, cement, textiles and motor vehicles were produced. The industry was intended to provide jobs and produce some of the goods that Nigeria had to import (this is called **import substitution**).

Further money was spent on road construction and armaments. The great expense of these projects was only partly met by oil revenues. Much of the cost was met by loans from banks in the developed countries. The government hoped to pay back the loans using future oil earnings. Unfortunately, the fall in oil prices was devastating for Nigeria's plans. The result was high unemployment, heavy debt and falling living standards. Nigeria knows that oil brings wealth, but it also brings problems (**F**).

---

2 Study **D** and **E**.
  a In which year was Nigeria's oil production highest?
  b How does **E** help to explain the changes in oil production?
  c What effects do you think the falling oil prices have had upon Nigeria?

3 a Where are most of Nigeria's oilfields located (**C**)?
  b Name the main oil exporting port in Nigeria.
4 a What is meant by **import substitution**?
  b Why would Nigeria be keen to have import substitution industries?
5 Explain how oil has brought both wealth and problems to Nigeria.

Advantages

* Big increase in government income from oil revenue
* Oil production and related industry provides many jobs
* Great improvements possible in education and health
* Through its oil Nigeria has a more important voice in African and world affairs
* Development of new industries such as oil refining

Disadvantages

* Government embarked on ambitious projects which needed huge loans. Nigeria now deeply in debt
* Many of the top jobs in the oil industry taken by foreigners
* Country became totally dependent upon oil (98% of export income in 1981). When oil prices fell Nigeria was badly hit
* Nigerian agriculture collapsed as people left the countryside to seek work and wealth in the cities. Agricultural exports fell from £200 million in 1971 to £95 million in 1981
* Nigeria's cities have grown far too rapidly. Lagos' population grew by 300 000 per year during the early 1980s
* Increased personal wealth caused a flood of imports of consumer goods which hit Nigeria's own industries, eg cars

F How oil has affected Nigeria

PEOPLE'S NEEDS

3.14 War in the Middle East

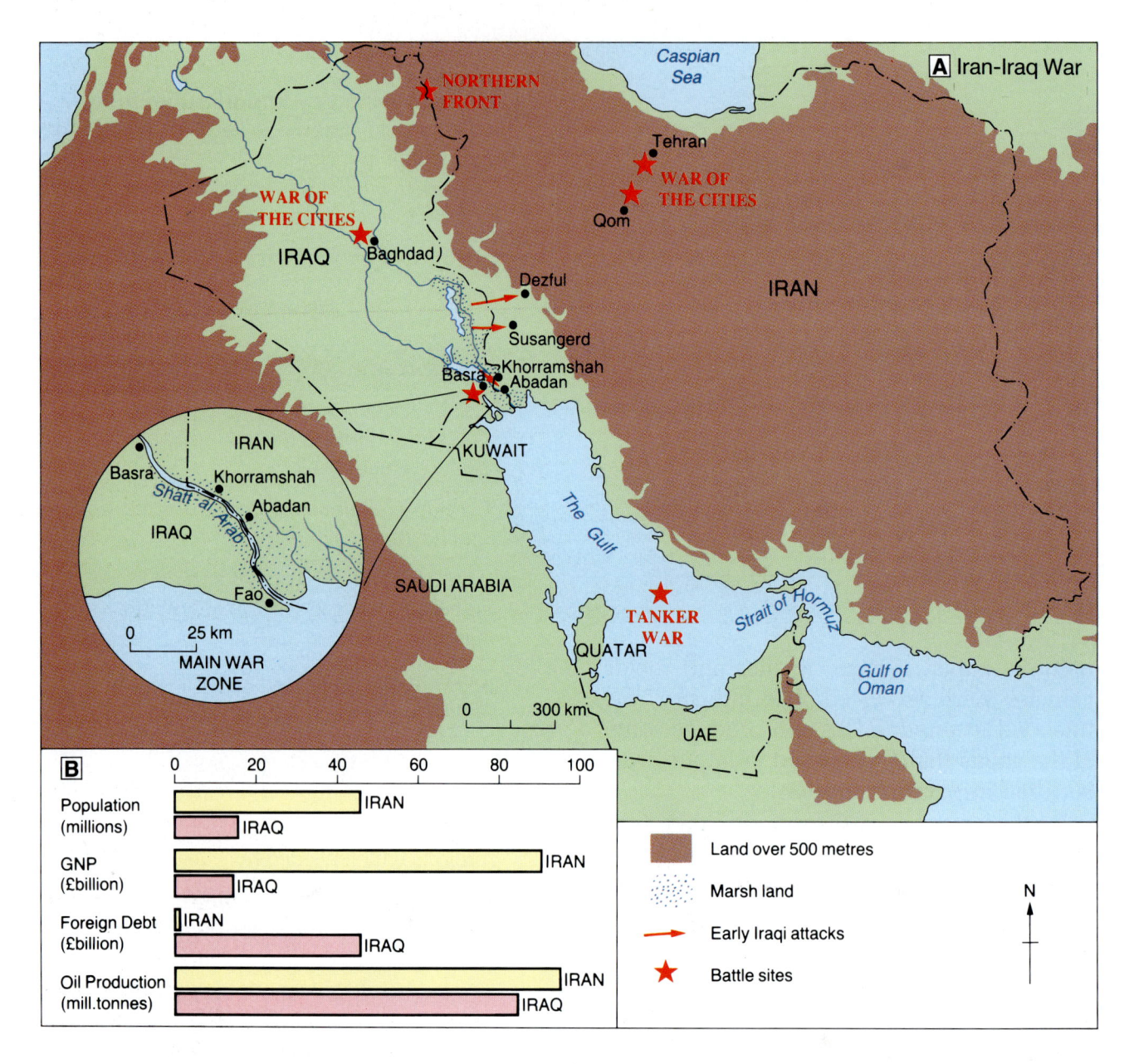

A Iran-Iraq War

Map legend:
- Land over 500 metres
- Marsh land
- Early Iraqi attacks
- Battle sites

Battle sites marked: Northern Front, War of the Cities (Baghdad), War of the Cities (Tehran/Qom), Basra/Khorramshah/Abadan area, Tanker War.

Inset: Main War Zone showing Basra, Khorramshah, Abadan, Fao along the Shatt-al-Arab.

B Comparison bar chart (scale 0-100):
- Population (millions): IRAN (larger), IRAQ (smaller)
- GNP (£billion): IRAN (larger), IRAQ (smaller)
- Foreign Debt (£billion): IRAN (very small), IRAQ (large)
- Oil Production (mill. tonnes): IRAN, IRAQ (similar)

The Middle East is often in the news. Unfortunately, the news is usually of warfare.

In the Middle East the 1980s were dominated by the war between Iran and Iraq.

This unit looks at the Iran-Iraq War as a case study of the geographical causes and effects of war.

Why was the war fought?

Iraq has only a short coastline. The Shatt-al-Arab waterway provides a route from Iraq's largest port, Basra, to the Gulf at Fao (**A**). It is a vital route for Iraq's exports of oil. The east bank of the Shatt-al-Arab forms the border with Iraq's powerful neighbour, Iran. Iran was able to control Iraq's major sealanes and tried to dominate the Gulf area.

In 1979 a revolution in Iran threw the country into confusion. Iraq seized its chance to become the dominant power in the Gulf.

In 1980 Iraq invaded Iran, aiming to grab the east bank of the Shatt-al-Arab and occupy the cities of Khorramshah and Abadan. The Iraqis made slow progress and

Skills	map work
Concepts	Conflict, superpowers
Issues	war, importance of oil

C An oil tanker ablaze in the Gulf, 1987

were surprised by the strength of the Iranian defence. The Iraqis were thrown back to the Shatt-al-Arab. Iran tried to invade Iraq but had no success.

Why did the war continue for so long?

The information in **B** suggests that Iran could have continued the war much longer than Iraq. But Iraq had superior weapons and air power, plus money from its Arab allies including Kuwait and Saudi Arabia.

The Iran-Iraq War became a 'war of attrition'. Neither side could win. Other Gulf countries, and the Superpowers (the USA and the former USSR) did not want any country to have sole control over the Gulf because of its importance for oil supplies. They wanted a 'balance of power' in the region. In 1988 the United Nations worked out a ceasefire agreement. Both Iran and Iraq accepted. The war had gone on for eight years. Over a million people had died and the economies of both countries were wrecked.

1 How do the following factors help to explain the causes of the Iran-Iraq War:
   a The border along the Shatt-al-Arab waterway
   b The inland location of the port of Basra
   c The Islamic Revolution in Iran in 1979
   d The desire to be supreme power in the Gulf?
2 Study **A**.
   a Where was the main war zone in the Iran-Iraq War?
   b Which country is larger in area?
   c How would the following physical factors affect the fighting:
     (i) the marshland of the main war zone
     (ii) the mountains of the Northern Front?
     (Think of the problems faced by tanks, vehicles and infantry.)
3 Study **B**.
   a What is the population of (i) Iraq (ii) Iran?
   b Which of the two countries should have been able to continue the war longest? Why?
   c Why were the Superpowers prepared to let the war continue?

PEOPLE'S NEEDS

3.15 Needs not being met – Apartheid in South Africa

In South Africa there are over 32 million people in an area four times the size of the United Kingdom. **A** shows the make-up of the South African population, in racial groups:

A

	% of total population
Africans/Blacks (Zulu, Xhosa, Tswana etc)	74
Whites	15
Coloured (people of 'mixed race')	8
Indians/Asians	3

South Africa is the only country in the world that classifies people according to their race and colour. Many non-white people prefer to be called 'blacks'.

Most white South Africans are rich and have affluent lifestyles similar to Europeans and Americans. Their white government is powerful and has military forces. The whites have a vote but black people are not allowed to vote. Because the blacks have no say in the political system they are not able to change South Africa. Over the last 100 years the white settlers have used cheap black labour to develop an advanced industrial economy. Diamonds, fruit, gold, coal and wine are among South Africa's main exports. But black people do not get a fair share of the wealth they help to create (**B**).

The South African government has constructed a system of **apartheid**. This offically means a policy of 'separate development' of the white and non-white populations. Apartheid maintains the **privilege** of the whites. It **separates** the black people from the whites; it controls where the blacks live and gives them the poorest land. **C** shows the unfair distribution of land and services in South Africa.

"I shall never forget my visit to Zweledinga, a resettlement camp near Queenstown where I met this little girl coming out of a shack in which she lived with her widowed mother and sister. I asked her "Does your mother receive a pension or grant or something?" "No," she replied. "Then what do you do for food?"
Then she said, "We borrow food." "Have you ever returned any of the food you borrowed?" "No," she replied. "What do you do when you can't borrow food?" "We drink water to fill our stomachs."

This is a conversation seared into my memory. More than anything I have experienced of the evils of apartheid, this encounter with the girl at Zweledinga made me determined to do all I could to stop such a vicious policy – which could let people starve, not accidentally, but by deliberate Government policy."

Archbishop Desmond Tutu. Christian Aid.

B

The South African government has established ten **'homelands'** or **bantustans** (**D**). Black Africans of a particular tribe are forced to live in their 'homeland'. They have little freedom of movement and jobs are few. Although the homelands offer some independence to the blacks, no-one outside South Africa recognises them. They are really a method of controlling black people (**E**).

C

Land distribution
White 87%   Black 13%

Pupil/teacher ratio
White 19 to 1   Black 46 to 1

Doctors per head
White 1 per 330   Black 1 per 12 000

Infant mortality
(number of children who die before their first birthday)
White 1 in 72   Black 1 in 12

Skills	map work, research
Concepts	apartheid, forced removals
Issues	racism, inequality

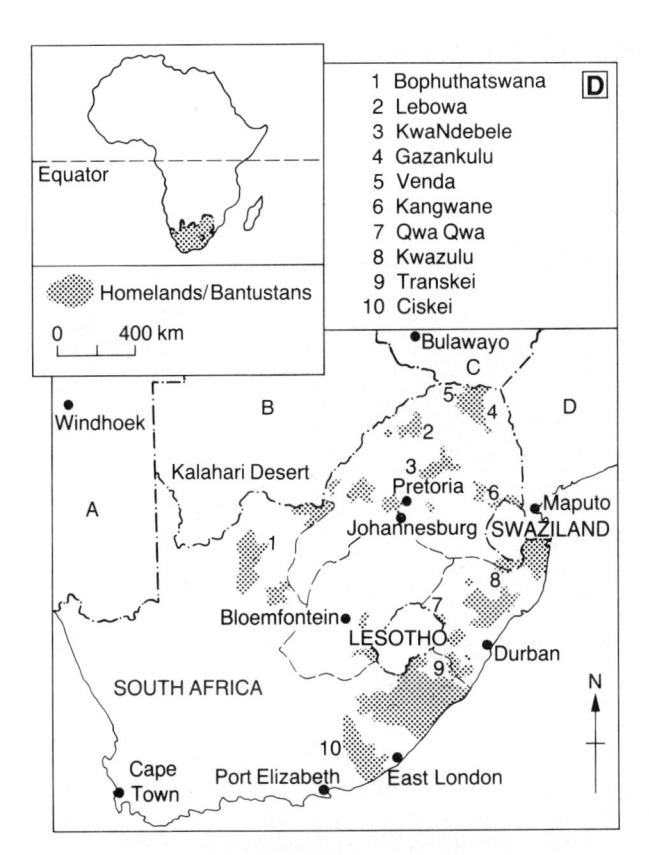

Many people all over the world are against apartheid. They put pressure on the South African government to relax the apartheid laws. In the early 1990s the apartheid policy was abandoned.

The leader of the main black political party, Nelson Mandela, was released from prison.

Plans were drawn up to give black people the vote. However, living standards for black people will be much lower than for whites for a long time.

1 Bophuthatswana
2 Lebowa
3 KwaNdebele
4 Gazankulu
5 Venda
6 Kangwane
7 Qwa Qwa
8 Kwazulu
9 Transkei
10 Ciskei

1 On an outline map of South Africa (there is one in the *Activity pack*), name: **a** The major cities; **b** The countries which have borders with South Africa; **c** The Transkei and Ciskei bantustans.
2 Read the story told by Archbishop Desmond Tutu in **B**. Write in your own words why the Archbishop was so affected by the little girl.
3 Read about forced removals (**E**). Why have black people been moved to 'homelands'?

Forced Removals: the Churches estimate that 3.5 million people, mainly black, have been forcibly removed from their homes as their labour is no longer needed, or as black and white areas have been redefined.

Christian Aid.

83

PEOPLE'S NEEDS

3.16 Needs not being met – Being a Foreigner in Britain

A

JAMAICA TO SHEFFIELD

"Winston and Eileen's Story"
by Ian Hunt

This is a true story. Winston and Eileen are real people, as are Cecil and Stephen and Martha.

Winston met Eileen in a well-to-do restaurant on Kingston High Street in Jamaica. They had known each other for a long time and had decided to get married. They hoped to build a good life together.

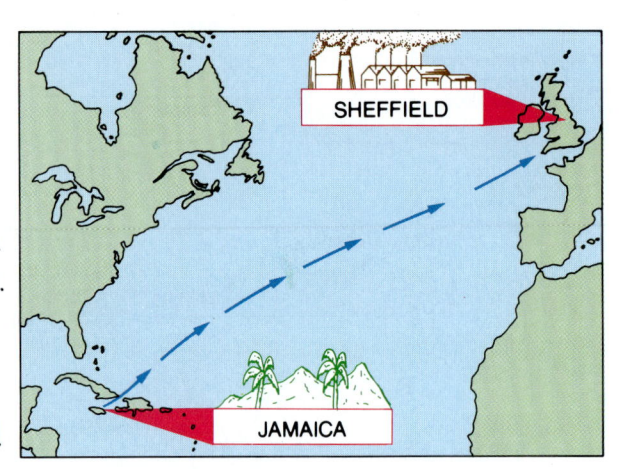

Eileen saw an advertisement asking for workers in Britain and thought, "We are needed in the mother country. Here is our opportunity for a good life in Britain."

Peter Williams was a friend of Winston who had emigrated to Britain two years earlier. He wrote to Winston saying that there were plenty of jobs in the Sheffield steelworks.

It was decided that Winston and Eileen would go to Sheffield and stay with Peter.

They caught the boat from Kingston and were welcomed when they arrived in Southampton.

They stayed with Winston's friend for two months by which time Eileen was working in the National Health Service and Winston was working in the steelworks. They then rented a flat in a converted Victorian house until they managed to put down the deposit on a place of their own.

Their children Cecil and Martha Thomson were both born in England as was Peter Williams' son. He was called Stephen and was great friends with Cecil and Martha.

Both Cecil and Martha did well at school and got 'O' levels and Cecil went on to get 'A' levels and a degree from University; but although Martha got a job as a nurse with the help of her Mum, Cecil found job-hunting more difficult.

At the same time things started to get a little more difficult for Winston and Eileen. Although they were both good at their jobs, reliable, trustworthy and worked hard, they were never offered promotion. This disappointed Winston because he knew he was good enough, but he kept working hard.

In 1982 the steelworks closed down and Winston was out of a job for the first time in his life. Jobs were now more difficult to get and Winston felt that others were getting jobs that he was better qualified for. He was upset by this but kept on trying. He also noticed that more and more of his Caribbean friends were unemployed and that their children couldn't find work. Nobody had actually said so but he knew that it was because they were black.

Skills	discussion, empathy
Concepts	prejudice
Issues	racism, prejudice

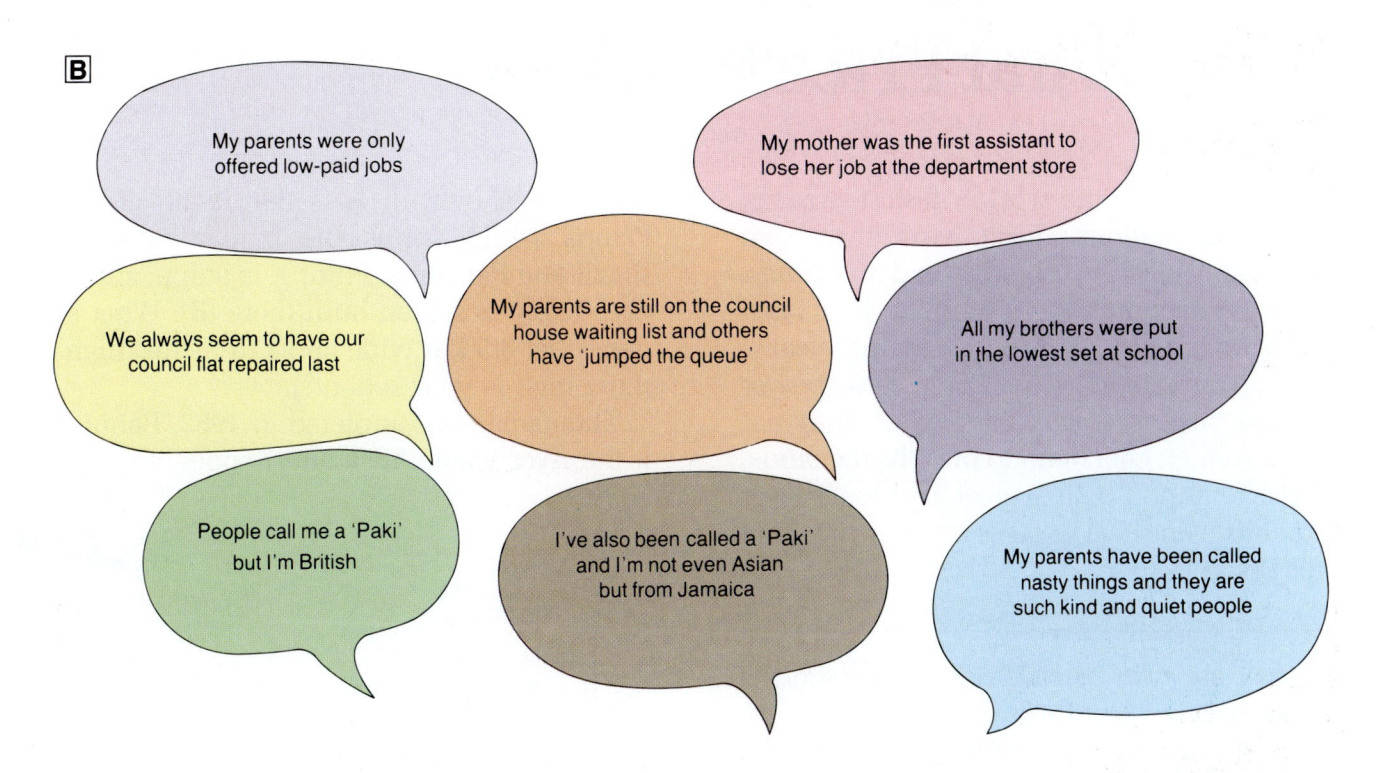

B

- My parents were only offered low-paid jobs
- My mother was the first assistant to lose her job at the department store
- We always seem to have our council flat repaired last
- My parents are still on the council house waiting list and others have 'jumped the queue'
- All my brothers were put in the lowest set at school
- People call me a 'Paki' but I'm British
- I've also been called a 'Paki' and I'm not even Asian but from Jamaica
- My parents have been called nasty things and they are such kind and quiet people

1. Why did Winston and Eileen emigrate from Jamaica to Britain?
2. What did Eileen mean by the 'mother country'?
3. a Where did Winston work?
   b Where did Eileen work?
4. Why do you think that Winston and Eileen were never offered promotion?
5. When and why did Winston lose his job?
6. What nationality are Cecil and Martha?

Racial Prejudice and Racism

Being a foreigner in Britain is difficult, especially for black people. Some white people are **prejudiced** against black people. Prejudice means **'pre-judge'** and people sometimes pre-judge other people who are different from themselves. They comment in a general way about them and do not base their judgements on fact.

When the decisions and actions of people are influenced by racial prejudice, often without them knowing it, this is known as **racism**.

C The mixed-race pop group UB40

FURTHER WORK

- Study **B**. These comments were made by black children. All of them have one or more parents who are immigrants into Britain from a developing country.
  List the examples of racial prejudice and racism they and their parents have experienced.
- What benefits can you think of that foreigners have brought to Britain (see **C**)? You can divide the benefits into economic and social/cultural.
- What can a country like Britain do to stop racial prejudice? How can schools help? What can the government do, eg to make employment fair?

PEOPLE'S NEEDS

3.17 What Price Progress?

Brazil is one of the world's fastest-growing industrial nations. Each year there are thousands of new factories and machines. Brazil's demand for electricity has been growing at over 2000 megawatts per year – that's equivalent to one large new power station needed every year! Brazil does not have enough coal or oil to meet its demands. It has to import both at great expense. Power stations using coal or oil as a fuel are no good for Brazil!

---

1 Why are coal or oil-fuelled power stations unsuitable for Brazil?

2 What other types of power station would be more suited to Brazil?

3 Map **A** shows part of a large river in Brazil. Over 20 000 people live on this part of the flood plain of the river and its tributaries. They live in small villages and farm the fertile soils of the flood plain. There are plans to build a dam across the river at point X.
  a Why do you think the dam is being built?
  b What effect will the dam have on the people living on the flood plain?
  c Do you think that the dam should be built?

The river shown in **A** is the mighty River Parana which forms the border between Brazil and Paraguay. Point X is Itaipu, and a dam really has been built there (**B**). What a dam it is! 8.5 km wide and 175 metres high (how high is your school?).

The dam was completed in 1982. Behind it the river waters rose and flooded an area

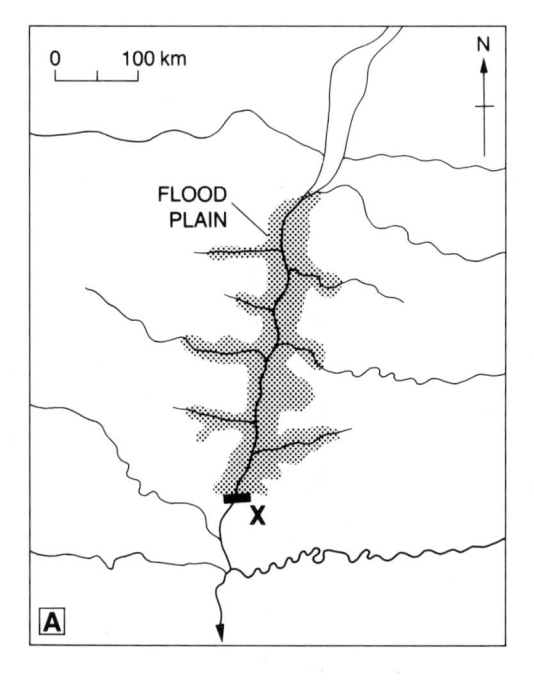

B Itaipu dam

Skills	map work
Concepts	HEP
Issues	scarce resources

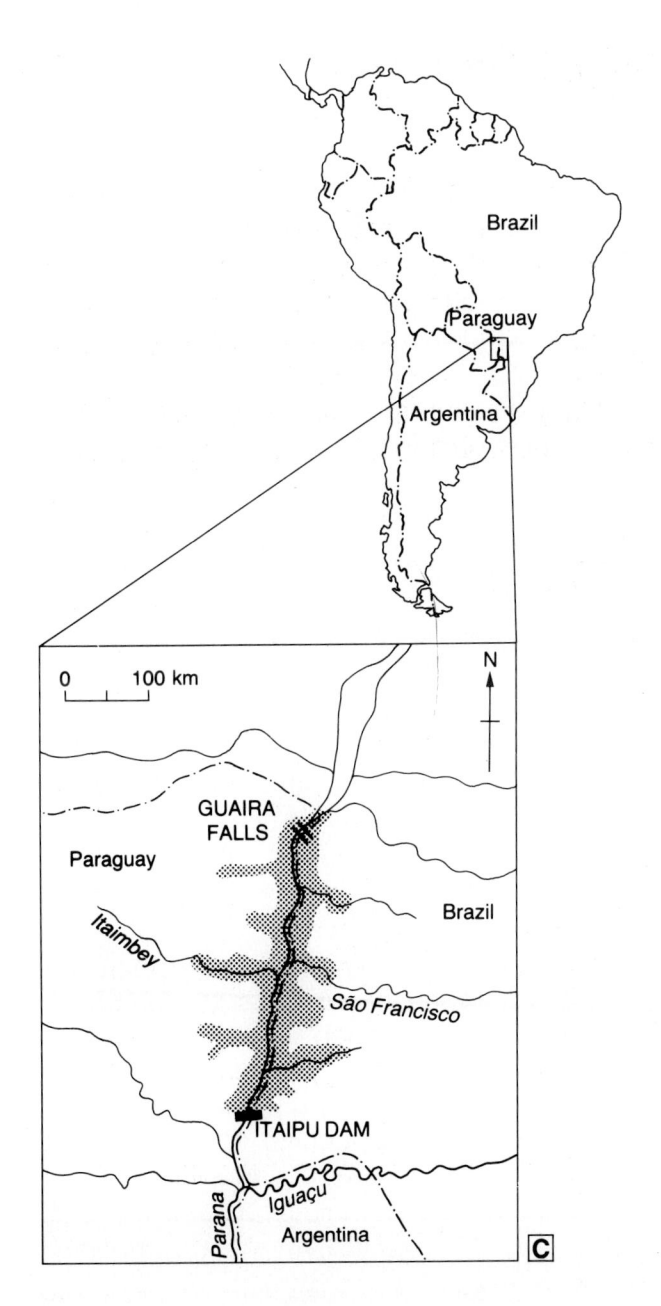

covering 1400 sq km (50 times the size of Lake Windermere, England's largest lake), making a reservoir over 200 km long (**C**). 20 000 people lost their homes when the valley was flooded. Some of the best farmland in the region was covered with water. Why was the dam built? Why was £8000 million spent on this project? **Hydro-electric power**. The Itaipu dam has eighteen huge turbines linked to alternators which generate 700 megawatts of electricity each (1 MW = 1 million watts) (**D**). This is a total capacity of 12 600 MW. Itaipu is the world's largest hydro-electric power station.

Who is the power for? It is carried away to the industrial towns of South East Brazil. Although half of the power belongs to Paraguay the Paraguayans use only about 500 MW and so they sell the rest to Brazil. Eventually it is hoped that an industrial centre will develop near Itaipu where new towns have been built on both sides of the river. These towns were built to house the construction workers and their families, plus the 20 000 people displaced by the reservoir.

---

4 Why is Brazil keen to develop hydro-electricity?

5 a Where is the Itaipu HEP project?
  b List the advantages and disadvantages of the Itaipu Project.

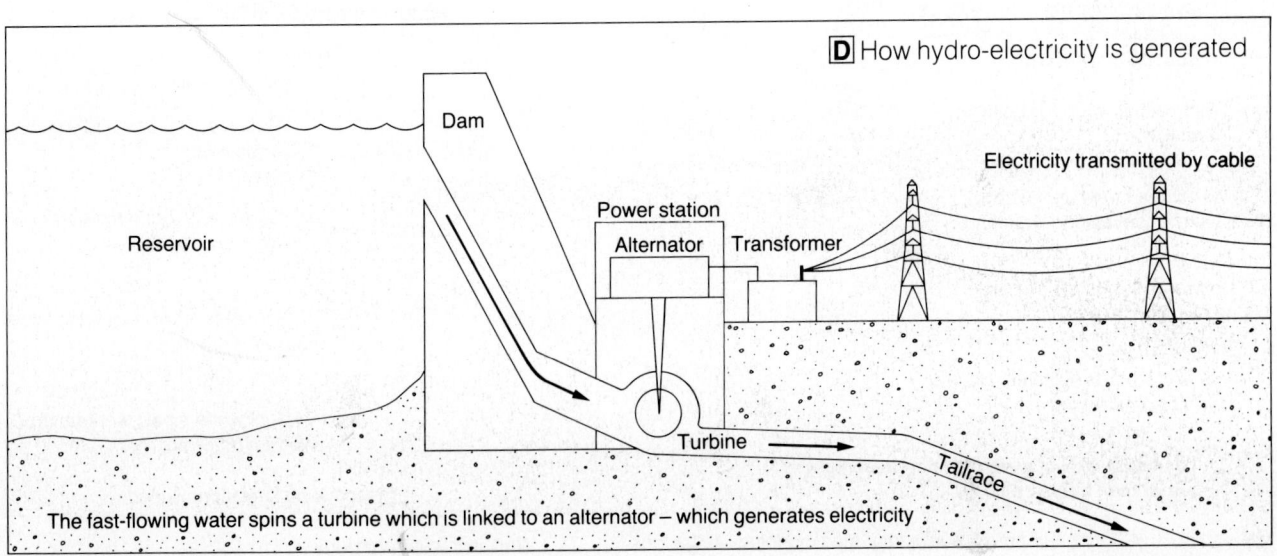

D How hydro-electricity is generated

The fast-flowing water spins a turbine which is linked to an alternator – which generates electricity

87

PEOPLE'S NEEDS

3.18 Half the World's People

Some of the facts in **A** may surprise you. Did you realise that you lived in such an **unequal** world? Boys and men seem to be favoured at the expense of girls and women.

1 Make a list of facts from **A** that shows the unequal treatment of women and men.

There are many reasons for the inequality you have just noted. One is **traditional attitudes** towards the **role of women**. For example, in most of the world's countries women do most of the **domestic work** (cooking, cleaning the home etc). Often this work is not valued and is unpaid. Yet this work is vital, for it involves caring for infants, looking after old people, running the house, cooking and feeding people, family health and welfare. Women need to be highly skilled, hard working and good managers ... Yet men, and society as a whole, expect them to do these things without payment.

2 What is domestic work?

3 Ask ten girls/women and ten boys/men what jobs they do at home. Who does the cooking, bedmaking, washing, ironing ..?

In the developing world domestic work is only part of a long and exhausting day for women (**B**). Often women tend the food crops; they have to work on the land using simple tools and a lot of energy. The men traditionally look after cattle and do the building work. Men tend to take over machinery and the production of cash crops. Domestic work also includes collecting firewood and water – which often means walking a long way and carrying heavy loads.

4 Look at **B**.
  a How many hours rest do rural women get?
  b Which of the jobs in **B** do not need to be done in developed world countries, for example Britain? Give reasons for your answer.
  c What would happen to an African girl's family if the mother became ill?

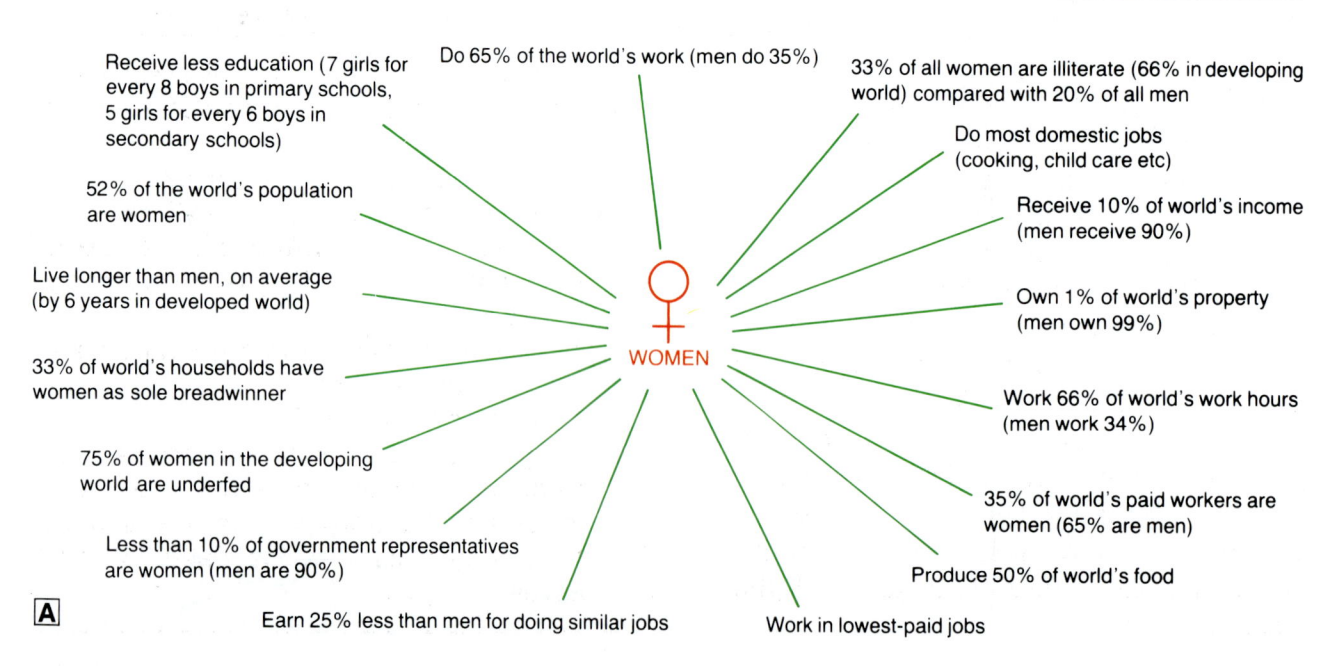

A WOMEN
- Receive less education (7 girls for every 8 boys in primary schools, 5 girls for every 6 boys in secondary schools)
- Do 65% of the world's work (men do 35%)
- 33% of all women are illiterate (66% in developing world) compared with 20% of all men
- 52% of the world's population are women
- Do most domestic jobs (cooking, child care etc)
- Receive 10% of world's income (men receive 90%)
- Live longer than men, on average (by 6 years in developed world)
- Own 1% of world's property (men own 99%)
- 33% of world's households have women as sole breadwinner
- Work 66% of world's work hours (men work 34%)
- 75% of women in the developing world are underfed
- 35% of world's paid workers are women (65% are men)
- Less than 10% of government representatives are women (men are 90%)
- Produce 50% of world's food
- Earn 25% less than men for doing similar jobs
- Work in lowest-paid jobs

Skills	discussion, keyword plan
Concepts	women's work, tradition
Issues	inequality

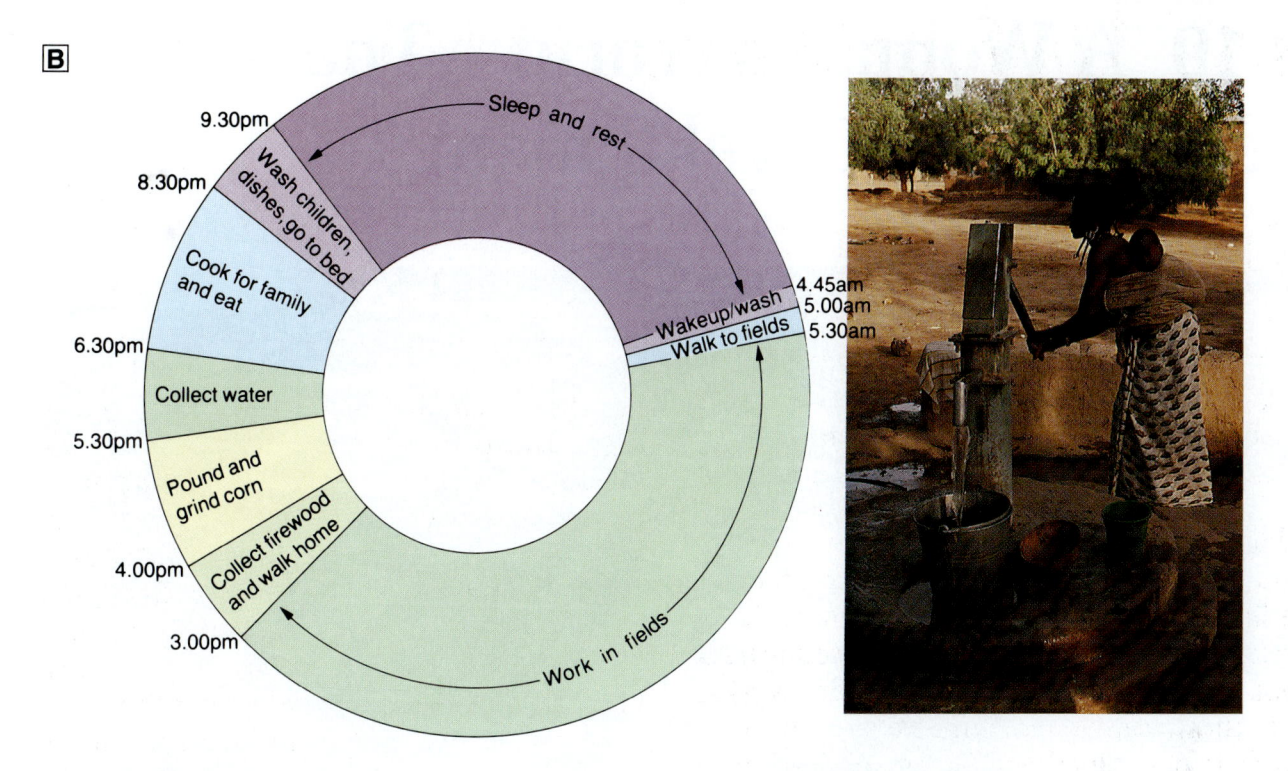

Education and health

Many development projects build on the traditional role of women. Projects on birth control and encouraging the breast feeding of babies have put women at the centre of health improvements in countries such as Cuba, Sri Lanka and Tanzania.

The future

Attitudes are slowly changing in the developed world. Boys and men are beginning to take responsibility for some domestic work. However, in the developing world **standards of living** need to be raised before there can be much progress towards equality. For example, a good supply of piped water would reduce girls' and women's chores. This might give them more time for education. Girls' and women's **expectations** need to be raised, so that they do not simply accept traditional roles. The burden of looking after large families needs to be relieved.

Some women in developing countries are fighting for equality. They argue that 'when a woman is educated then the whole family is being educated' – because women will then teach their children.

In Unit 3.19 you will see how women are making major contributions to development.

5 Draw up a keyword plan to show how women in the developing world could be helped to improve their lives.
6 Why would it be wise for developing world governments to give women and men equal opportunities in education?

FURTHER WORK

Ask three boys/men and three girls/women:
- What does being a girl/woman mean to you?
- What difficulties do women face?
- Do women need to earn money? Why?
- What aspects of girls'/women's lives would you want to change? Give reasons for your answer.

Now compare the answers given by boys/men and girls/women.
How are they different?
Imagine you are a newspaper reporter. You have to write an article about attitudes towards girls and women. Use the answers to your questions as the basis for your article.

PEOPLE'S NEEDS

3.19 A Woman's World – The Role of Women in Development

A

In Unit 3.18 you read about the **inequality** between women and men. In many of the newly-industrialised nations of South-East Asia (see Unit 4.8) it is mostly women who provide cheap labour. They are prepared to work long, boring hours on assembly lines, for example in textiles and electronics factories (**A**). There is often no protection, safety or health care and wages are low. The women are **exploited** because these jobs are the only ones open to them and their families rely on their wages for survival.

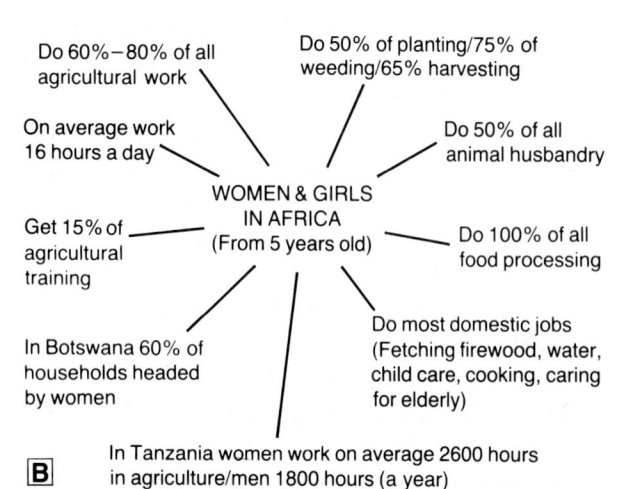

B WOMEN & GIRLS IN AFRICA (From 5 years old)
- Do 60%–80% of all agricultural work
- Do 50% of planting/75% of weeding/65% harvesting
- On average work 16 hours a day
- Do 50% of all animal husbandry
- Get 15% of agricultural training
- Do 100% of all food processing
- In Botswana 60% of households headed by women
- Do most domestic jobs (Fetching firewood, water, child care, cooking, caring for elderly)
- In Tanzania women work on average 2600 hours in agriculture/men 1800 hours (a year)

The United Nations Decade of Women (1975–85) revealed that women make a major contribution to **development**. The UN aimed to tell people of the important role of women and to give them a better life.

1 Copy and complete the sentences below

In the newly industrialised nations of _____ ____ Asia women provide _____ labour. They work ____, _____ hours on assembly lines. There is often no safety or _____ care. These women are _____ because their families need the low wages they earn for survival. The _____ _____ recognised that women make a major contribution to _____. There is a need to give women a better life.

Look at **B**. In rural areas of Africa, men tend to concentrate on cash crops or take jobs in towns. The women are left to grow the much-needed food crops. However, they are also expected to help with cash crop production, often for lower pay than men. This

| Skills | empathy, designing poster, role play |
| Concepts | women's role in development |

means women find it difficult to increase food production. Cash crops also take up more and more of the most fertile land. Banks will often not give women farmers loans to buy seed or tools because much of the land is owned by the men. Usually it is the men who inherit land in Africa.

---

2 Make a table of the ways in which women are treated less fairly than men in Africa (**B**).

3 Imagine you work for the United Nations in Africa. You are asked to design a poster to show how important women are to African farming. Draw a poster to bring this idea to the attention of people in the developed world.

The role of women in Africa's development is now being recognised. In Burkina Faso (Upper Volta) women took part in a survey to find out which trees were most useful for fuel, fodder, food, medicine and building materials. This small Agro-Forestry survey has now led to better fuel and food production. In Zimbabwe women are being given land and are encouraged to be leaders in rural areas. Food production is increasing. Aid agencies are beginning to realise the important role of women and avoid past mistakes. For example, under a scheme, in Gambia, land was taken away from the women who traditionally owned and worked on it. The land was irrigated and given over to rice production. Then it was divided up, but the aid agency did not consider the important role of women and men got most of the land. As a result, food production fell.

Women need to be heard at national levels, so that their needs are understood. They should have the same opportunities as men (education, land ownership and pay). They should share equally in all aspects of their nation's development.

---

4 How did aid agencies make mistakes in Gambia?

5 How has the Government of Zimbabwe helped women?

6 What evidence is there that aid agencies now recognise the role of women in development?

7 Do the exercise in the *Activity pack* on women in agricultural development.

FURTHER WORK

● Form a group of six or eight. Divide into equal numbers of 'women' and 'men' (where possible, girls should play men and boys women).

● You all live in a village in Africa. You are called to a meeting to discuss how to increase food production. In village meetings like this, the men tend to ignore the women's ideas.

● Prepare your arguments for what should be done. Role-play the meeting (remember, women find it difficult to make themselves heard). Appoint someone to make notes of what is said.

● When you have acted out your meeting, vote to decide what to do. How did the boys feel about not being given a fair hearing? What did you do to get your ideas heard? What else could you have done?

PEOPLE'S LIVES AND WORK

4.1 Farming Systems

Introduction

Most people in developing countries live in the countryside and work on the land. They work on many different types of farm, but most of them are **subsistence farmers**. This means that they work on small farms and grow food mainly to feed themselves and their families.

Many developing countries depend upon the export of a few crops. Often, trade in these **cash crops** was started by Europeans when the developing countries were colonies. The European colonists often forced the local people to stop growing subsistence food crops and to grow crops which the Europeans themselves wanted. For example, in Tanzania sisal replaced millet, in Ghana cocoa replaced sweet potatoes and in the Gambia groundnuts replaced rice.

Plantations

Cash crops are often grown on **plantations** which are large farms growing a single crop for sale (**A**). Plantations often have their own processing factory, houses for the plantation workers, shops and services such as clinics. The first plantations were developed by Europeans in Brazil and the West Indies for sugar cane. Later rubber, coffee, tea, cocoa, tobacco, palm oil and sisal plantations were developed.

The workforce needed for the plantations was not always available. In such cases the Europeans transported people to work in the plantations. For example, the British shipped hundreds of thousands of Chinese to Malaysia's rubber plantations and thousands of Indians to Fiji's sugar plantations. The workers had very low pay; the system was tightly controlled for the benefit of the Europeans. In many countries there has been trouble between the descendants of these 'imported' workers and the local population. In Fiji descendants of the Indian migrants outnumber the native Fijians; in 1987 the Fijian army overthrew the government to prevent the Indians gaining power.

When developing countries became independent some of the plantations were broken up and the land given to local farmers. Other plantations were taken over by the new governments. Some others remained in the control of multinational companies based in the developed countries.

Why do some developing countries maintain the colonial farming system? The export earnings are vital; it is easier to achieve consistent delivery and high quality from large farms rather than small farms. However, part of the profits go to the foreign multinationals and the plantations take the best land which could be used to grow food for the people.

---

1 What is subsistence farming?
2 What is a plantation?
3 Study photographs **B** and **C**.
   a Describe carefully the scenes in the two photographs.
   b What would it be like to live and work in the plantation(s) shown?
4 Copy and complete the passage below, using the wordbank:

Europeans introduced plantations into developing countries when they were .... The plantations grew crops which could not be grown in ...., such as sugar cane, ... and .... If .... labour was not available the Europeans brought in workers from elsewhere.
Workbank: Europe   rubber   colonies   local   coffee

5 What problems have been caused by the movement of people from one country to another to work in the colonial plantations?
6 Draw up a table giving two advantages and two disadvantages of plantations for independent developing countries.

Skills	interpreting photographs and charts
Concepts	farming, subsistence, cash crops
Issues	colonialism

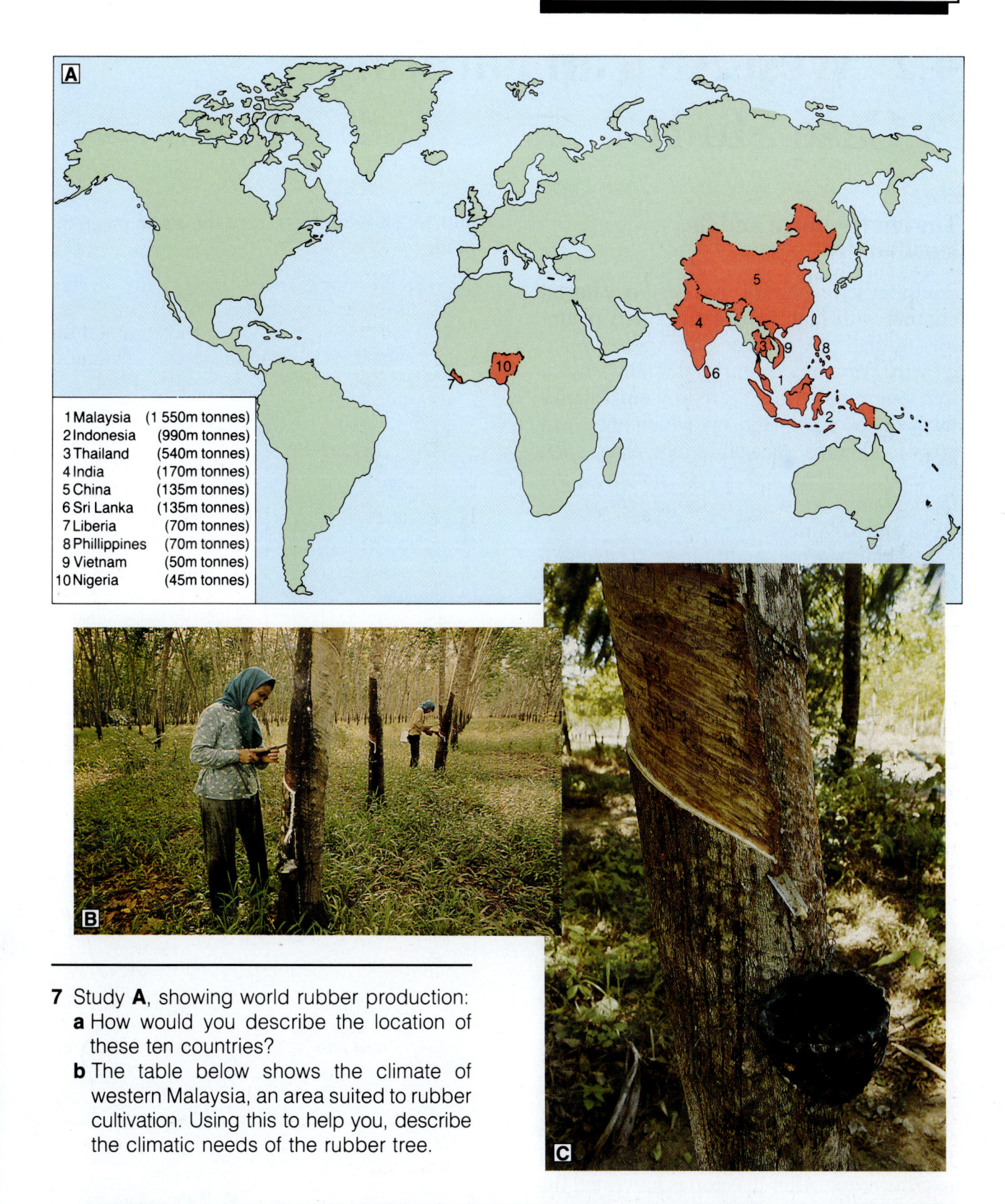

A

1 Malaysia (1 550m tonnes)
2 Indonesia (990m tonnes)
3 Thailand (540m tonnes)
4 India (170m tonnes)
5 China (135m tonnes)
6 Sri Lanka (135m tonnes)
7 Liberia (70m tonnes)
8 Phillippines (70m tonnes)
9 Vietnam (50m tonnes)
10 Nigeria (45m tonnes)

7 Study **A**, showing world rubber production:
 a How would you describe the location of these ten countries?
 b The table below shows the climate of western Malaysia, an area suited to rubber cultivation. Using this to help you, describe the climatic needs of the rubber tree.

Month:	J	F	M	A	M	J	J	A	S	O	N	D
Temperature (°C):	26	27	28	28	28	28	28	27	27	27	27	26
Rainfall:	248	185	188	190	175	180	170	200	180	210	245	220

93

PEOPLE'S LIVES AND WORK

4.2 West African Farming – A Case Study

The environment and the smallholder

South-Eastern Nigeria has an **equatorial climate** with high temperatures and plentiful rainfall (**A**). This encourages plant growth. For many centuries the rainforest of this region has been cleared by **subsistence farmers** to create land on which they can grow food crops. As well as food crops such as yam, cassava and sweet potatoes, the farmers also grow cash crops: cocoa, oil palm and kola nuts.

Most farmers are **smallholders**. They use a traditional system of farming the rainforest environment, using simple tools. Their farming knowledge has been passed on over the centuries.

---

1 Find a map of Africa in an atlas, and locate Nigeria. On the outline map in the *Activity pack*:
  a Mark the states of South-Eastern Nigeria: Rivers, Imo, Cross River and Anambra.
  b Name the rivers, seas and major cities.
  c Give the map a title: South-Eastern Nigeria (West Africa) and add a northing arrow.
2 What crops do the subsistence farmers grow in the equatorial rainforest?

Plan **B** shows a typical smallholding. Plots (fields) of different shapes surround the village/family compound. Soils are not very fertile and so a system of **rotational bush fallowing** is used: a plot is cleared and used to grow crops. After the crop is harvested the plot is left to rest for up to six years to recover its fertility. In the next year the smallholder will move on to a plot that has been rested. A system of **intercropping** helps smallholders make the best use of land. For example they grow beans between maize and so get two crops from the same piece of land.

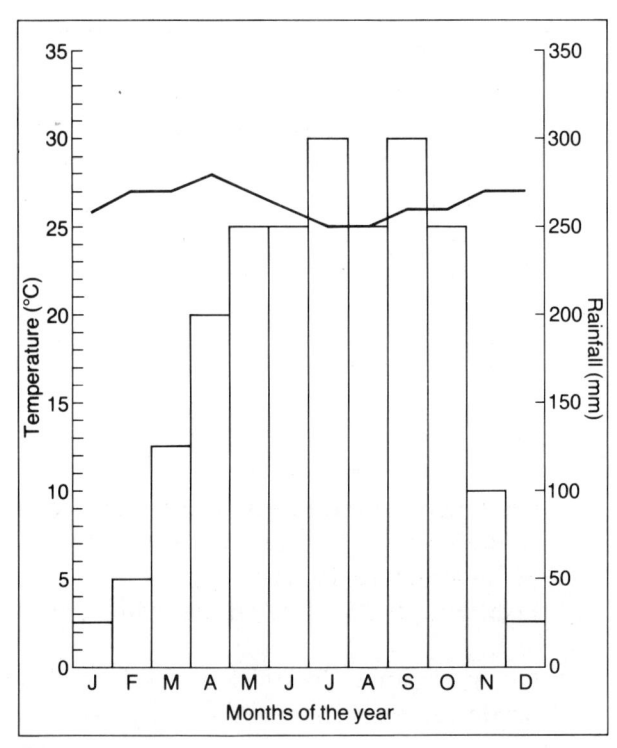

A Climate of Nigeria

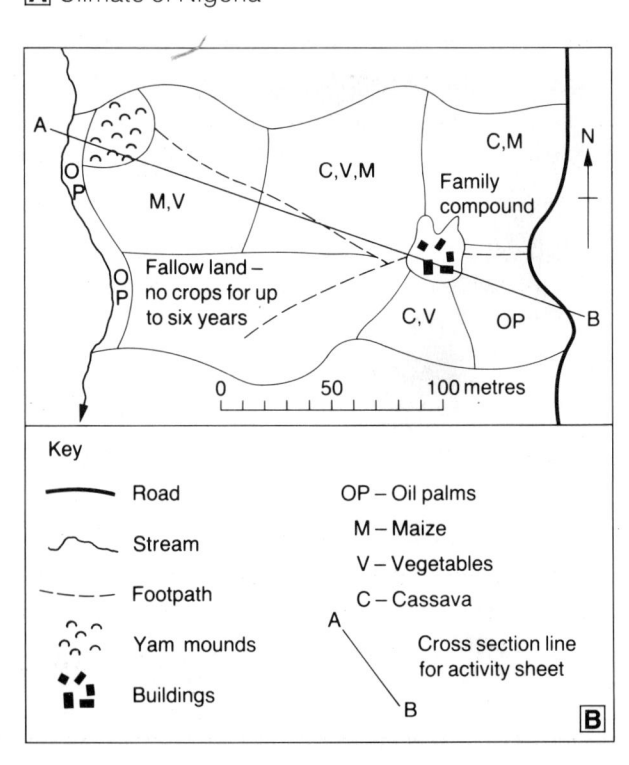

B

Skills	atlas and map work
Concepts	climate, farming systems
Issues	natural hazards, self-sufficiency

Life is not easy for the smallholder. Subsistence farming is often a struggle for existence. **C** shows some of the problems a Nigerian farmer might face.

3 Use plan **B** and complete the transect drawing of the smallholding in the *Activity pack*.

C
1. Flash floods wash away crops
2. Plant diseases cause lower cocoa production
3. Pressure to feed a growing population means that fields are not rested – soils become exhausted
4. Waterlogging of some crops (yams are grown on mounds to avoid this)
5. Heavy rainfall washes nutrients deep down into the soil so that plants cannot get them (leaching)
6. Traditional farming systems cannot produce enough food to keep pace with increasing demand
7. Tsetse fly limits areas where cattle can be kept
8. Young people leave the land and farming knowledge and skills are lost

4 In your own words, explain what is meant by rotational bush fallowing, and intercropping.

5 Look at **C**. What are:
  a The natural pressures on smallholders?
  b The human pressures on smallholders?

6 Design a poster for the Nigerian Government to encourage smallholders to grow extra food to feed the nation

The Nigerian Government wants the country to be self-sufficient in food (able to produce enough to feed all its people). **D** shows some of the problems the government faces, and some possible solutions.

FURTHER WORK

- Look back at Unit 1.5.
  Make a list of similarities and differences between the village in Unit 1.5 and a smallholding in South–Eastern Nigeria. Write a newspaper article for the *New Nigerian* pointing out the similarities and differences of people's lives in rural areas North and South of the country.

Problem	Cause	Solution
Need to import food	Not enough food grown in country. Focus on cash crops	Encourage production of food crops
Traditional farming methods do not produce a surplus	Traditionally, people only grow enough food for their own family	Agricultural education and cash support for new methods
Increasing urban population that needs feeding	Migration to the cities (See Units 1.6, 1.7, 1.8)	Encourage more extensive use of existing farmland
Loss of land	Urban people return to the land to grow own food as could not survive in the city	Improve urban areas
Lack of cash crop production for home market	Concentrate on just growing food for family	Rison Palm Enterprise buys oil fruits from farmers
Need for better yields	Disease and poor seed	Government supplies disease-resistant seed and fertilisers.

D

PEOPLE'S LIVES AND WORK

4.3 Cash Crops Cost Lives

Sudan is a very poor country in Africa. The area suffered appalling drought during the 1970s and 1980s. Then in 1988 there was serious flooding in Khartoum (the capital) and the Gezira area. Rich world governments and charities sent food aid to Sudan (**A**). Yet Sudan is not short of **arable** (crop) land.

The **Gezira Scheme** is a major success story (see Unit 2.5). Thousands of hectares of cotton are grown on rich soils between the Blue and White Nile rivers. The cotton is exported. This earns foreign currency.

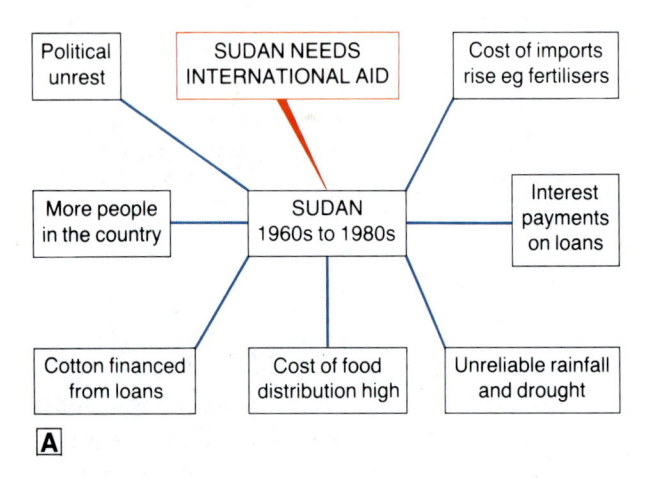

A

- Political unrest
- SUDAN NEEDS INTERNATIONAL AID
- Cost of imports rise eg fertilisers
- More people in the country
- SUDAN 1960s to 1980s
- Interest payments on loans
- Cotton financed from loans
- Cost of food distribution high
- Unreliable rainfall and drought

The Gezira Scheme depends on irrigation to grow cotton for export. If Sudan had used irrigation for food crops, thousands of people might not have starved in the droughts. It sounds an easy solution – but it is not so simple.

Developing world countries need to earn money to buy imports such as fertiliser, oil and machinery. Earnings from cash crops can also be used to build local fertiliser and tractor plants. To grow cash crops is an obvious way to boost export earnings. These cash crops are **primary products**. They are usually exported in a 'raw' state. **B** gives some viewpoints on cash crops grown by developing countries for export.

Food crops – a priority

There is nothing wrong with growing cash crops – as long as food crops are also grown.

B

We don't want to grow cash crops for you – what happens if the price falls? Then cash crops will cost us our lives!

We'll give you aid to help you grow your export crops.

But often, land that could have grown food is used to grow export crops. Tea and sugar are important cash crops. Africa's tea production has quadrupled since 1970 and its sugar production has doubled!

European aid was sent to Senegal (in West Africa) for a project to irrigate desert areas. But instead of food, aubergines and mangoes were grown on the irrigated land, and exported by air to Europe! This bizarre scheme did not survive, but similar schemes continue elsewhere in Africa.

Maize and millet (**C**) are basic food for millions of Africans. Both are rich in energy-

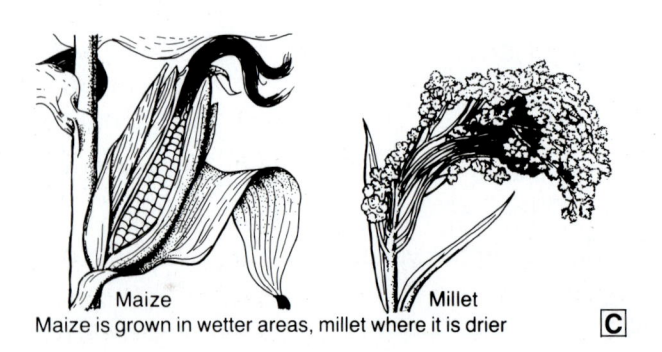

C

Maize is grown in wetter areas, millet where it is drier

Skills	decision making
Concepts	cash crops, primary products, irrigation
Issues	aid, conflict of interests

giving carbohydrate. In southern Africa people make maize meal porridge (**putu**). It can be eaten for breakfast – with milk, if it is available. In the evening it is mixed with vegetables to provide a main meal. The remains of both crops are fed to animals. These are the crops that Africa needs to grow.

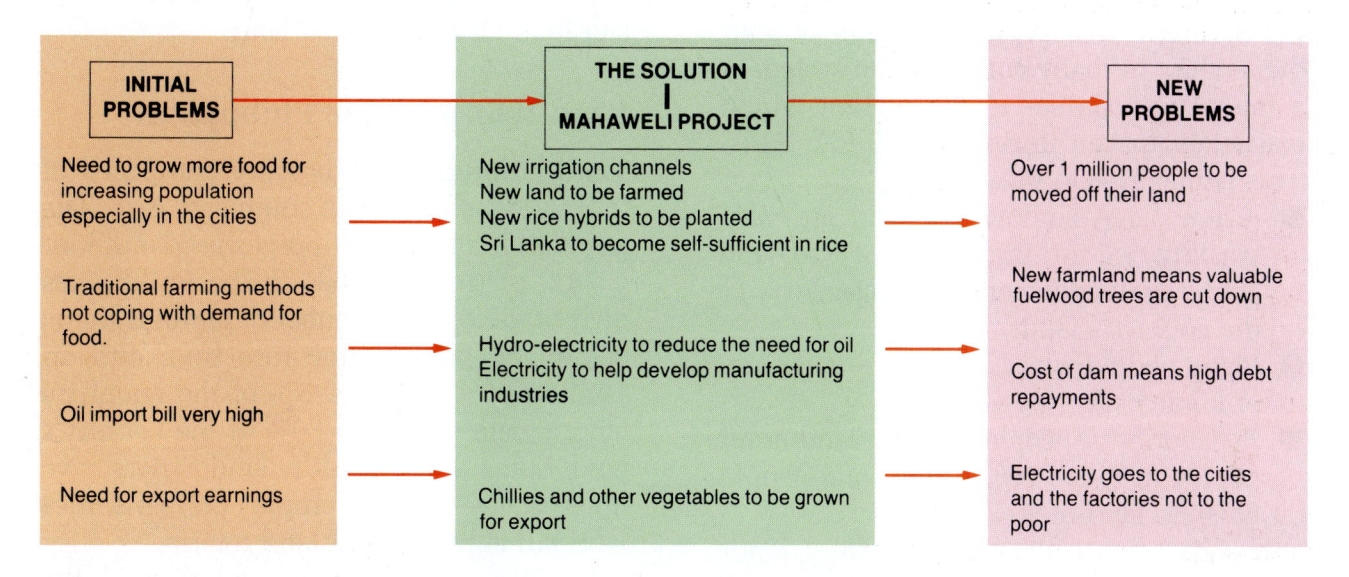

INITIAL PROBLEMS	THE SOLUTION — MAHAWELI PROJECT	NEW PROBLEMS
Need to grow more food for increasing population especially in the cities	New irrigation channels New land to be farmed New rice hybrids to be planted Sri Lanka to become self-sufficient in rice	Over 1 million people to be moved off their land
Traditional farming methods not coping with demand for food.		New farmland means valuable fuelwood trees are cut down
Oil import bill very high	Hydro-electricity to reduce the need for oil Electricity to help develop manufacturing industries	Cost of dam means high debt repayments
Need for export earnings	Chillies and other vegetables to be grown for export	Electricity goes to the cities and the factories not to the poor

D

Mahaweli Project in Sri Lanka

It is not only in Africa that new products can cost lives. A massive hydro-electricity and irrigation scheme has been started in Sri Lanka. Four main dams will control the Mahaweli Ganga river. The Victoria Dam is funded by Britain. The Mahaweli Project aims to solve some of Sri Lanka's problems. But it is not a perfect solution. The project is creating many new problems of its own (**D**).

1. **a** Why do developing world countries grow cash crops?
   b Give four examples of cash crops grown in developing world countries.
   c What are the problems for a developing country if it depends too much on one cash crop?
   d What is the problem for a developing world country if it does not grow enough food crops?
2. In pairs, use the ideas in **B** and make up your own conversation. One of you is an African and the other a European. The African wants to grow crops for export. In return, the European is offering good payment and other help for development.
3. Study **D**. Over 75% of Sri Lankans live on the land.
   a List the ways many of these people have suffered because of the Mahaweli Project.
   b Who do you think has benefited from this massive water scheme?

FURTHER WORK

- 'If there is enough food in the world, why are so many people still starving?'
  'Why does Europe have food surpluses while people in the developing world go hungry?'
  How would you answer these questions?
- Try the decision-making exercise on 'cash crops or food crops' in the *Activity pack*.

PEOPLE'S LIVES AND WORK

4.4 Land Ownership and Land Reform

One of the major causes of poverty in developing countries is the system of land ownership. In many countries the system is a **feudal** one similar to the pattern which existed in Britain during the Middle Ages. This feudal system involves:
- A few large landowners who are very wealthy (eg in Brazil just 2% of the country's landowners own over 60% of the country's land!)
- Many people who have only small plots of land
- A majority of people with no land at all (**A**) (eg in Brazil 70% of the rural people have no land of their own!)

In Britain, just 1% of the country landowners own 52% of the country's land; most Britons own no land at all. However, this is not very important for the wealth of the people since most Britons live in towns and earn their living in industry or services. This is not the case in most developing countries. The majority of people, who do not own land, have low standards of living. Many live in poverty. The answer to the unfair distribution of land is **land reform**. When this happens big estates are broken up and the land is redistributed to the peasants who can then farm their own land.

Land reform in the Philippines

The Philippines is a country composed of thousands of islands in south east Asia. The population of the Philippines is 57 million.

78% of rural families in the Philippines own no land. The number of families living below the poverty line rose from 48% in 1971 to 63% in 1985. 5% of the country's landowners own over 80% of the country's land. Some of the wealthy landowners have huge estates (**B**). They employ private armies who kill supporters of land reform.

In 1986 there was a revolution in the Philippines. The corrupt president Ferdinand Marcos was overthrown. The new president Cory Aquino said that land reform was essential, but she was unable to overcome the power of the landowners (her own family has one of the largest sugar cane plantations in the country). In July 1987 Mrs Aquino launched a land reform programme. But many people felt she was trying to do too little, too late.

Mrs Aquino's land reform programme included the following:
- Compensation for landowners for the land they had to give up. The amount of the compensation was fixed *by the landowners!*
- Peasants receiving land would have to pay for it over thirty years at a high rate of interest. If they were unable to pay, their land would immediately be taken over by the government.

This type of land reform was unacceptable, and many people were against it, especially the landless peasants. For years peasants have supported a rebel, communist army: the New People's Army (NPA) (**C**). The

Country	Percentage
Bolivia	85
Guatemala	85
Indonesia	80
Philippines	78
Sri Lanka	77
Bangladesh	75
Peru	75
Brazil	70
Colombia	66
Mexico	60

A Percentage of the rural population which owns no land in certain developing countries

Skills	graph work
Concepts	land ownership
Issues	land reform

NPA is fighting a guerilla war against the Philippine government forces. It has promised to set up a real programme of land reform if it wins control. The US Government is worried by the threat of a communist revolution. It supports the Philippines Government – but the USA, too, is pressing the Philippines Government to bring in real land reform and improve living standards.

The example of the Philippines shows that land reform is not easy, yet there have been successes. For example in China the communist government enforced a programme of reform after the revolution of 1949 (see Unit 4.14). South Korea also went through a successful land reform. Over half of the land was redistributed between 1948 and 1957. The USA paid generous compensation to the landowners in an attempt to rebuild the country's economy after the Korean War of 1950–53.

Perhaps a similar policy is needed if the Philippines is to avoid a long and bloody war.

1. What is meant by a feudal system of land ownership?
2. a What should happen when land is reformed?
   b What are the advantages of land reform?
3. Study **A**.
   a Draw a bar graph to illustrate the statistics in the table.
   b How do the rural people without land earn a living?
4. a Where are the Philippines?
   b Why is land reform needed in the Philippines?
   c Why has little progress been made in land reform policies in the Philippines?
5. Why did land reform succeed in South Korea and China?

PEOPLE'S LIVES AND WORK

4.5 Industrialisation or Alternative Technology?

Clothes for people

A group of 14-year-olds were asked the following question?
'How should a developing country provide more clothing for its people?'

The group gave three possible answers:

Answer 1 Import clothes from the Far East eg Hong Kong or Taiwan
Answer 2 Import cloth and make it into clothes in a factory.
Answer 3 Set up a modern factory that can make cloth and clothes.

Which of these ideas is the best? **B** shows the pupil's attempts to work out the advantages and disadvantages of each scheme.

---

1 What has to be imported for Answer 1?
2 Why does Answer 1 not provide employment?
3 What must be imported for Answer 2?
4 How could a poor country obtain the expensive machinery needed to manufacture cloth or clothes?
5 Write in your own words what is needed for Answer 3.
6 a What are the advantages with Answer 1?
  b What are the problems with Answer 1?)

As you can see in **B**, there are problems with each of the schemes the pupils suggested:

- Local people are not employed in great numbers
- Local materials and technology are not used
- A lot of money has to be spent on imports of raw materials, capital and equipment
- Clothes are made at a high cost

What seems to be needed is a method of producing clothes at a smaller scale, using local people and local technology. In 1973 E F Schumacher wrote a famous book called *Small is Beautiful – A Study of Economics as if People Mattered*. In it, he talked of **intermediate technology**. He wanted developing countries to use simple equipment which could be maintained and repaired on the spot. It would be **labour intensive** – employing local people and materials.

Which is the most **appropriate technology** for the developing world (**C**)? Poorer countries do need some modern technology eg large scale electricity plants and modern ports. But often it is a form of intermediate technology that is most appropriate. Countries will become **self-reliant** more quickly if they can develop a technology that they can understand and control themselves. Advanced technology obtained from the West or the Communist countries is not always appropriate in the developing world.

---

7 Study **C** and compare the advantages of each loom for a developing world country. Which loom would you choose for a poor African country? Give reasons for your choice.
See *Activity sheet 44* for an exercise on Appropriate Technology.

| Skills | problem-solving |
| Concepts | industry, appropriate technology |

B	**Answer 1**	**Answer 2**	**Answer 3**
raw materials	none	only buttons, zips and cotton thread	cotton, wool, synthetic fibres, button, zips, dyes etc.
capital/money (technology)	import facilities eg docks, roads	cutting machinery, sewing machines, factory	spinning and weaving machines, cutting and sewing machines, large factory
land	none	factory site	large factory site
labour	none	mainly female labour	mainly female labour
energy	only transport fuel	electricity for machines	a lot of electricity for machines
success?	may not suit local fashions: high import bills	provides some employment but expensive machinery, costly cloth imports, possibility of some exports	provides employment: very expensive equipment, export material

NB. All the options will require transport and import facilities (ports).

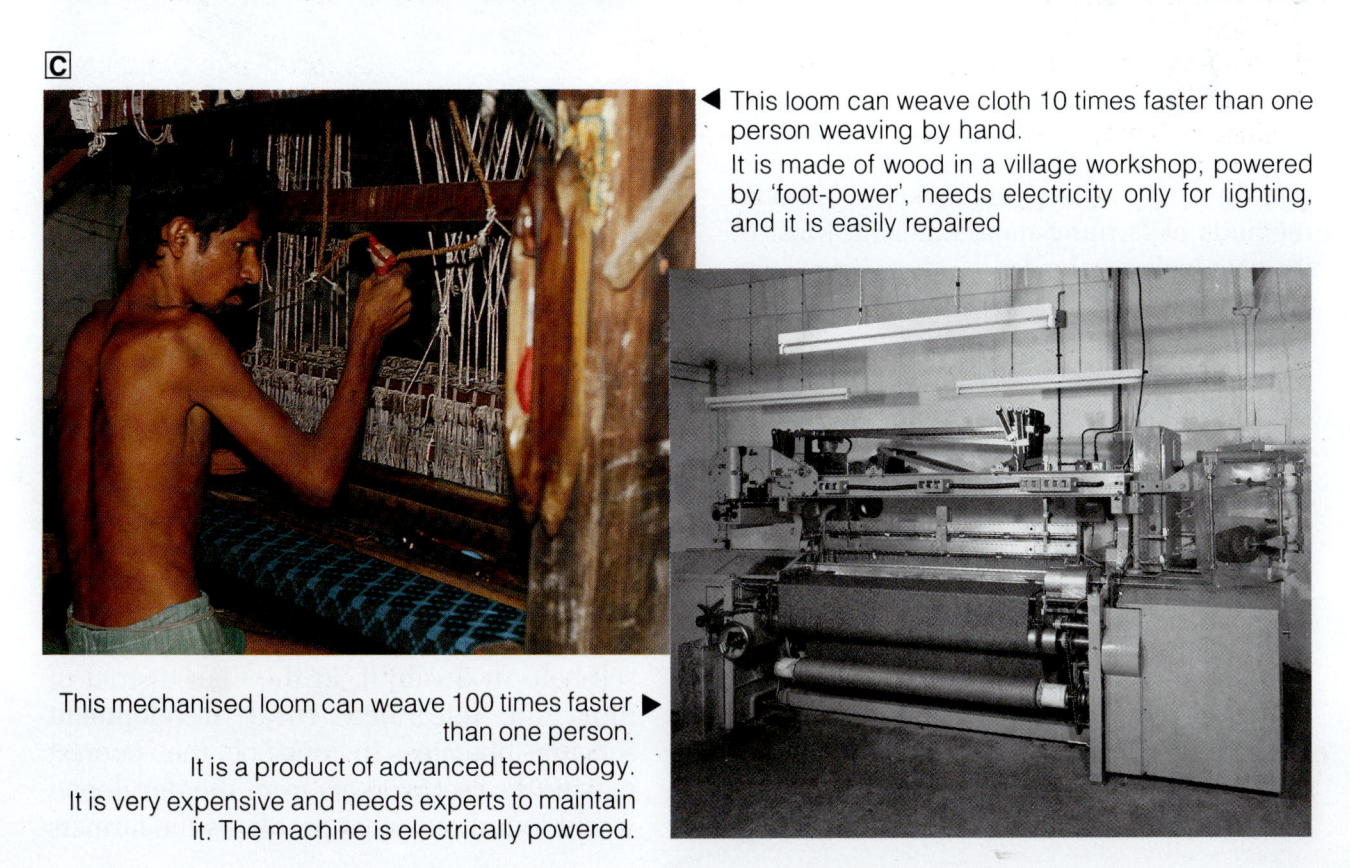

C

◀ This loom can weave cloth 10 times faster than one person weaving by hand.
It is made of wood in a village workshop, powered by 'foot-power', needs electricity only for lighting, and it is easily repaired

This mechanised loom can weave 100 times faster ▶ than one person.
It is a product of advanced technology.
It is very expensive and needs experts to maintain it. The machine is electrically powered.

PEOPLE'S LIVES AND WORK

4.6 Appropriate Technology

Would the people living in the Hausa village (Unit 1.5), the Sahel (Unit 2.3) or the rainforest (Unit 4.2) really benefit from large-scale industrial development? In Unit 4.5 you began to look at the issue of **industrialisation** or **appropriate technology**.

An appropriate approach to development.

Many developing countries have realised the problem of using imported technology (**A**). is on a small scale it does not damage the environment.

---

1. Look at **A**. Why might a country not want to import a lot of tractors to help its farmers?
2. What does 'Ujamaa' mean?
3. Give examples of how people work together on Ujamaas.
4. Make a keyword plan of the advantages of Ujamaas to a developing country like Tanzania.

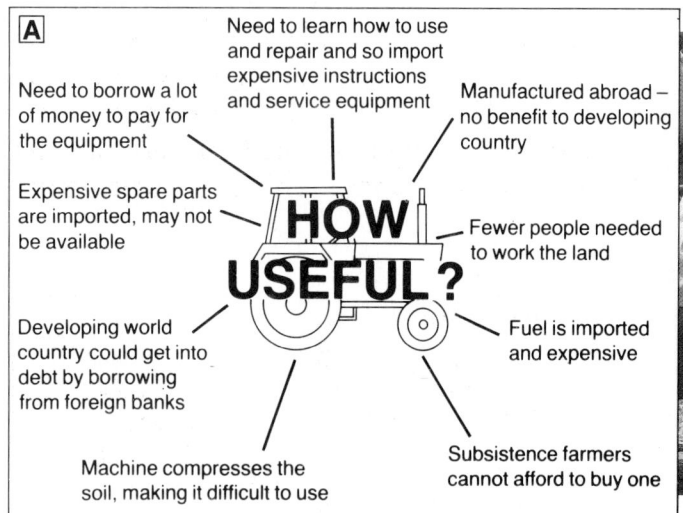

A HOW USEFUL?
- Need to borrow a lot of money to pay for the equipment
- Need to learn how to use and repair and so import expensive instructions and service equipment
- Manufactured abroad – no benefit to developing country
- Expensive spare parts are imported, may not be available
- Fewer people needed to work the land
- Developing world country could get into debt by borrowing from foreign banks
- Fuel is imported and expensive
- Machine compresses the soil, making it difficult to use
- Subsistence farmers cannot afford to buy one

Tanzania is trying to make traditional methods of farming more efficient. Most of its people farm the land. They have been encouraged to work together in **self-help** groups called **Ujamaa villages** (**B**). Ujamaa means 'familyhood'.

The villagers use oxen to pull their ploughs. They dig wells together when new supplies of freshwater are needed. Some people **specialise**, for example, in making and repairing ploughs. The cost of development is low and everyone is employed. A **communal** farming scheme like this can develop anywhere in the country. Everyone is involved, so people can understand the changes. People are not dependent on foreign imports. The villagers use whatever is around them, but because the development

---

5. Imagine you have been asked to help a village improve its water supply. How would you convince the people that working together would be better than bringing in outsiders to do the work?

There are many other examples around the world of developing countries encouraging self-help using appropriate technology. In Kenya there are Harambee schools and workshops which promote education, self-help and development (harambee means self-help in Swahili). In the Etah district of India an **integrated rural development** scheme operates in one of the poorest regions. Project workers from the developed world found out what problems the farmers

Skills	poster design, sketching, problem solving
Concepts	appropriate technology, self-help
Issues	small scale versus large scale development

faced. They set up demonstration plots to show what could be done. Farming, health, education and local crafts are all being developed together.

Cattle dung and vegetable waste are converted into fuel at bio-gas plants, providing gas for cooking and lighting. Villagers have been trained as health workers. Farmers use improved seed and can get loans to pay for the advice and equipment they need. At present, the multinational company Unilever supports the project, but in future farmers will run things for themselves.

C
- Wind pump (Equipment)
- Silo for grain storage (Equipment)
- Fish farming (Working idea)
- Cooperatives (Working idea)
- Solar powered cookers (Equipment)
- Soil conservation using fences etc (Idea)
- Making gas from animal waste (Equipment)

6 Design a poster to encourage farmers in Etah district to join in the Integrated Rural Development scheme.

7 Look at **C**. Choose one of these examples of appropriate technology. Sketch the example, and around it add your ideas about why and how it is appropriate to the developing world. (Think about cost, use, energy, what it's made of, local conditions . . .)

How can the developed world help?

Many developed countries now support self-help development using appropriate technology (**C**). They provide money and education. Some groups try to encourage governments to adopt small-scale approaches to development. Others get people to find out what countries really want, rather than telling developing countries what they need. Conservationists and ecologists (people who study the natural environment) believe that appropriate technology will help to save the world's resources.

The company Project Equipment Ltd, in Oswestry, designs **implements** (tools) for farmers in developing countries. The designs take local conditions into account. They are simple enough for local people to make the implements with the minimum of equipment and skill.

D shows Project Equipment's 'Pecotool'. This can be operated by people or by animals (such as oxen or donkeys). Many developing world farmers are illiterate, so most of the instructions are drawings. The company also advises farmers to pass on their skills and knowledge by word of mouth. Implements like the Pecotool can be bought as part of a 'package deal scheme'. Project Equipment sell the tool and workshop equipment so that people in the developing country can manufacture more for themselves.

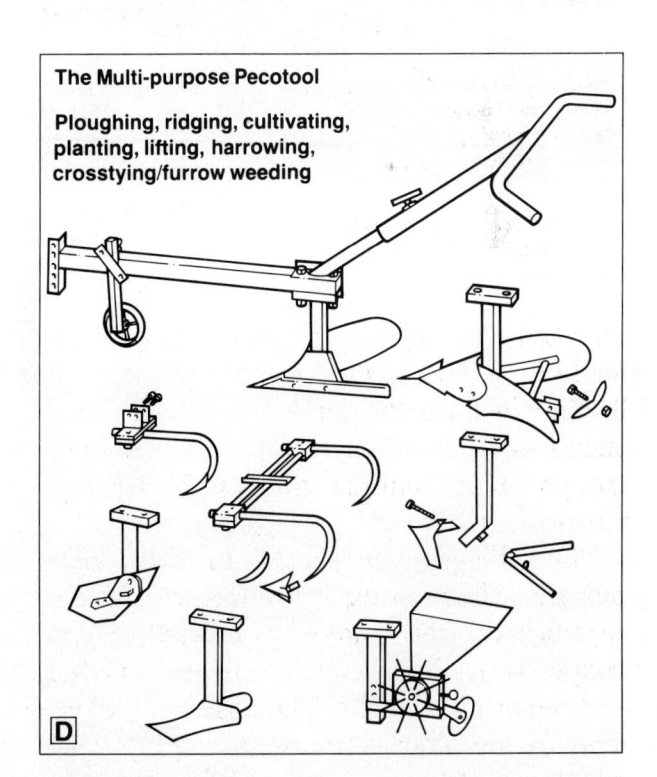

D

The Multi-purpose Pecotool

Ploughing, ridging, cultivating, planting, lifting, harrowing, crosstying/furrow weeding

7 In what ways do Project Equipment Ltd consider local conditions in developing countries?

PEOPLE'S LIVES AND WORK

4.7 The NICs – Newly-Industrialising Countries

High-rise buildings, crowded central business districts, luxury hotels, advanced industry and agriculture. People with money to spend on consumer goods and fashionable clothes. These are typical images of rich developed world countries.

Skills interpreting photographs
Concepts NICs, industrialisation

1. For each photograph (**A**, **B** and **C**) decide if you think it was taken in the developed or developing world. Write down your reasons under the headings: Buildings, Activities, Transport.
2. The photographs are in fact from the developing world. Suggest where they were taken. (Clue: two places are in the Far East, one is in the Middle East.) The answers are on page 129.

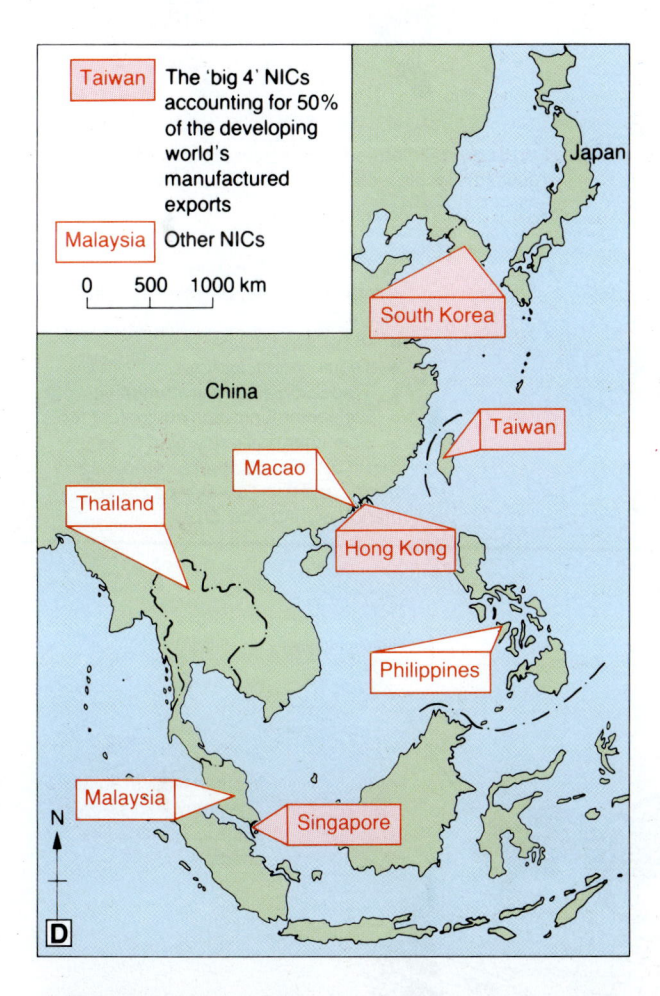

E Made in South Korea / Made in Hong Kong / Made in Taiwan

D Map showing: Taiwan, Malaysia (the 'big 4' NICs accounting for 50% of the developing world's manufactured exports), Other NICs — South Korea, Taiwan, Macao, Hong Kong, Thailand, Philippines, Malaysia, Singapore; also Japan, China.

Map **D** shows the locations of the fast-developing countries of the Far East. Some Middle East countries are also developing rapidly: Saudi Arabia, Kuwait, the United Arab Emirates and Bahrain. These fast-developing countries are called **NICs** (**newly-industrialising countries**). Check their location in an atlas.

Why have some countries developed so quickly? In the case of the Middle East countries, growth has been based on oil and gas resources. These countries have exported their oil and gas and invested their profits in new roads, harbours, cities and industry.

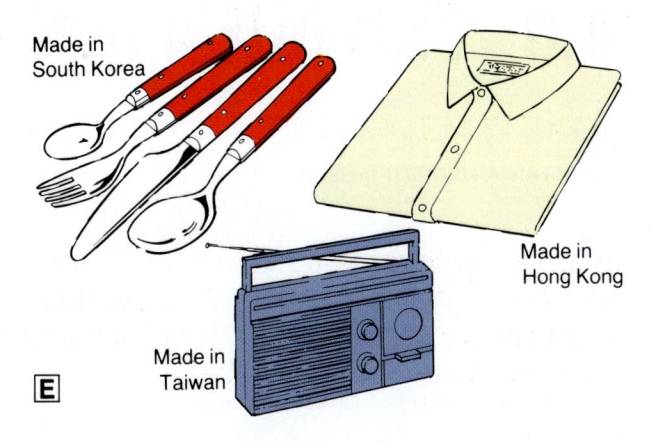

The Far East countries had no raw materials. They developed using hard-working and cheap **labour**. There is also a lot of **enterprise** (ideas) in these countries. They have borrowed money from developed countries to invest in manufacturing industry. Today, households throughout the developed world contain products from the Far East (**E**). **F** is a keyword plan which shows some of the reasons for the development of NICs.

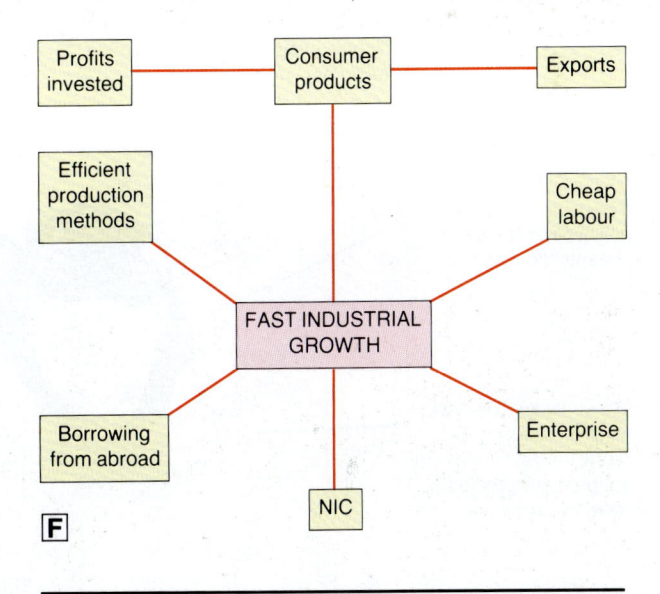

F Keyword plan: FAST INDUSTRIAL GROWTH — Profits invested, Consumer products, Exports, Efficient production methods, Cheap labour, Borrowing from abroad, Enterprise, NIC.

3. Look at some of the items you have at home. How many of them were made in a Far East NIC?
4. Draw up a keyword plan and fill in your own definitions of the words used in **F**.

105

PEOPLE'S LIVES AND WORK
4.8 Taiwan – A NIC

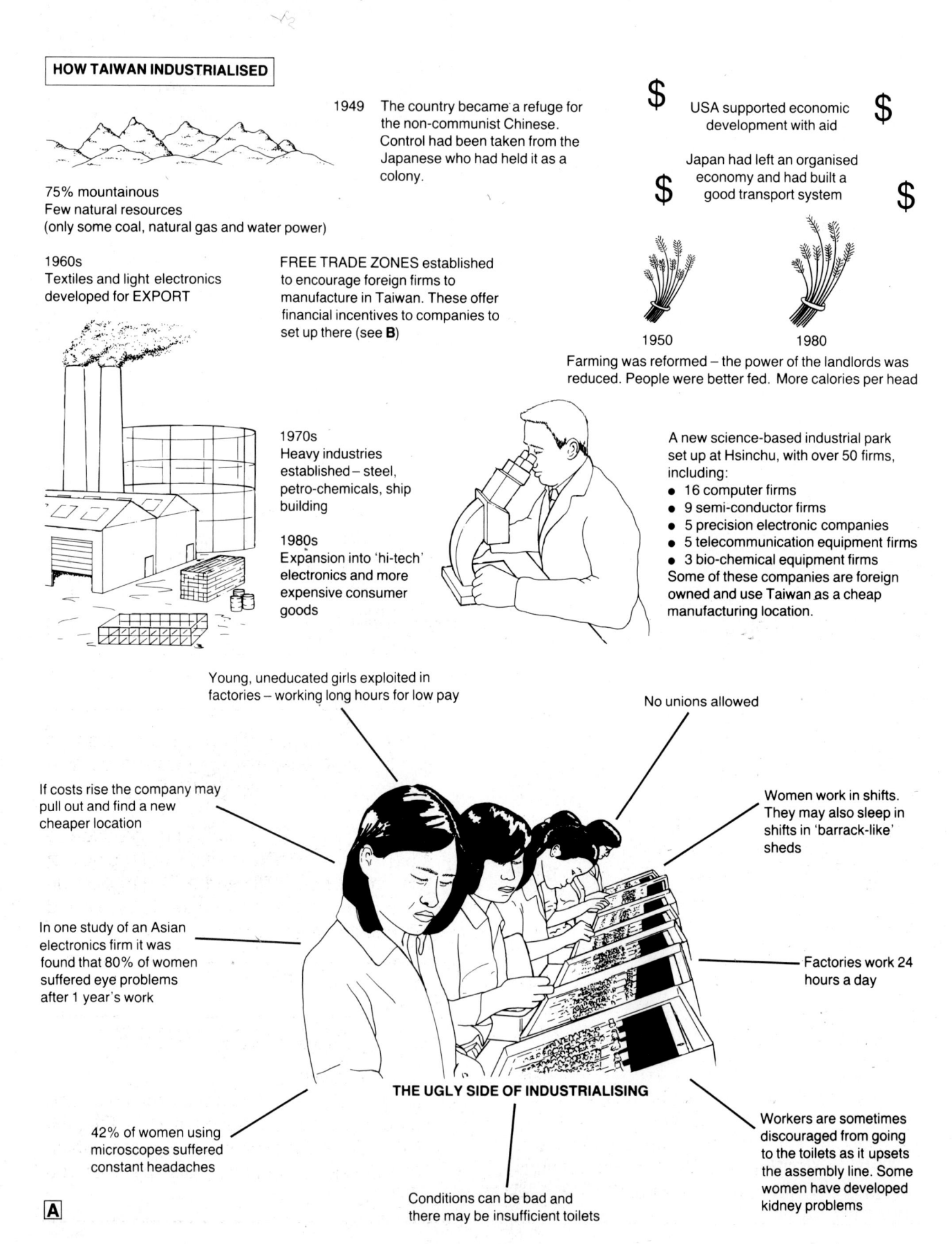

HOW TAIWAN INDUSTRIALISED

75% mountainous
Few natural resources
(only some coal, natural gas and water power)

1949 The country became a refuge for the non-communist Chinese. Control had been taken from the Japanese who had held it as a colony.

USA supported economic development with aid

Japan had left an organised economy and had built a good transport system

1960s
Textiles and light electronics developed for EXPORT

FREE TRADE ZONES established to encourage foreign firms to manufacture in Taiwan. These offer financial incentives to companies to set up there (see **B**)

1950   1980
Farming was reformed – the power of the landlords was reduced. People were better fed. More calories per head

1970s
Heavy industries established – steel, petro-chemicals, ship building

1980s
Expansion into 'hi-tech' electronics and more expensive consumer goods

A new science-based industrial park set up at Hsinchu, with over 50 firms, including:
- 16 computer firms
- 9 semi-conductor firms
- 5 precision electronic companies
- 5 telecommunication equipment firms
- 3 bio-chemical equipment firms

Some of these companies are foreign owned and use Taiwan as a cheap manufacturing location.

THE UGLY SIDE OF INDUSTRIALISING

Young, uneducated girls exploited in factories – working long hours for low pay

No unions allowed

If costs rise the company may pull out and find a new cheaper location

Women work in shifts. They may also sleep in shifts in 'barrack-like' sheds

In one study of an Asian electronics firm it was found that 80% of women suffered eye problems after 1 year's work

Factories work 24 hours a day

42% of women using microscopes suffered constant headaches

Conditions can be bad and there may be insufficient toilets

Workers are sometimes discouraged from going to the toilets as it upsets the assembly line. Some women have developed kidney problems

A

Skills group work, research, display
Concepts NICs, incentives

THE FREE TRADE ZONE A CARROT FOR FOREIGN COMPANIES

- Cheap loans
- No taxes
- Anti-strike laws
- Subsidised facilities
- Cheap labour
- No threats of nationalisation
- No customs duties
- 100% foreign ownership

B

C — Map of Taiwan showing Science-based industrial park (Hsinchu), Free trade zones, main cities (Keelung, Taipei, Taoyuan, Hsinchu, Ilan, Taichung, Chunghua, Hualien, Chiai, Tainan, Pingtung, Kaohsiung, Taitung), Pescadores Islands, Formosa Strait (to mainland China), 25°N, airports. Scale 0–100 km.

1 Copy and complete the sentences below using the **Wordbank**.

Wordbank: Taipei, Japan, non-communists, electronics, mountainous, island, heavy, resources, 25° North, textiles, north

Taiwan is an .... off the coast of mainland China. It lies at latitude .... Its capital city is .... which is in the .... of the country. Taiwan was once a colony of .... From 1949 it became a refuge for the .... Taiwan is a .... country and has few natural ....
During the 1960s light electronics and .... were developed for export. Later .... industries were established. Today Taiwan is a leading .... producer.

2 What type of **incentives** are available for foreign companies in Taiwan (see **B**)?

3 a Name three different types of firms that have set up in the Hsinchu Science Park.
  b How would you describe the types of firms which have set up in the Park?

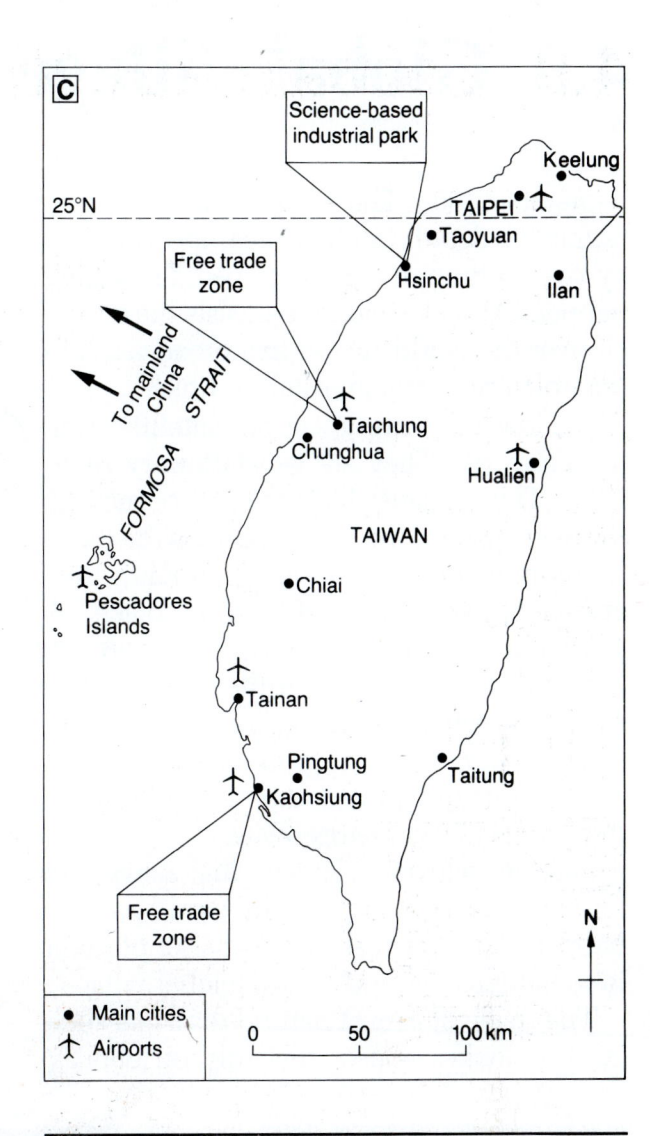

4 Describe the background to industrialisation in Taiwan – what made Taiwan favourable for economic development? (Refer back to Unit 4.7).

5 Work in a small group and produce a display which shows the 'ugly side' of industrialising. Think of the working conditions such as the long hours, low pay and dangerous materials used.

FURTHER WORK

● *A class activity*
Collect a series of advertisements and product labels from goods made in Far East NICs. (This does not include Japan, which is a developed country.) Display what you collect.

PEOPLE'S LIVES AND WORK

4.9 Global Village

September 1988. The events of the Olympic Games in Seoul, South Korea, are watched by over a thousand million people as they happen (**A**). Television broadcasts the events all over the world. These live broadcasts are possible only through satellite links.

A series of communications satellites ring the Earth (**B**). They are **geostationary** satellites. This means that they are moving through space at the same speed as the Earth is spinning. So to an observer on Earth they appear to remain in the same place. A geostationary satellite is positioned 36 000 km from the Earth, above the equator. The satellite receives the television pictures and sound track from a ground station and re-transmits them to another ground station, thousands of kilometres away.

Satellite television means that news and ideas can be sent around the world as they happen. The world seems a smaller place, it is sometimes referred to as a 'global village'.

The tragic effects of natural disasters such as earthquakes appear instantly on our TV screens. People all over the world are shocked and upset (a **global response**) and want to help. Aid agencies often use television to raise money for appeals. Satellite TV also makes it easier for people to gain a

Skills	research, discussion
Concepts	satellite communication
Issues	'global village'

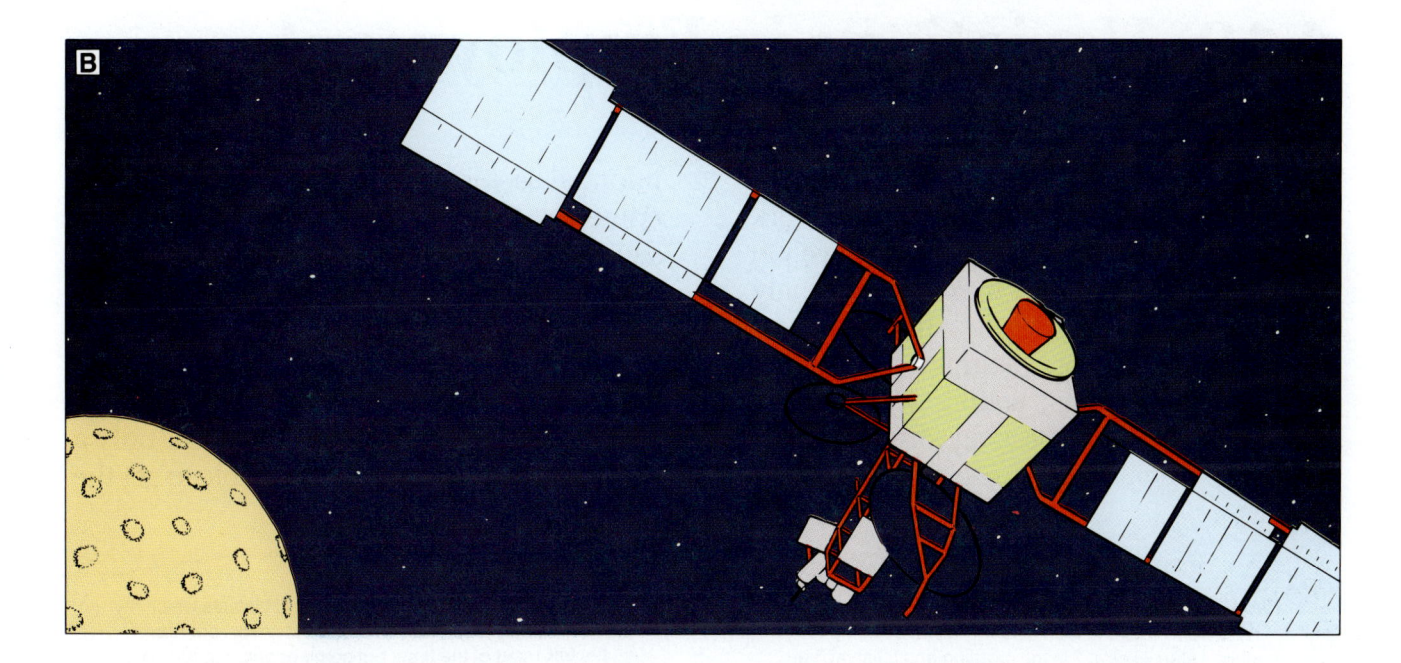

world audience; for example terrorists hijacking airliners know that their demands will be heard across the globe.

Satellite communication is dominated by developed countries, especially the USA. American ideas and attitudes are broadcast to the world. The effect of American television programmes has been called 'cultural imperialism'. American programmes can influence opinions and fashions, breaking up local traditions and culture and replacing them with an imitation of American culture. Coca-Cola and Macdonald's hamburgers are just two American products that have spread throughout the world.

Many developing countries would like to launch their own communications satellites but the sophisticated technology and equipment needed is very expensive.

Satellites over India

India is one of the few developing countries to have its own satellite communications system. Seven satellites have been placed in orbit over India. Since the launch of the satellites the number of television broadcast stations has increased from 12 to 187. Over 2000 community television sets have been placed in remote villages. Most of the programmes broadcast are educational; they use entertainment and folklore to get their message across.

India is a vast country. Different regions have different languages, customs and traditions. It is difficult for Indian TV producers to show programmes that suit everyone. But despite the problems, television means that people who have hardly travelled beyond their village are now in contact with the world.

1 How has India used satellite communications?
2 What problems may be caused by the domination of satellite communications by a few developed countries such as the USA?

FURTHER WORK

- Satellite communication is very expensive. Should developing countries spend the money on simpler projects which are more suitable for local needs?
- Make a list of all the satellite television broadcasts which occur over a period of a week on television. Where were the broadcasts from? What were the purposes of the broadcasts?

PEOPLE'S LIVES AND WORK

4.10 Variations in Employment

The aid agency OXFAM estimates that over 25% of the people in São Paulo, Brazil, work in the **informal sector** (**A**). They have no full-time paid job; they make a living any way they can, often illegally. 'Informal' jobs include shining shoes, selling food, selling toys and handicrafts, selling water, child minding and so on. Begging, drug-pushing, theft and prostitution are also part of the informal sector. Some people are forced into crime as they struggle to survive in the slums. There are no tax demands in the informal sector, but there are no sickness or pension benefits either.

Unemployment is a major problem in the developing world. Under-employment is also a problem: some people work for only a few weeks a year; others are unable to get the

> I work in a small factory in São Paulo. I make shoes. It is hard work. I have to lean over the table, stitching the leather. I start work at 7 in the morning and finish at 7 at night, with half an hour for lunch and a short tea break. There isn't much light in the factory and it's hot and stuffy. I always get headaches and my back is killing me by the time I go home. I earn £9 a week; most of it goes to my parents to help support my family.

ROBERTA
16 YEARS OLD

> I don't have a paid job. I sell sweets and biscuits which my mother makes. I sell them on the streets near our home. It's OK most of the time, but some people frighten me. The drug dealers have tried to get me to sell drugs. They say they'll pay me well. I might do it, just once, to get some real money...

MARIA
17 YEARS OLD

> I've finished school and I'm soon starting a course at university. I'm hoping to get a management job with an aerospace company. My father is a bank manager. I've had to work hard to get my qualifications so I haven't had time to get a job. My parents give me enough pocket money anyway.
> Yes, I know about the poor. It's bad luck, but they don't help themselves as much as they could. They keep missing school, for one thing. They'll never improve themselves without qualifications. I don't understand it...

MARCO
18 YEARS OLD

> Well, there weren't many opportunities in my town so I applied to join the army along with several friends. Only two of us got accepted, the others weren't fit enough. It's a good life in the army but I must admit I don't like having to break up the street riots: some of the rioters used to be my friends. At least I've got a home and plenty to eat...

THALIS
20 YEARS OLD

A

kind of job for which they are qualified and so have to settle for a less skilled job. Even if they do get a paid job, the wages for most workers in developing countries are very low. Conditions at work are often bad (**C**). Many workers in developing countries are **exploited** by their employers, which may include multinational companies based in developed countries. Low wages mean higher profits for the employers. There are no trade unions, so workers are afraid to strike for better conditions.

1 Read the statements in **A**.
  a How many of the people speaking have paid jobs?
  b (i) Which of the four is likely to be most successful in life?
  (ii) Give reasons for your answeer.
  c (i) What problems face Roberta at work?
  (ii) Why doesn't she get a better job?
  d (i) How does Maria earn a living?
  (ii) What problems might she face on the streets?
  (iii) What might happen if Maria did try to sell drugs, 'just once'?
  e Marco says that poor children 'keep missing school'. Why do you think they do this, and what problems may it cause?
  f Why are many developing countries prepared to pay good wages to their soldiers?

Country	Percentage of the workforce employed in:		
	Agriculture	Industry	Services
UK	2	34	64
Brazil	35	21	44
Japan	9	36	55
India	60	13	27
USA	4	28	68
Burkina Faso	80	5	15

B The composition of the workforce in selected countries

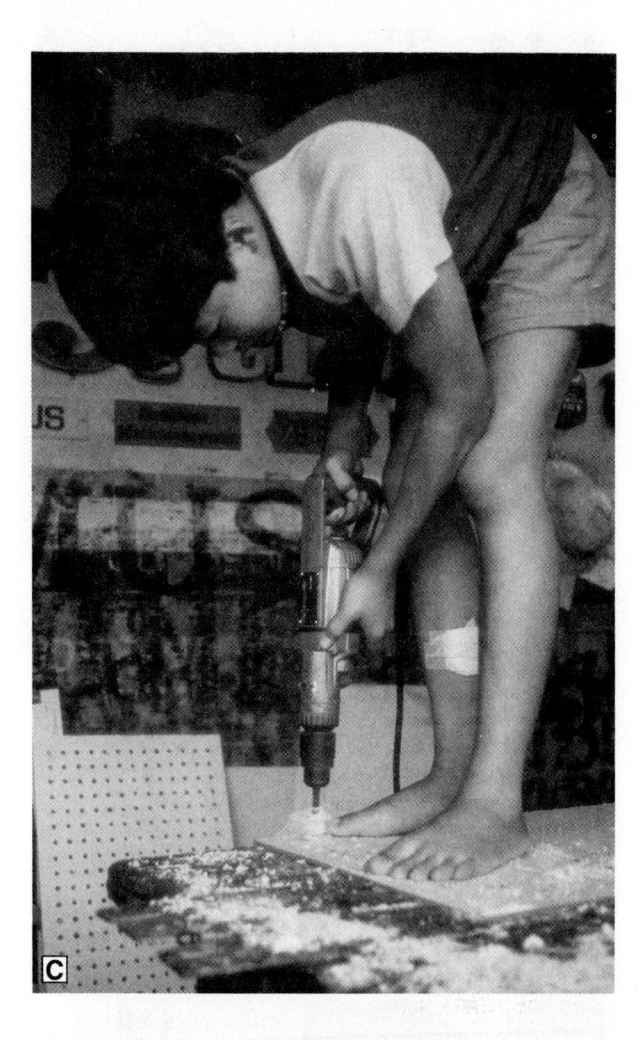

Skills	empathy, interpreting data
Concepts	informal employment
Issues	exploitation

2 a What is meant by the 'informal sector' of employment? (see also Unit 1.7)
  b Give five examples of jobs in the informal sector.
  c What does under-employment mean?
3 Study **B**.
  a Copy the table, but this time place the three developed countries first, followed by the three developing countries.
  b How does the structure of employment in the three developing countries compare with that of the three developed countries in the table?
  c What does the table suggest about variations in employment between developing countries?
4 Why are companies based in the developed world attracted to a developing country as a site for a factory?

PEOPLE'S LIVES AND WORK

4.11 Tourism – A Way Forward

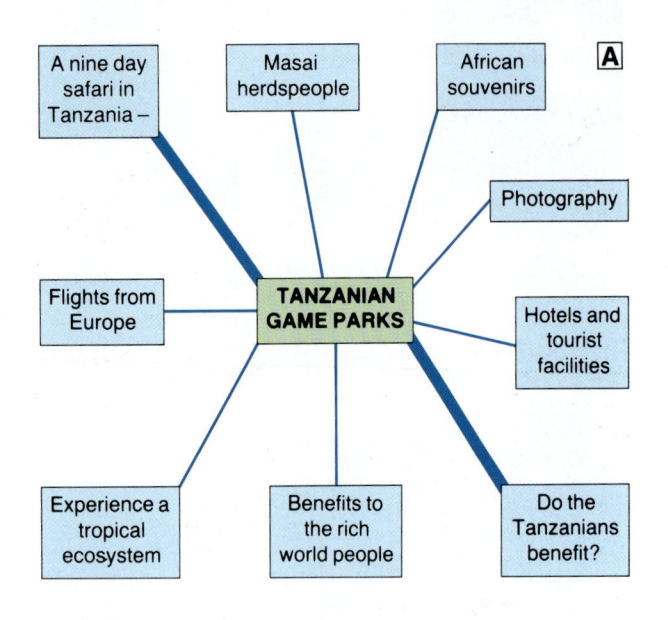

A

Spider diagram centred on **TANZANIAN GAME PARKS** with connections to: A nine day safari in Tanzania; Masai herdspeople; African souvenirs; Photography; Hotels and tourist facilities; Do the Tanzanians benefit?; Benefits to the rich world people; Experience a tropical ecosystem; Flights from Europe.

- An **economic benefit** is the cash income received from tourists by local shopkeepers, farmers, garages, airport workers and people such as safari drivers and game wardens.
- A **cultural benefit** is the meeting of peoples of very different lifestyles: for example, the increased understanding of African dance music experienced by a travelling European. The cultural benefits also extend to people in the host country who learn about life in the tourists' home countries.
- An **environmental benefit** is, for example, where the controls on poaching in an African Game Park are strictly enforced. Animal and plant species are conserved for the future. If tourists have experienced the 'big game' environment they are likely to make efforts to help preserve it.

Tourism – a way forward

The benefits of tourism can be grouped into economic, social/cultural and environmental categories:

THE BENEFITS OF TOURISM

Income from tourist spending
Pool attendants
Building and construction jobs
Jobs as barstaff
Hotel staff

Minibus and Landrover drivers
Conserving wildlife

Increased understanding of other people's lifestyles

Local foods sold to tourists and hotels

B

Skills	planning, flow diagrams
Concepts	tourism
Issues	benefits of tourism

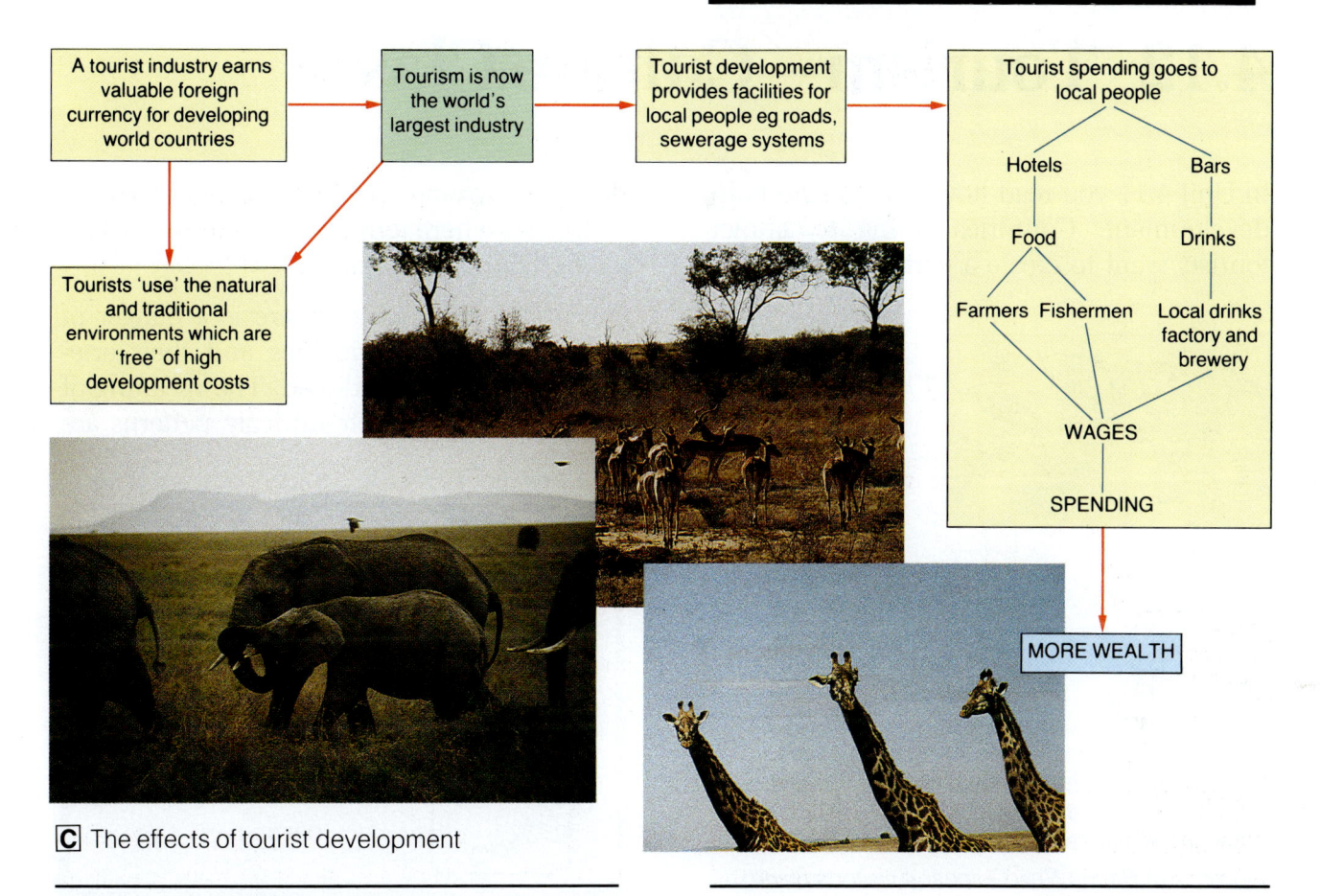

A tourist industry earns valuable foreign currency for developing world countries → Tourism is now the world's largest industry → Tourist development provides facilities for local people eg roads, sewerage systems → Tourist spending goes to local people

Tourists 'use' the natural and traditional environments which are 'free' of high development costs

Tourist spending goes to local people: Hotels, Bars, Food, Drinks, Farmers, Fishermen, Local drinks factory and brewery → WAGES → SPENDING → MORE WEALTH

C The effects of tourist development

1 The Game Park Development

Read the following development plan and answer the questions. A base map for this exercise is on Activity Sheet 49.

Development of New Zebra Village Complex

To extend the metalled road from the airport to a new Game Village complex. The village will cater for 30 tourists. There will be a restaurant and bar development and small outdoor heated swimming pool with associated shower facilities.

No arable farmland or good quality grazing land will be lost for the development. Local farmers will be encouraged to grow vegetables for the restaurant. Labour for construction will be recruited locally. 'Hotel' staff will be part locally recruited and part advertised regionally. Local drivers will be particularly sought for 'safari' expeditions.

a List the construction jobs that will be created because of the development of the Game Village.
b List the jobs that will be created at the final tourist 'hotel'.
c How will local farmers benefit from the development?
d How might the wild animal environment be protected once the development is established?
e In what ways might the local people benefit socially and culturally from the visiting tourists?
f How will the tourists benefit from contact with the local workers and farmers?

2 Imagine you go on a holiday to an East African country.

a What economic benefits will the country gain from your visit?
b What understanding of the African environment might you gain?
c How might your awareness of other people's lifestyles be raised?

3 Study **A** and **B**. Construct your own 'flow diagram' to show how tourism benefits a local area.

113

PEOPLE'S LIVES AND WORK

4.12 Tourism – Culture Clash?

In Unit 4.11 you read how tourism can help development. Countries trying to attract tourists want to create a particular **image**.

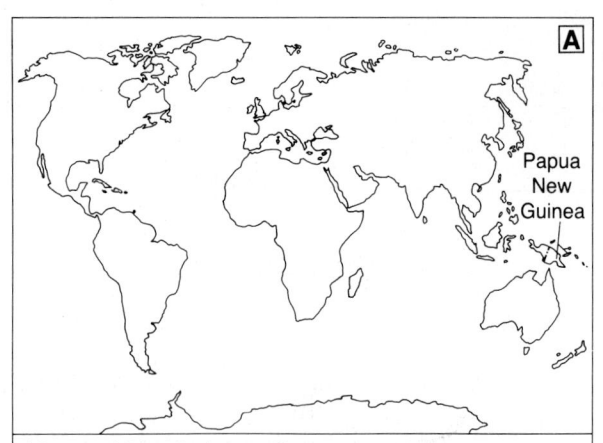

A

'Papua New Guinea offers a combination of scenic beauty and culture, a distinct variety of fauna and flora, marine tourism, village style and modern hotels.'

(*Discover Papua New Guinea: A visitor's guide*)

1. What is Papua New Guinea selling? List all the features in **A**. (Look up the meaning of any words you don't understand.)
2. What is being sold to tourists in **B** and **C**?
3. How are Papua New Guinea people used in **B** and **C**?

Who do you think is right in **D**? Sometimes tourism can bring **social problems**:

- local religious/cultural centres become shopping centres for souvenirs
- tourists introduce local people to alcohol and gambling. Playing cards were banned in Papua New Guinea for a time because of gambling
- imported food and drink for tourists become attractive to local people but are expensive to buy.
- the environment can be upset by building new hotels.

- many young people are attracted to places where tourists stay and leave their traditional ways of life.

In Papua New Guinea there is a danger of tribes becoming curiosities and their artefacts being mass produced. The meaning of the artefacts and their intricate patterns are lost.

B

PNG ART

Spring Garden Road, Hohola
P.O. Box 9264, Hohola
PAPUA NEW GUINEA.
Phone: 25 3976
(a.h.): 25 7803

THE BIGGEST SHOWROOM OF ARTIFACTS IN PAPUA NEW GUINEA.

We supply both the public interested in Papua New Guinea art forms and the dealer interested in something special.
We distribute worldwide and are major PNG exporters.

OPEN 7 DAYS A WEEK
MONDAY - FRIDAY — 9am - 4.30pm
SATURDAY — 9am - 4.00pm
SUNDAY — 11am - 4.00pm

C

114

Skills	empathy, role play
Concepts	culture clash, tourism
Issues	problems of tourism

WHAT DO YOU THINK?

(Scene: Mum, Dad and the children are on holiday.)

Come on, we're off to the museum today.

Oh, Dad! We wanted to go fishing today.

We haven't come all this way to go fishing. There are lots of interesting historical things to see in this town.

History! Who wants to see that boring old stuff? Holidays are meant to be fun.

It's part of your heritage. You ought to see it.

It's our holiday too, you know. You always try to make us do what you want. It's not fair.

Yeah, we're people too you know.

That's enough, you two! If your father says we're going, we're going.

D

4 Imagine you are a local person worried about the effect of tourism in Papua New Guinea. Write a letter to your local newspaper expressing your concern. Include examples of the problems you think tourism brings.

Australia	1421
New Zealand	120
Japan	133
UK	182
USA	435
Others	64
Total	2355

E Visitor arrivals (per month)

Most tourists are from the rich, developed world (**E**). They expect high standards of accommodation. Most of the visitors' money is spent on getting to Papua New Guinea and on their accommodation. The airlines and hotels are mostly owned by foreign companies and managed by foreigners. Local people usually get low-paid jobs as waiters, cleaners and entertainers. So most of the profits from tourism go out of New Guinea.

5 What developed countries did visitors come from in **E**?
6 What did visitors expect to find in Papua New Guinea?
7 Who gets most of the profits from tourism?

Papua New Guinea was once an Australian colony. Now the country is independent. It is developing, but still feels the influence of nearby Australia. With the growth of tourism, some people fear that the influence of foreign culture will increase. Papua New Guinea is aware of this problem; local culture and traditions are promoted through education, so that people can continue to pass on their culture to future generations.

FURTHER WORK

- Look at **D**. Find a partner. Imagine one of you is a young Papua New Guinean and the other their parent. Act out the scenes in the cartoon, adding any other arguments you can think of.
- Use the *Activity sheet* to research images of other tourist attractions.

PEOPLE'S LIVES AND WORK
4.13 China

China covers a large part of south eastern Asia (**B**). It is the third largest country in the world. Western and northern China consists mainly of high land and mountain ranges. Most of the best farming regions are in the eastern lowlands and most Chinese live in this area (**B**). The fertile flood plains of the rivers Hwang-ho and Yangtze Kiang are amongst the most densely populated areas in the world.

China is one of the world's most important countries. Its civilisation dates back over 5000 years. While the peoples of Europe lived in simple tribal societies, the Chinese had developed a national system of government and a sophisticated culture. Poetry, painting, sculpture and literature thrived in China. Many of the world's most important inventions originate in China (**C**).

China's history is long and glorious. But, as in most countries, it was only glorious for some. For most people, life was hard and short. Many were treated as slaves by the rich and powerful. From the 1800s the country was plagued by rebellion, civil war and foreign intereference. In 1949 the Communist party finally won the civil war. There were many years of turmoil, but gradually China began to make progress once again. You can read more about this development in the next unit.

China's rulers aim to restore the country to what they consider to be its true role: one of the world's most powerful nations.

---

1 a What is the present population of China?
 b What is the population density of China?
 c The population of the world is 5.5 million. What percentage of the world's population lives in China?
2 What is the GDP per capita of China?
 (i) £254 (ii) £127 (iii) £1250 (iv) £485?
3 Draw a pie graph to show the percentage of the Chinese workforce in agriculture, industry and services.
4 a Why is Hong Kong the most important destination for Chinese exports?
 b Why is Japan the major source of imports to China?

A **Database**

Area:	9597 sq km (third largest country in the world)
Population:	1100 million (highest in the world)
Population density:	112 persons per sq km
Birth rate:	22 per thousand (third lowest in Asia – 42 countries)
Death rate:	8 per thousand (sixth lowest in Asia
Life expectancy:	69 years (fifth highest in Asia)
GDP:	£140 000 million (second largest in Asia)
Workforce:	45% in agriculture, 42% in industry, 13% in services
Urbanisation:	24% of population lives in cities 34 cities over a million population – more than all of the countries of Europe put together
Capital city:	Peking (Beijing) population 9.4 million
People per doctor	1740
Major exports:	Textiles, food products, oil, clothing, arms
Major imports:	Machinery, transport equipment, manufactured goods, grain.

Skills	research
Concepts	culture, change, communism

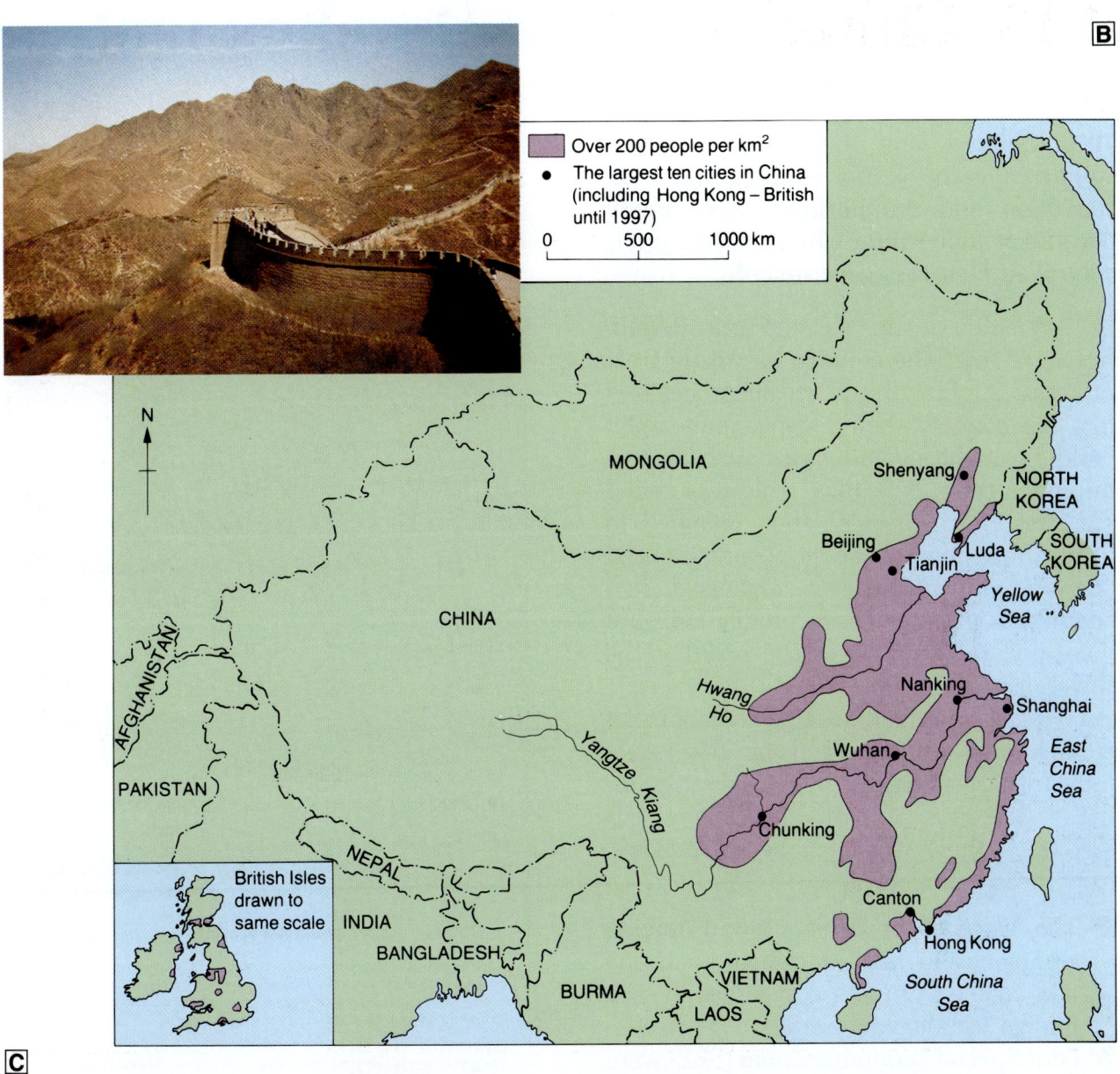

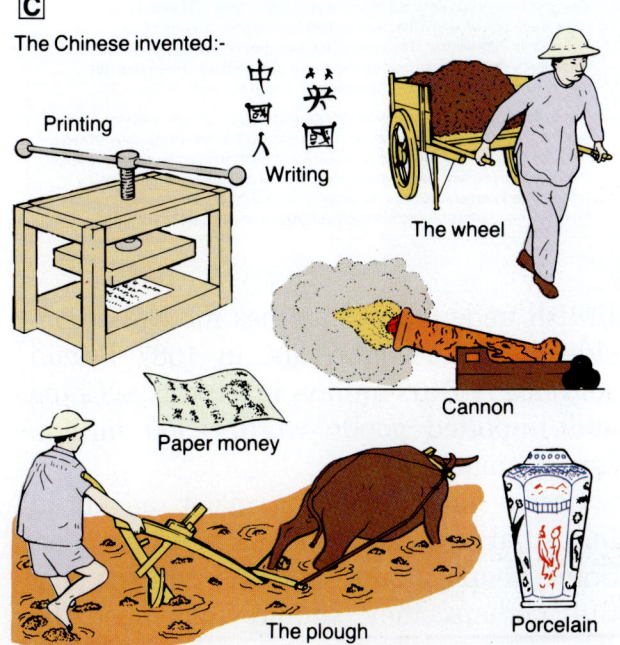

B

Over 200 people per km²

● The largest ten cities in China (including Hong Kong – British until 1997)

0   500   1000 km

British Isles drawn to same scale

C

The Chinese invented:-
- Printing
- Writing
- The wheel
- Cannon
- Paper money
- The plough
- Porcelain

FURTHER WORK

Try to find out more information about the history of China and its civilisation (your school or local library may be able to help). Who was Kublai Khan? Who built the Great Wall, and why? What was 'Cathay'? Where is the Forbidden City and who had it built? What was the Opium War of 1839–42? What connections do the Chinese have with paper, the compass and porcelain? Write and illustrate a report on what you discover or draw up a timeline of China's history.

PEOPLE'S LIVES AND WORK

4.14 China's Road to Development

1949. *China is one of the most deprived countries in the world. Millions die from starvation and malnutrition. After many decades of civil war the Chinese mainland is controlled by a new government.*

In 1949 China became a Communist Republic. Since then, the country has made great progress. At first the government decided that the country should concentrate upon building up heavy industries such as coal mining, steel and textiles. This was called the 'great leap forward'; they intended to turn China into a modern industrialised country. Agriculture was organised into **communes** (**A**) to boost production. But these policies were not as successful as the Government hoped.

Living standards did not rise enough. Not enough jobs were created by the heavy industries. Farm production was disappointing.

In 1978 there was a change of policies. New ideas included:

- **The Open Door** This allowed foreign companies to sell equipment to China and enabled Chinese companies to seek foreign technical assistance.
- Four **Special Economic Zones** (SEZ) were established on the Chinese coast. Foreign companies were encouraged to open factories in these areas (**D**). The foreign companies were attracted by cheap labour, tax reductions and other special deals.
- In 1984 14 more coastal cities were designated **'open cities'** with many of the incentives of the SEZs.
- **Agricultural reforms** involved breaking up the communes and replacing them with townships. People could now retain any surplus from farming for their own use or for sale.

A number of large factories have been built by foreign companies. An example is the Volkswagen plant at Shanghai (**C**). This is a **joint venture** between the Chinese government and Volkswagen. It assembles Santana cars from kits imported from West Germany.

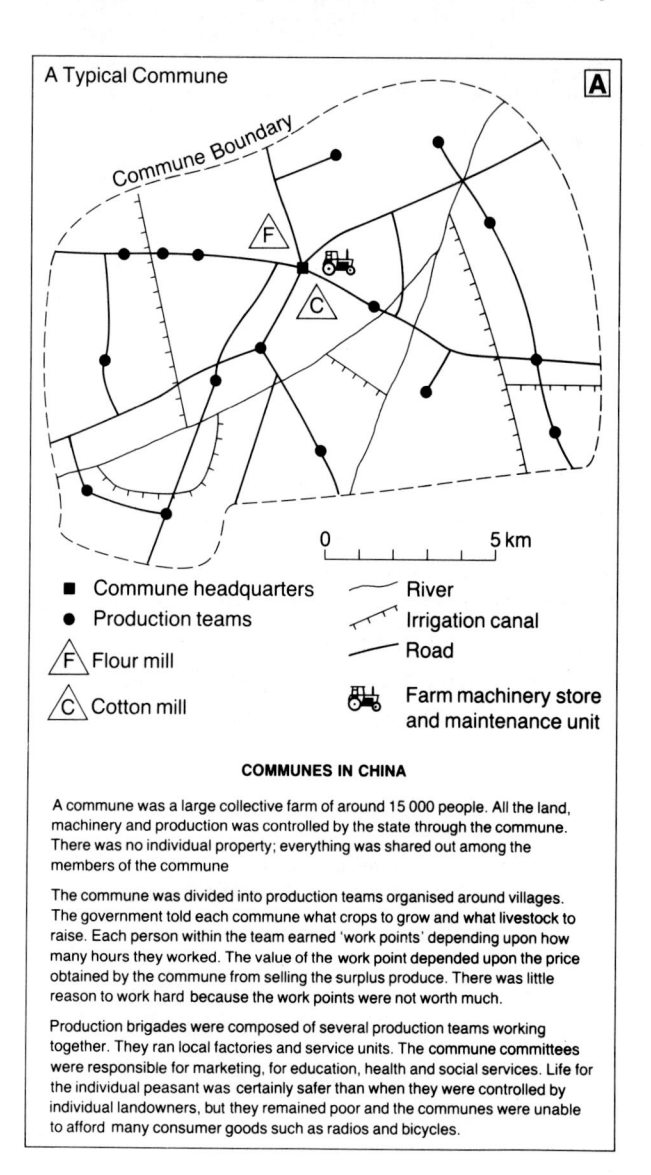

A Typical Commune

- ■ Commune headquarters
- ● Production teams
- ⬡ F Flour mill
- ⬡ C Cotton mill
- River
- Irrigation canal
- Road
- Farm machinery store and maintenance unit

COMMUNES IN CHINA

A commune was a large collective farm of around 15 000 people. All the land, machinery and production was controlled by the state through the commune. There was no individual property; everything was shared out among the members of the commune

The commune was divided into production teams organised around villages. The government told each commune what crops to grow and what livestock to raise. Each person within the team earned 'work points' depending upon how many hours they worked. The value of the work point depended upon the price obtained by the commune from selling the surplus produce. There was little reason to work hard because the work points were not worth much.

Production brigades were composed of several production teams working together. They ran local factories and service units. The commune committees were responsible for marketing, for education, health and social services. Life for the individual peasant was certainly safer than when they were controlled by individual landowners, but they remained poor and the communes were unable to afford many consumer goods such as radios and bicycles.

British trade with China has increased considerably in recent years. In 1987 Britain sold nearly £400 million in exports to China and imported goods worth £300 million from China.

China aims to be a major advanced industrial nation within a few decades. Some people doubt that this will happen. But perhaps they should remember the

Skills interpreting charts
Concepts change, communism, joint venture

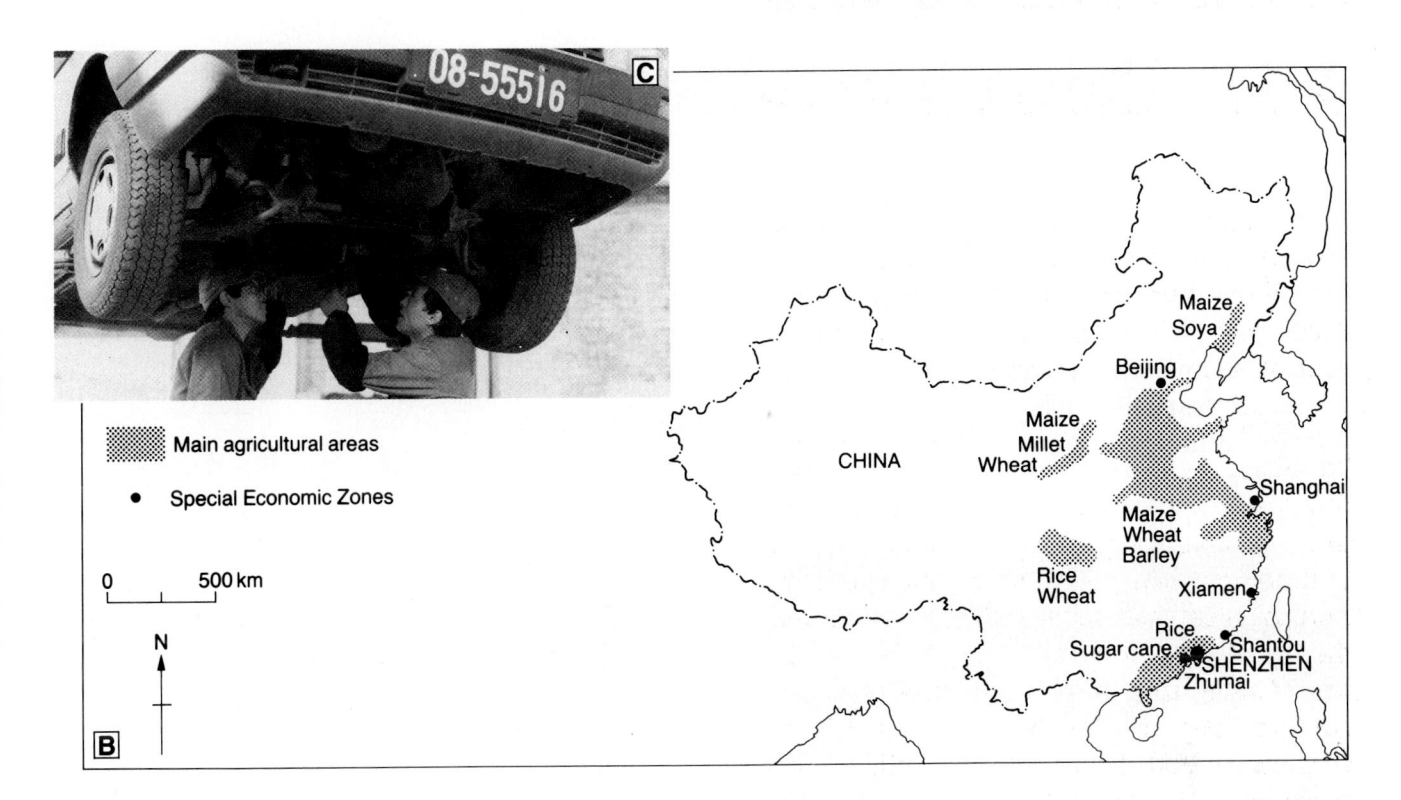

B (map legend)
- Main agricultural areas
- Special Economic Zones

Map labels: CHINA, Beijing, Shanghai, Xiamen, Shantou, SHENZHEN, Zhumai; Maize, Soya, Millet, Wheat, Barley, Rice, Sugar cane

example of Japan (see Book 2 of this series) and consider China's three big advantages:

- A huge domestic market;
- Raw materials, minerals and high quality farmland in abundance;
- The determination to regain China's past role as a leader in science and technology.

Shenzhen is an area bordering the British colony of Hong Kong. In 1978 Shenzhen had a population of 25 000; by 1988 the population was over 400 000. Over 4000 factories have been built here, including a Pepsi-Cola bottling plant, petro-chemicals, furniture and electronics. The road and rail systems have been improved. An airport and a deepwater seaport are planned.

D Shenzhen SEZ

---

1 What was the 'great leap forward' in China?

2 a What was a commune?
   b How were the communes changed after 1978

3 What caused the change of policy after 1978?

Country	Exports from China %	Imports to China %
Hong Kong	27	12
Japan	23	35
USA	9	12
Singapore	8	1
The former USSR	4	2
Germany	3	6
Brazil	2	2
UK	1	2
Italy	1	2
Canada	1	3
Others	21	23

E China's Trading Partners

4 Study **E**
   a Name the country which is the largest importer of Chinese goods. Why do you think that country imports so many Chinese goods?
   b Name the country from which China imports most goods. Why do you think that country is such an important source of imports for China.
   c Does the table provide evidence for the success of 'the open door' policy?

PEOPLE'S LIVES AND WORK

4.15 One World – Sporting Links

What did you do on Saturday afternoon? Go to a football match? Play tennis? Watch sport on TV? Millions of people all over the world take part in, or watch, sporting events. Hundreds of millions watch TV broadcasts of major contests such as the World Cup, World Athletics Championships, or Olympic Games.

A

In 1988 and 1992 one third of the world's population watched the opening ceremony of the Olympic Games. Satellite technology made this communications link possible (see Unit 4.9). Such worldwide links are unusual for television broadcasting.

The Olympic Games of the modern era began in Athens on 6 April 1896. The idea behind these Games is that sport can bring

1936 medals (Summer Olympic Games)

	Gold	Silver	Bronze
Germany	33	26	30
United States	24	20	12
Hungary	10	1	5
Italy	8	9	5
Finland	7	6	6
France	7	6	6
Sweden	6	5	9
Japan	6	4	8
Netherlands	6	4	7
Great Britain	4	7	3
Austria	4	6	3
Czechoslovakia	3	5	–
Argentina	2	2	3
Estonia	2	2	3
Egypt	2	1	2
Switzerland	1	9	5
Canada	1	3	5
Norway	1	3	2
Turkey	1	–	1
India	1	–	–
New Zealand	1	–	–
Poland	–	3	3
Denmark	–	2	3
Latvia	–	1	1
Romania	–	1	–
South Africa	–	1	–
Yugoslavia	–	1	–
Mexico	–	–	3
Belgium	–	–	2
Australia	–	–	1
Philippines	–	–	1
Portugal	–	–	1

B

1896 medals

	Gold	Silver	Bronze
United States	11	7	1
Greece	10	19	17
Germany	7	5	2
France	5	4	2
Great Britain	3	3	1
Hungary	2	1	2
Austria	2	–	3
Australia	2	–	–
Denmark	1	2	4
Switzerland	1	2	–

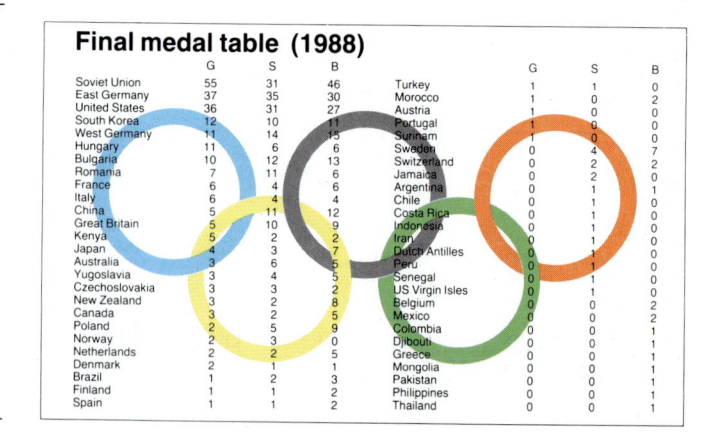

Final medal table (1988)

	G	S	B		G	S	B
Soviet Union	55	31	46	Turkey	1	1	0
East Germany	37	35	30	Morocco	1	0	2
United States	36	31	27	Austria	1	0	0
South Korea	12	10	11	Portugal	1	0	0
West Germany	11	14	15	Surinam	1	0	0
Hungary	11	6	6	Sweden	0	4	7
Bulgaria	10	12	13	Switzerland	0	4	2
Romania	7	11	6	Jamaica	0	2	0
France	6	4	6	Argentina	0	1	1
Italy	6	4	4	Chile	0	1	0
China	5	11	12	Costa Rica	0	1	0
Great Britain	5	10	9	Indonesia	0	1	0
Kenya	5	2	2	Iran	0	1	1
Japan	4	3	7	Dutch Antilles	0	1	0
Australia	3	6	5	Peru	0	1	0
Yugoslavia	3	4	5	Senegal	0	1	0
Czechoslovakia	3	3	2	US Virgin Isles	0	1	0
New Zealand	3	2	8	Belgium	0	0	2
Canada	3	2	5	Mexico	0	0	2
Poland	2	5	9	Colombia	0	0	1
Norway	2	3	0	Djibouti	0	0	1
Netherlands	2	2	5	Greece	0	0	1
Denmark	2	1	1	Mongolia	0	0	1
Brazil	1	2	3	Pakistan	0	0	1
Finland	1	1	2	Philippines	0	0	1
Spain	1	1	2	Thailand	0	0	1

Skills	reading statistics, making comparisons
Concepts	sporting links, Olympic Games
Issues	'one world'

people together no matter what their race, beliefs, politics or nationality. This sporting event is just one of many that seeks to bring people together in friendly but competitive situations.

1 Where and when did the modern Olympic Games begin?
2 What is the idea behind the Olympic Games?
3 Why was it possible for a third of the world's people to watch the opening ceremonies in 1988 and 1992?
4 Look at **B**.
   a What changed in the medals tables between 1896 and 1988?
   b Why was there a great increase in numbers of countries competing between 1936 and 1988? (Think about independence).

Some countries refuse to play sport with others because they disagree with their actions or policies. For example, many countries refused to play sport with South Africa to protest against their policy of apartheid (see Unit 3.15). Some countries, for example the USA and the former USSR, use their sporting success as an advertisement. They invest large amounts of money in training their sporting representatives. Sports like athletics take place in almost all countries of the world. Others, like skiing, are popular in only a few countries.

5 In what ways do some countries use sport?

Sporting heroes – national heros

C shows a number of sports stars who are the pride of their countries. People respect them and follow their exploits with great interest. These sporting figures feel responsible for representing their country and all that is good about it. **D** shows the jubilation of a triumphant team. It is a time for people to celebrate their country's achievement.

6 How do sports stars bring the people of their country together?
7 Name some of your favourite sports stars. What countries do they represent? What sports do they play?

121

Backtrack What to do in Igrinea?

Igrinea is a developing country in Africa. The new government has to decide how best to spend money set aside for development. If you were a government minister, what would you do? The information in this section and on the related Activity Sheet will help you decide.

Proposals
- Build a new network of roads and railways to improve transport of people and goods (look at the Northern Belt on the map)
- Improve industry, building new steelworks and high technology factories (proposed site in the South, on the map)
- Improve agriculture with irrigation schemes and new laws about land ownership (look at the Middle Belt and Northern Belt on the map)
- Improve education of the people with more schools, teachers, buildings and equipment (this could help people in the Northern Belt)
- Promote tourism in your country (could provide work in the Northern Belt).

In groups of five:

Study the map of Igrinea. There are three Belts. Each of them has certain features. For example, population in the Middle is low compared with the North and the South.

The following people meet to discuss the proposals:

Minister for the South Belt – your region is wealthy and you want to keep it that way.

Minister for the Middle Belt – your region is poor and has not benefited from past development.

Minister for the North Belt – your region is poor and you are upset at the inequality with the Christian south.

Leader of Igrinea – you worry about the divisions in your nation and want to see a better life for all your people.

United Nations Advisor on development – you have been invited to give your opinion as an outsider. Your experience will prevent mistakes being made in how development takes place.

Decide which person you want to be. Study the map carefully and note how the proposals could help your region or the whole country. Consider each proposal and put them in order of priority from **your** point of view. In each case follow this question route to help you decide.

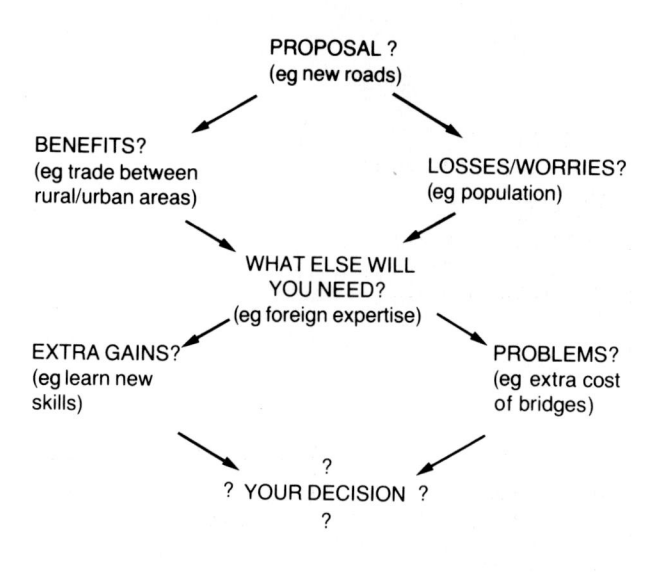

```
                PROPOSAL?
               (eg new roads)
              ↙           ↘
   BENEFITS?              LOSSES/WORRIES?
   (eg trade between      (eg population)
   rural/urban areas)
              ↘           ↙
            WHAT ELSE WILL
             YOU NEED?
           (eg foreign expertise)
              ↙           ↘
   EXTRA GAINS?            PROBLEMS?
   (eg learn new           (eg extra cost
   skills)                 of bridges)
              ↘     ?     ↙
               ? YOUR DECISION ?
                     ?
```

BE CAREFUL: There are hidden problems. For example if you invite foreign countries to help, this may cause problems such as culture clash.

When you have decided on the most important proposal argue your case with the other people in your group. Remember they will have their own priorities. You will need to convince them. It is best if you prepare a report with all of your arguments. You could set it out like the question.

Take it in turns to express your views. Then each of the other people can question you with their worries.

When each of you has done this vote and decide which proposal is to be adopted.

Now answer these questions
1 What did you do?
2 What did your group do?
3 What did you learn?
4 What did you enjoy?
5 What do you value about this type of work?
6 How can you improve?

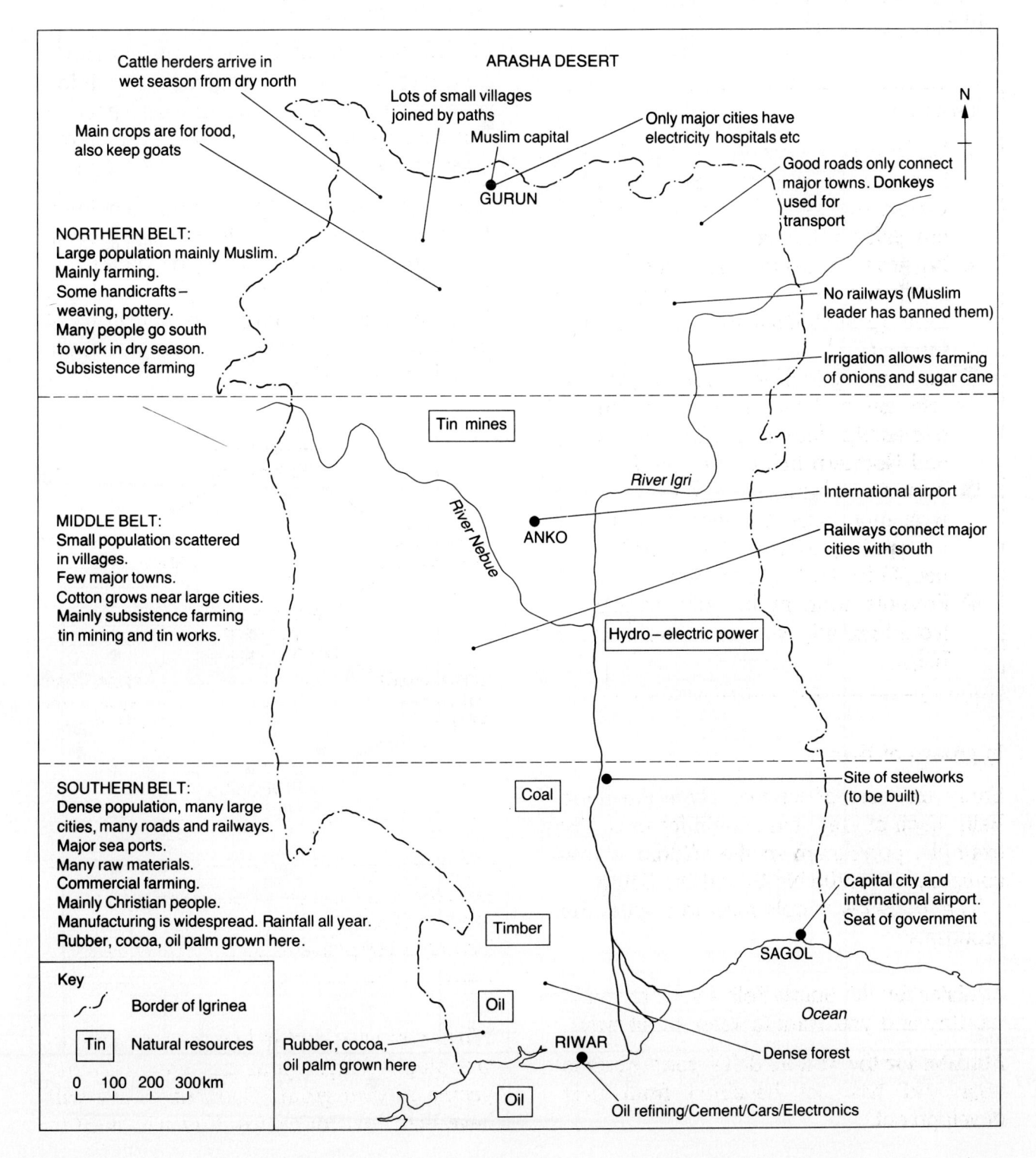

ARASHA DESERT

Cattle herders arrive in wet season from dry north

Lots of small villages joined by paths

Muslim capital

Only major cities have electricity hospitals etc

Main crops are for food, also keep goats

GURUN

Good roads only connect major towns. Donkeys used for transport

NORTHERN BELT:
Large population mainly Muslim.
Mainly farming.
Some handicrafts – weaving, pottery.
Many people go south to work in dry season.
Subsistence farming

No railways (Muslim leader has banned them)

Irrigation allows farming of onions and sugar cane

Tin mines

River Igri

River Nebue

International airport

ANKO

Railways connect major cities with south

MIDDLE BELT:
Small population scattered in villages.
Few major towns.
Cotton grows near large cities.
Mainly subsistence farming tin mining and tin works.

Hydro – electric power

Site of steelworks (to be built)

Coal

SOUTHERN BELT:
Dense population, many large cities, many roads and railways.
Major sea ports.
Many raw materials.
Commercial farming.
Mainly Christian people.
Manufacturing is widespread. Rainfall all year.
Rubber, cocoa, oil palm grown here.

Capital city and international airport.
Seat of government

Timber

SAGOL

Ocean

Oil

Key

Border of Igrinea

RIWAR

Dense forest

Tin Natural resources

Rubber, cocoa, oil palm grown here

0 100 200 300km

Oil

Oil refining/Cement/Cars/Electronics

Matrix of Concepts and Issues

UNIT NO.	1.1	1.2	1.3	1.4	1.5	1.6	1.7	1.8	1.9	1.10	1.11	1.12	2.1	2.2	2.3	2.4	2.5	2.6	2.7	2.8	2.9	2.10	2.11	3.1	3.2	3.
Issues																										
equality/inequality	○	○	⊕			⊕	●			●										●					●	
quality of life		⊕	●		●	⊕	●	●		●	⊕	●					●	●								
pollution																					⊕				●	
planning								○	⊕		●						●					●	●		●	
conflict																	○	○			○	⊕	●			
unemployment							○																			
perception/viewpoint	⊕	●	●	●			●				●	●									●					
interdependence	⊕				●													●	●					●		●
colonialism/neo-colonialism				○								○									○					
desertification																⊕		●								
resource depletion														⊕												
racism																										
reform									○																⊕	
famine																		○								
Major Concepts																										
scale		○		○		○		○		⊕	●						○	●	●	●					⊕	
change				○	○		⊕		⊕	⊕	●			●	●	●			○		●	○				
symbols			○								●															●
system					⊕			○						●			⊕			●		⊕	⊕	⊕	⊕	
cause/effect					○	⊕	○	○	⊕			●	●	⊕	⊕	⊕		⊕	⊕	⊕	⊕	⊕	●		⊕	
time/distance			○	●	●			○				○					●		○				⊕			
interaction	○			⊕	●											⊕					●	●	○			●
evidence		○			○			⊕											⊕	⊕						
development		○	⊕	●	○	○				●							⊕			●	⊕				●	
location	○	○	○	○			○			⊕			⊕	○	○	○	⊕	●	●	●	○	●	○			●
distribution/pattern		○	⊕	○			○	⊕	●	⊕			⊕	●	⊕	⊕		●	●	●				○	⊕	⊕
Geographical Topics/Concepts																										
region		○		○	○		⊕	●				●	⊕	●	●	●	●	●						→		
population						○		○	⊕	⊕	⊕	●					●									
welfare		○	⊕			⊕			●	●								●		●					⊕	
culture			⊕	●						●														●		
survival				○													○		⊕	●	●		●		⊕	
trade	○			○																				○		○
food					○												○		○							
work					○		⊕														○					
natural hazards					○											○	○	⊕	⊕	⊕				⊕		
rural life				⊕	⊕			●									●								●	
urban life					○	⊕	⊕	●		⊕															●	
migration/movement						⊕			○	○	⊕													→		
infrastructure						○		○	○		⊕														⊕	
weather/climate					○								⊕		⊕	⊕		⊕		⊕						
farming					⊕												○	⊕						○		○
landscape																⊕										
government			○					⊕	○								⊕	●		○	⊕				●	
erosion/deposition															○		⊕	●			●					
natural environment					○								⊕	⊕	⊕	⊕						→	●			
communication			○							○																
accessibility																	⊕								⊕	
conservation														○		○						⊕				
ecosystem														⊕	●	●						●				
human interference														⊕	●	⊕		●			⊕	⊕				
aid																	○	○							⊕	
irrigation															○	⊕					⊕					
water supply					○										○	○								○	⊕	
co-operatives																○										
reclamation															○	⊕					●					
technology																										
industry				○																⊕						●
transport							○			○																
multinationals																						○				
resources																○										⊕
remote sensing																										
capitalism/communism																										
tourism																						○				
energy/fuel																	○				⊕					●

Key ○ concept/issue/skill introduced or mentioned ⊕ concept/issue/skill focused on ● concept/issue/skill reinforced and taken as part of students'

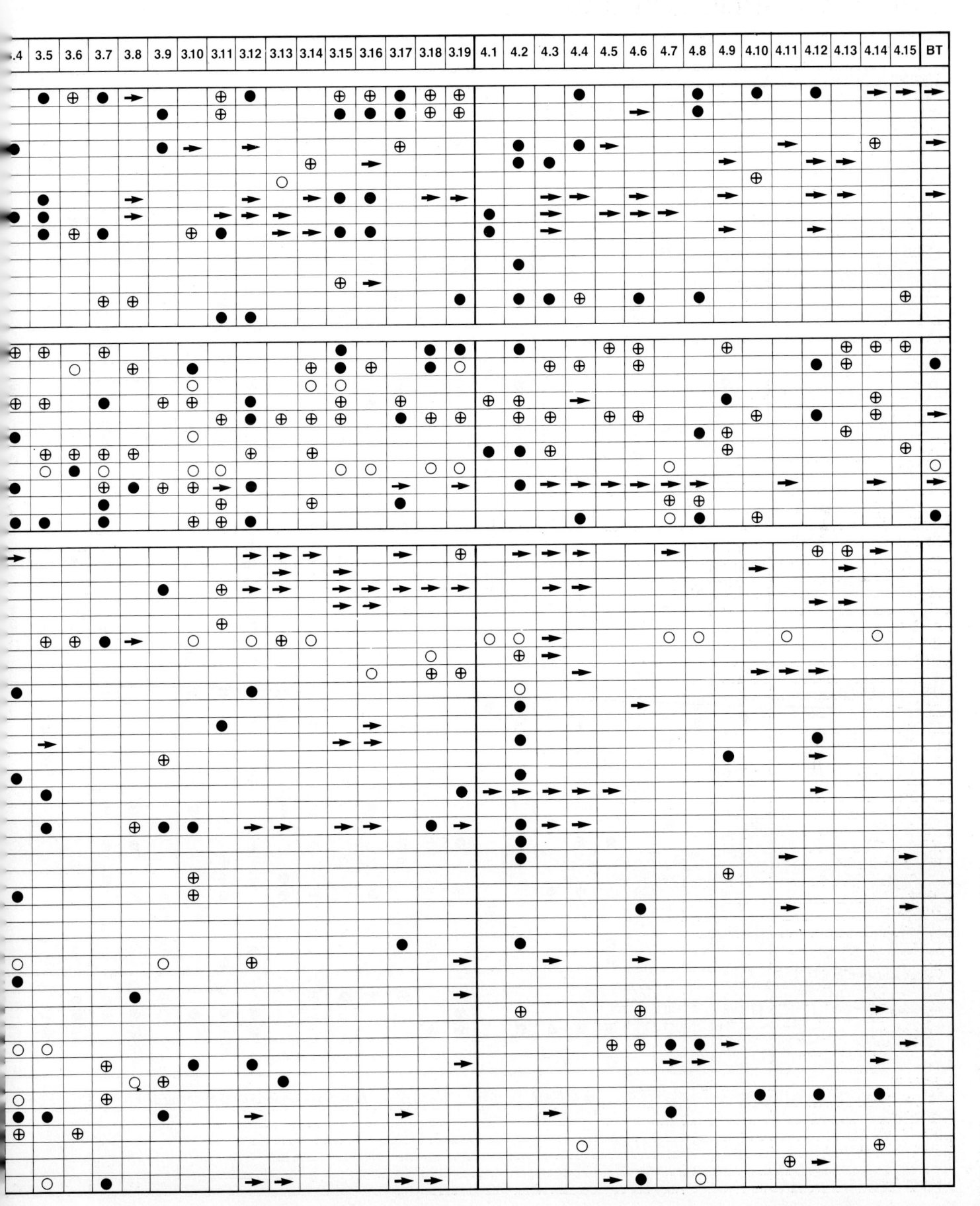

	3.5	3.6	3.7	3.8	3.9	3.10	3.11	3.12	3.13	3.14	3.15	3.16	3.17	3.18	3.19	4.1	4.2	4.3	4.4	4.5	4.6	4.7	4.8	4.9	4.10	4.11	4.12	4.13	4.14	4.15	BT

→ concept/issue/skill expanded and developed into new area

125

Matrix of Skills

UNIT NO.	1.1	1.2	1.3	1.4	1.5	1.6	1.7	1.8	1.9	1.10	1.11	1.12	2.1	2.2	2.3	2.4	2.5	2.6	2.7	2.8	2.9	2.10	2.11	3.1	3.2	3.
Communication and Numeracy																										
advertising																		O						●		●
assessment/evaluation								O		O											⊕					
calculating mean					⊕													●								
collecting data	O																									
discussion						O	O											O				⊕				
enquiry/research	O			⊕				⊕	⊕									●				O				
explaining					O	O		⊕						●	●	●		⊕		●				●		
imaginative writing				O				⊕										⊕						⊕		
keyword planning		⊕																●							●	
measuring				●																						
observing																										
presenting results																										
recording													●							⊕						
report writing						⊕								⊕				●								
questionnaires																										
rank order				⊕																						
Map and Graphicacy																										
atlas work		●						●					●					●								⊕
cross-section/transect													⊕	●												
direction										O														⊕		
flow/systems diagram				●				O				O		⊕						●		●	→	O		
drawing graphs — line					●																					
drawing graphs — bar					●					→	O															
drawing graphs — scatter			⊕																							
drawing graphs — pie																										
interpreting graphs — line					●			●							⊕			●								
interpreting graphs — bar					●				O	O					⊕			●								
interpreting graphs — scatter			⊕																							
interpreting graphs — picture											O															
interpreting graphs — pie																										
map interpretation		●		●	O			●	⊕				⊕		O			●	O	●		O		●		●
map making/design	●						●											●					→			●
satellite false image																										
sketching/perspective																										
timeline					⊕																					
using block diagram																		●	●		→					
using statistics			⊕						●																O	O
using photographs		O	●		⊕		●						⊕	O	O	●	●	⊕		O	O			●	●	
using scale					●					O								●		●						
Decision making/problem solving																										
deciding on locations		●	●															●								●
deciding on priorities								O						O												
finding solutions						O								⊕		O	⊕			●		●	●			
forming opinions	⊕			●			●													⊕	●					
grouping/categorising	O	O				●	●				●	⊕	●									●	●			O
planning																		⊕								
predicting/forecasting					O												●	⊕	⊕							
recognising problems					O	O	●	●	O		⊕		●	O	⊕	●		●	●	●	●	⊕	⊕			
weighing up evidence		O					O		⊕											⊕						
Social																										
group work						●					⊕									O						
co-operation/sharing						●					●							●								
Values and attitudes																										
awareness of environment													⊕	⊕	●	⊕					⊕			●	●	
awareness of others	⊕	⊕		⊕	⊕	⊕			●									●	●	●	O	●	●	●	⊕	
empathy				O	O	⊕	●	●			●	●						●	⊕	O		⊕	●	⊕	●	
game/simulation																			⊕			⊕				
role play						⊕																⊕				

Key   O concept/issue/skill introduced or mentioned   ⊕ concept/issue/skill focused on   ● concept/issue/skill reinforced and taken as part of students' k...

→ concept/issue/skill expanded and developed into new area

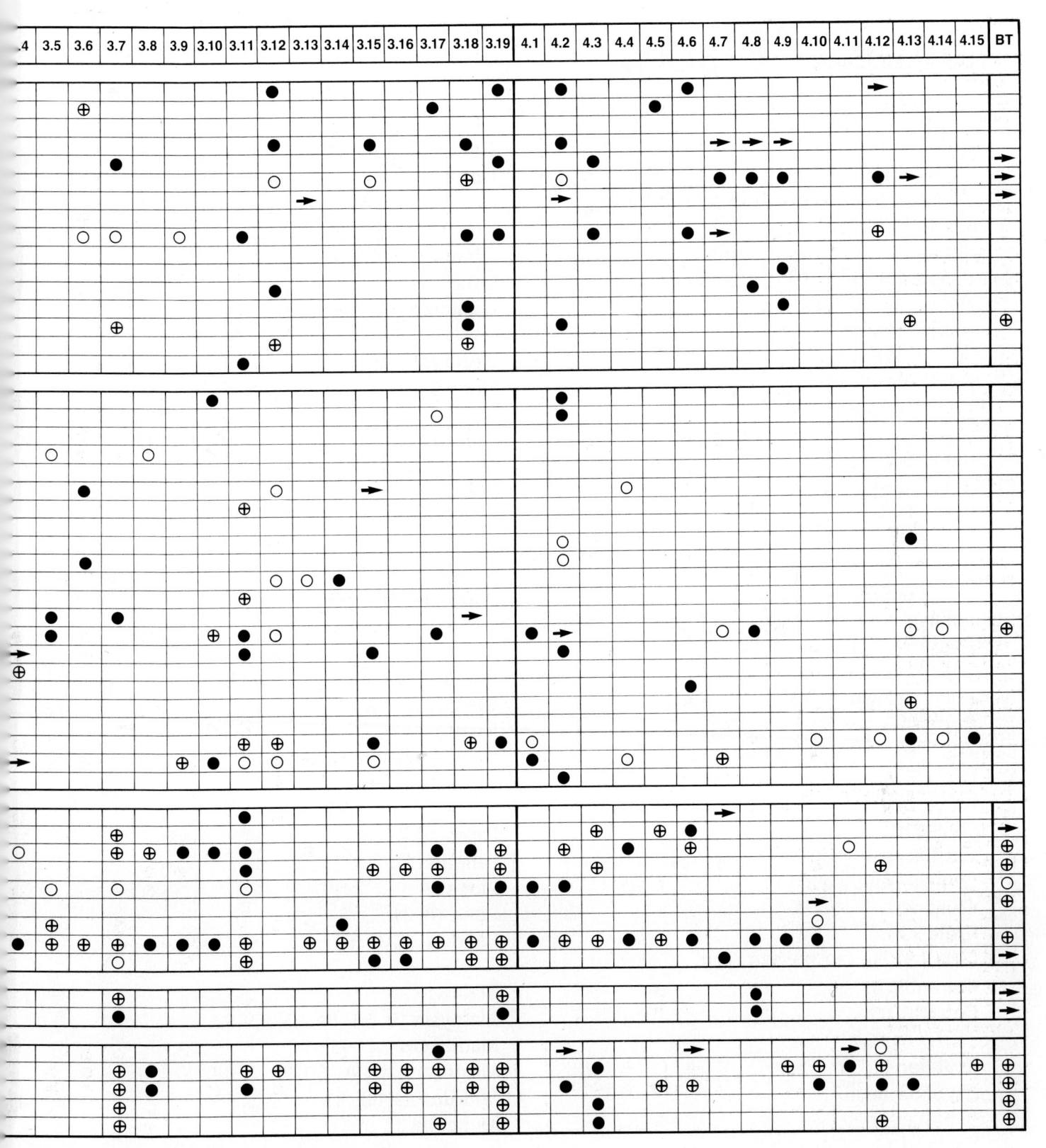

Index of Places

Abidjan 18–19, 21
Afghanistan 32
Africa 8, 14–15, 28, 32–33, 52–53, 76, 90–91, 96–97
Alps 55
Amazonia 24, 34, 61
Asia 8, 14, 28, 32
Aswan 50–51
Atlantic Ocean 37
Australia 46, 58–59
Australasia 8, 10, 28

Bahrain 105
Bangladesh 59, 98
Basra 80
Bhopal 48
Bolivia 58–59, 98
Bombay 18, 21, 49
Botswana 62, 63
Brazil 9, 13, 19, 22–28, 30–31, 34, 58–59, 65, 69, 86–87, 92, 98, 110–111
Burkina Faso 91, 111
Burma 59

Cairo 57
Cameroon 33
Canada 10
Caribbean 46–47
Central America 8
Chad 33
Chile 32
China 32, 58–59, 99, 116–119
Colombia 59, 98
Cuba 46, 89

Ecuador 44, 59
Egypt 33, 50, 57
El Salvador 59
England 14, 34, 46
Ethiopia 43, 59, 76
Europe 8, 18, 28, 78, 96

Fao 80
Fiji 92
France 14

Gabon 33
Gambia 92
Gao 43
Gezira 40, 96
Ghana 37, 92
Greece 10, 13
Guatemala 59, 98

Honduras 59
Hong Kong 100

India 13, 18, 48, 57, 59, 76, 102, 109, 111
Indian Ocean 47
Indonesia 58–59, 69, 98
Iran 69, 80–81
Iraq 80–81
Itaipu 86–87
Ivory Coast 18, 59

Jamaica 46, 84, 85
Japan 10, 13, 59, 78, 107, 111
Kenya 52, 102
Khartoum 96
Kuala Lumpur 19, 21
Kuwait 12, 81, 105

Lagos 19, 21, 73
Lebanon 33
Libya 78
Lima 18, 21
London 30, 31, 61

Malawi 57
Malaysia 19, 58–59, 65, 92–93
Manila 46
Mexico 10, 21, 46, 59, 98
Middle East 80–81
Mongolia 32

New Zealand 10
Nigeria 14, 16–17, 19, 59, 73, 78–79, 94–95
Nile Delta 50
North America 8, 10, 18, 28

Pacific Ocean 47